BLANTYRE
AN HISTORICAL DICTIONARY

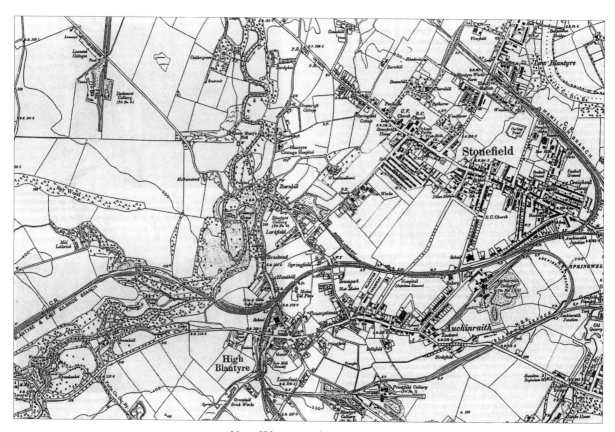

Map of Blantyre, eatly 20th century.

BLANTYRE
AN HISTORICAL DICTIONARY

Neil Gordon

PHILLIMORE

2006

Published by
PHILLIMORE & CO. LTD
Shopwyke Manor Barn, Chichester, West Sussex, England

© Neil Gordon, 2006

ISBN 1-86077-395-8
ISBN 13 978-1-86077-395-2

Printed and bound in Great Britain by
CAMBRIDGE UNIVERSITY PRESS

This book is dedicated to my dear wife, Elma,
my daughters, Lynne and Julie,
my son, Barry, and his wife, Pauline,
and grandchildren, Emma, Euan and Drew.

CONTENTS

Contents

List of Illustrations

Frontispiece: Map of Blantyre, early 20th century.

LIST OF SUBSCRIBERS

Lillias and Arthur Addison
Beth Ahmed
Francis Aitken
René and Sheila Aitkenhead
George Allan
Ina Allan
Mrs Agnes Allen (née MacDonald)
Donna M. Anderson (née Young)
William Anderson
Ella and Allan Andrew
Jean Arbuckle
John and Agnes Armstrong
Anne Arthur
Greta and Joe Ashbridge
Margaret Auchintibber
Iain Averell
Margaret and Eric Averell
Barbara Baillie and Paul Goyda
Neil and Jean Baillie
Elsie and Alex Balneaves
Joyce Barclay
Jean Barr
Jock Barrie
Bobby Beaton
James Beaton
Janette Bell
Robert Bell
Ryan Edward Bell
Mr and Mrs J. Berry
Blantyre Psychological Service
    Centre
Isobelle Bordon
Mr and Mrs R.S. Borland
Mr Andy and Mrs Betty Boyd
William Brawley
Claire Breen
Rachel Breen

James B. Brown
John Robertson Brown
John and Marion Brownlie
Isobel Burnett
Betty Burns
John Calderwood
William Cameron
Anne and David Campbell
Elizabeth Campbell
Essie Campbell
Nan Campbell
Elizabeth Cardoo (née Anderson)
M.P. Carpenter
J.W. and E.A. Cassells
Mary Caulder
Mrs A.D. Chalmers
Susan and Lester Chilcott
George Chisholm
Miss Elspeth Christie
Dr Gordon Christie
Dr Sandy Christie
Kathy and Dan Clarke
Lesley Clarkson
Ian Cleland
Michael and Fiona Coates
Janet B. Cochrane
Anne and Douglas Coke
Gladys Colston
Helen MacKenzie Conner
Rose Anne Conroy
Alex Cook
Anne Cook
David Cook
Gordon Cook
Ian L. Cormack M.A.
Tommy and Margaret Corrigan
Stewart B. Cox

James Craig
Jim Craig
John Craig
Mrs Marion Craig
Carol Croft
Phyllis Crossan
Bill Cunningham
John Cunningham
Ann Cushley
Evelyn Dalziel
John Dalziel
Robert and Margaret Dalziel
John Darcey
Edie and Ned Davidson
Margaret Devlin
Peter Dillon
Alexander and Andrea Dobbins
Jim and Liz Docherty
Mary Dodd (Kay)
Stuart Dodd
Arthur Donnelly
Mary Ann Donnelly
John Dowie
Thomas Downie
Archie and Flora Duncan
Susan and Robert Duncan
Anne and Jim Dundas
Jean Dunsmoir
Betty Dunsmuir
East Kilbride Psychological Service
    Centre
Derek and Susan Farlow
Betty Farmer (née Lynch)
Steven and Leanne Farquhar
Tommy and Rena Farr
Bill and Janette Farrell
Robert Feelie

Alex O. Ferguson
Elizabeth and Jim Ferguson
Robert C. Ferguson
Annette Flannigan
Daniel Fleming
James Fleming
John Flynn
Michael Flynn
Bill Foley
Ford City, Pennsylvania Public
    Library
Neil Ford
Neil J. Ford
Louise Forrest
Betty and Robert Forsyth
Elsie (McCall) Fotheringham
Phil Foye
Charlie 'Chick' Frame
Kathryn Mary Freer
Matilda Fulston
Billy Gallacher
Harper Cole Gallacher
Bill Galloway
John Galloway
Tom Gibson
M. Gillespie
Cissie Carol Gilmour
Alan J. Glen
David D. Glen
Mr David K. Glen
Douglas K. Glen
John and Ann Glen
Mrs Margaret B. Glen
Robbie Glen
Alan and Andrea Gordon
Amy Gordon
Barry and Pauline Gordon
Brenda and Robert Gordon
Craig, Chantal, Dan and
    Ben Gordon
Drew Gordon (Grandson)
Elizabeth Gordon
Elma Gordon (Wife)
Emma Gordon (Grand-daughter)
Eric Gordon
Evan Gordon (Grandson)
Helen McIntosh Gordon
Ian Gordon
Ian D. Gordon
Julie Gordon (Daughter)

Lynne Gordon (Daughter)
Martin D. Gordon
Molly Gordon (Aunt)
Charles and June Gorrance
Joe Gorrance
John Gorrance
Jack Gourley
Peggy Goyda and Chuck Hileman
Helen Marion Gray
Sandy and Bete Gray
Albert Gregory
Jane Gregory
Alan Hambley
Edwin A. Hambley
Edwin and Irene Hambley
J. Hamilton
P. Hamilton
William Hamilton
Jean and Gordon Hart
Mary Izat Hawkins
John W. Henderson
Sheena Henderson
Sandy Henry
Karla Hewitt
Barbie Goyda Hileman
Terri Hileman and daughter
    Kira Lynn
Luke and Lauren Hitchen
Margaret Hougham
Margaret Houldsworth
William G. Houldsworth
Miss Catherine Houston
Gordon and Norma Hull
Mark and Elaine Hull
Catherine Hunter
Jessie R. Hunter
Louise Inglis
John Irvine BSc
Douglas and Margaret Izett
Robert and Nora Izett
William and Margaret Izett
Andrea Jackson
John and Alice Jackson
William and Janette Jackson
David Marshall Jarvie
James and Flora Jeffrey
Angela Johnson
Mrs Avril Taylor Johnston
Rev. Peter Johnston
Rita Johnston

Mrs Annie Johnstone
Derek and Jillian Jones
Agnes G. Kalinsky
Andrew Kalinsky
Michael Keenan
Alexandra Kelly
Eddie Kelly
Eleanor Kelly
Mary Rose Kelly
Patrick Kelly
Sarah Kelly (Miss)
Jean Kelso
Eileen Kennedy
Patrick Kerr
John L. Kirkland
Nancy and Peter Krastev
Geoff and Val Krawczyk
Marion and James Laidlaw
Marion Lambie
Scott Lambie
Dr W. George Lanyon
Bridie Larkin
Alexander Latimer
Marjorie and Gordon Leckie
Martha Doris Lee
Margaret and George Lees
Gordon Liddell
Barbara Little
James Little
William Little
David Livingstone Mem. P. School
Neil Gordon Loggie
Tom and Jill Loggie
Catherine Lomond
David Henderson Lowe
James Connelly Lowe
John (Ian) Lusk
Jim Lynn
Sheana MacDonald
Margaret Macfarlane
James Dawson MacGregor
Peter Mackie
William Mackie
Catriona Macleod, D.N.
Tony Madden
Marian and John Maguire
Patricia C. Mahon (née Loughran)
Eric Malley
Brian Martin
William and Jean Mason

Ian and Marjory Maxwell
Jimmy Maxwell
Mrs Mary A. Maxwell
Maureen Mays
Robert McAuslin
John and Netta McBain
Janet McBean
Joe McBride
John and Moira McCall
David McCallum
Kathleen McCartney
Bill and Jean McCorkindale
Ian and Ina McCorkindale
Jim and Alison McCormack
Jimmy and Rose McCormack
Jeanette McCourt
John McCourt
Mr Edward McCready
Chris McDonald
Patricia L. McDonald
Mrs Sharlene McElhill
Jean McEwan (Kelso)
Patrick McGaulley
Brendan McGhee
Dennis McGilligan
James McGilligan
McGowan Family
Harry McGowan
Tom and Margaret McGregor
Tom and Margaret McGregor (née
    Wilson)
Henry McGuigan
Mrs Irene Kane McGuinness
Charlie and May McGuire
Mary McGuire
Alastair and Elizabeth McHendry
Lorna and Kenny McIlvaney
Jim Beck McInerney
Margaret McInerney
Catherine McInulty
John McKay
Anne McKillop
Margaret McKinlay
Myra Orr McKinlay
Ishbel McKinlay-Wilkie
Eric McLachlan
Geraldine McLachlan
Joe McLachlan
Thomas Andrew Mclachlan
Jean McLaren

Jane McLaughlin
Malcolm Taylor McLean
Mary McLean
Edward Daly McLernon
Sandy and Liz McMillan
Mrs Sarah McNamee
Isobel McNeil
Arthur McNulty
Patrick McPartlin
Eliza McQuade
Tom McVey
A.E. McWilliam
Bobby McWilliam
Sarah and James Millar
Jane Milligan (Mrs)
Mr and Mrs K. Milligan
Christine B. Mitchell
Jack and Betty Mitchell
Moira Monk
Sarah Hamilton Montgomery
Jim Moodie
Jimmy Moore
Beth Mortimer
Mary Morton
Barbara Muirhead
Joann Mulholland
Greta Munro
Margaret Chassels Munro
William Murdoch
James Murphy
Margaret Murphy
Nancy Murphy
Carol Mary Ann Murray
Mr Peter Murray
Ronnie and Ellen Murray
Sharon Murray
Matthew Nash
Mrs Isobel Neeson
Ian and Isobel Neil
Morag Summers Neil
Andy Neilson
Mr and Mrs Ross and
    Eleanor Nelson
Elise Niven
K.E. Norris
Fr Charles O'Farrell
James O'Neill
John O'Neill
Nicholas O'Neill
Stuart and Megan Orr

Jack Owens
Gillian Parker
Mrs J. Pate
Neil T. Pate
Bert Paterson
Carol Paterson
George S. Paterson
Herbert Paterson
John Paterson
Nan Paterson
Shaunna Paterson
Mrs and Mrs William F. Paterson
Ailsa M. Phelps (née Simm USA)
Mr John Polockus (Snr)
Mary (Duddy) Poole
Elizabeth Potter
Maria B. Proudfoot
Jillian Pye
David Rance
H.T. Rankine
Daniel Ross Reddiex
Glenn Reddiex (N.Z.)
Jim Reddiex
John Reddiex (N.Z.)
Robert Reddiex (N.Z.)
James and Maureen Reid
Jean Reid
John and Helen Reid
John Richardson
Esther Richmond
Christine Robertson
Elizabeth (Duddy) Robertson
Hugh W. Robertson
Iain Robertson
John W. Robertson
Kate and Alan Robertson
Robert Robertson
Stuart Robertson
The Roche Family
John Rodger
Jimmy and Peggy (Carabine)
    Rooney
David Rouse
Elizabeth M. Roxburgh
John and Fay Russell
Harry Ryan
Mrs Bridget Rynn
Jerry L. Sanders (USA)
Margaret Scott (née Kelly)
Neil and Christine Scott

Joan C. Sempie
Drew Semple
Duncan Shaw
Reverend Duncan Shaw
Violet Shaw
Peter Sheppard
Archibald A. Simm (USA)
Heather L. Simm (USA)
Hugh Simm
Lindsay A. Simm (USA)
Susan M. Simm (USA)
Sadie Simpson (née Fulston)
Nancy Sinkinson (née Beveridge)
Doris Skinner
Jim McGaulley Slaven
K.J. Smart
Frances Sneddon
South Lanarkshire Library Service
Bob Speirs
Charlie Speirs
E. Sportt
Barry Stewart
Karen Stewart
Mrs Monica Stewart
Robert Stewart
Tom Stewart

Robert Stirling
Mary Dickson Stuart
Mr and Mrs James and
    Elizabeth Syme
Eileen Tait
Daniel Taylor
John Taylor
Jeanette Thomson
Robert J. Todd
Georgie Toomey
Jim Travers
David Tremble
Mrs Irene Tremble
Stuart Tremble
Bill Valentine
Janet and Josef Veverka
Evelyn Walker
Alison Walker-Hill
Miss Margaret Wands
Charles Ward
James and Elizabeth Ward
John Ward
Mary Ann Ward
Richard Ward
Drew and Isabel Wardlaw
Walter Wardlaw

Anne Watson
James Watson
Mr John Watson
Tom Watson
Mr W. Watson
Henry Watters
Robert Watters
William Watters
Elizabeth C. S. Weaver
Sherry and Bill Weir
Irene Welsh
Jimmy Whelan
James A. White
Don Wilkie
Andrew and Catherine Williamson
C. and A. Williamson
Janet and David Willis
Christine Wilson
Mrs E. Wilson
Margaret Wilson
Robert Wilson
Ewan Wotherspoon
Janette Wotherspoon
Anthony Yates
Evelyn and John Young

FOREWORD

This book was written by my dear brother, Neil Gordon. Sadly, Neil passed away on Sunday, 5 December 2004, in Hairmyres Hospital, East Kilbride, aged 67 years.

He was born at our parents' home, 56 Station Road, Blantyre and lived all his life in the town. After his marriage in March 1958, Neil and his wife, Elma, initially lived at 1 Clark Street. They moved to 14 Centre Street then subsequently to 74 Broompark Road. In 1971 they finally moved to 18 Stonefield Crescent which was their home for the rest of his life. With the redevelopment of Blantyre in the 1970-80s, both Clark Street and Centre Street disappeared. Such occurrences seemed to fire Neil's fascination for recording the Blantyre of old.

Neil was well known as a local artist and historian. He had an extensive collection of old, and not so old, photographs depicting the changing vistas of the town. The collection grew over a 25-year period with many of the images being gifted by people in the town. However, he did extensive photographic work himself; he even climbed up a ladder on the outside of the steeple of Livingstone Memorial Church just to get some unusual 'aerial' views. But his interest in all things Blantyre went further than photographs. He was almost fanatical in seeking out obscure facts about the town's historical connections – some obvious, others most certainly not so.

He was renowned for his presentations and slide shows about Blantyre's history. Many readers of this book will have attended them. The content of the book replicates the approach which he adopted in these sessions: factual historical events are included alongside nostalgic descriptions of how the town once looked not so long ago. His love of local anecdotal stories is also addressed.

His pet subject was the Dixon's pit explosion, which occurred on 22 October 1877. Such was his interest in this catastrophic event that the centenary memorial of the disaster, which is sited at High Blantyre Cross, was built to his design and is now an iconic image of the town.

Over the four years or so before his passing, he used his computer to record all the fascinating facts which he had collected about Blantyre. This resulted in the compilation of this document. It is sad that he did not see this book published, but, as his brother, I am greatly honoured that he requested that I see his project through to its completion.

Robert Gordon

PREFACE

Over the last 25 years I have had the pleasure of being invited to present my 'Blantyre Past and Present' slide and talk show to many organisations, groups and individuals within Blantyre and the surrounding districts. I was asked on many occasions if I intended to write a book on the subject and my reply was always the same – 'I am a story teller not a writer' – which you will probably agree with when you see this effort to present myself as a writer!

Nevertheless, the content of this book is an attempt to draw together the various historical notes regarding the history of Blantyre, which have always been available to the public – if one knew where to look. The information is scattered around in various books and booklets but the information contained within them has never really been logged together as a whole, and was sometimes not accurate. The only book written about Blantyre in great detail, as far as I am aware, is *The Annals of Blantyre*, which was written in 1885 by the Rev. Stewart Wright. Other brief presentations regarding the town's history are contained in various journals such as *Stothers* and the *Lanarkshire Illustrated*, which were published in the early 1900s, and a fine book named *A Contribution to the History of Lanarkshire*.

This book contains not only my researched history of our town but also stories, memories, recollections given to me by various individuals, many of whom attended my talk shows over the years, and passed on their 'unimportant' stories about family and friends. These unimportant anecdotes are in fact the very fabric that made Blantyre what it is today, which in my opinion deserve a mention in a book such as this. There must be many more tales and anecdotes out there in the community that I am not aware of.

I never imagined in my wildest dreams that one day I would attempt to write a book on the subject. Unfortunately, after collecting picture postcards and photographs of Blantyre, off and on, for over 25 years, I now find that I cannot remember with any accuracy who willingly donated their precious photographs to extend the collection for the benefit of the town. To them I offer my sincere apologies for being unable to record their contributions to this book. The names of all the photographic contributors that I can recall are acknowledged.

Postcard publishers over the last hundred years have produced many wonderful photographs of Blantyre and it is thanks to them that we can look into the past and see how our town has developed over the years. Many of the old postcards did not show the name of the publisher and most of them do not exist today. Valentine of Dundee was regarded as the best and most prolific company in the picture postcard industry and it is thanks to them that a book such as this can be illustrated.

My interest in all things Blantyre really began in earnest in 1977 after my involvement with the efforts of a dedicated group to construct the Blantyre Explosion Centenary Monument, in memory of those who died in that terrible catastrophe. At that time my curiosity was raised as to why persistent doubts existed regarding the number killed on 22 October 1877, and it was my involvement with a group researching the subject that kindled my interest in all things Blantyre.

I have made every effort to secure permission to include certain material in this book and I apologise for any errors or omissions.

Neil Gordon
2004

Acknowledgements

Mrs C.G.W. Roads, Court of the Lord Lyon, HM New Register House, Edinburgh; Dr McHugh, Archivist, Catholic Archdiocese, Glasgow; Glasgow University Archives; HM Records Office, Glasgow and Edinburgh; Scottish Mining Museum, Newtongrange; South Lanarkshire Cemeteries, Administration, East Kilbride; Mitchell Library, Glasgow; Lennoxlove House, Haddington; Pearl Murphy, Hamilton Reference Library; Hamilton Reference Library; Blantyre Library; Motherwell Heritage Centre; John McLeish, East Kilbride Library; Father Darcy, St Joseph's Church; my brother, Robert Gordon; Mrs May McLean, Millerdale; Andrew Reid; Jim Hamilton; Mrs B. Walsh; Walter Kerr; the late Mrs Elizabeth Parry; Alex Rochead; Robert Craig; Mrs Susanna Slivinski; Martin Lennon; Mrs M. Beggs; Mrs Bell; Bill Green, Miner's Welfare; Mrs Agnes McDade; Ella Gibson; Mrs Dick; George Cochrane; Mrs Betty Spiers; Mrs May McLean; Mrs Fleming; James Seaton; George Cochrane; the Rev. William Mackie, Nazarene Church; the late Mrs Meg Irvine; Mrs Potter; William Chassells; Mrs Wilkie, Bardykes; Andrew Reid; Allan Walker; Alex Russell; Mrs B. Walsh; Mrs Irene Hamley.

Many photographs are from the major archive of monochrome topographical views by James Valentine & Co. which is held by the University of St Andrews Library. My thanks go to Mrs C. Jackson there. Further details of this collection can be obtained via the internet at http://specialcollections.st-and.ac.uk or by contacting the Library direct:

Special Collections Department,
Library and Information Services,
University of St Andrews,
North Street,
St Andrews,
Fife KY16 9TR
(Tel : 01334 462326)

Blantyre

An Historical Dictionary

Auchentibber, c.1920.

Adam's 'Laun'/Adam's Sawmill

Tenements were usually known by the name of the owner of the land upon which they stood. The word 'land' was pronounced in the local dialect as 'laun' (pronounced lawn). In this case, since William Adam owned the land, the tenement was known locally as Adam's 'Laun'.

In the photograph, looking east along Main Street to High Blantyre Cross, Adam's 'Laun' was the tall building on the left. The gate to Adam's Sawmill is between the left lamppost and the tenement gable. Adam's Sawmill and yard was situated directly opposite the gates of the Old Parish Church on land now occupied by the west end of Kirkview Sheltered Housing.

Adam owned the land as far as the church halls, which stood on the corner of Hunthill Road and Main Street. Adam's Building was demolished in January 1989.

Main Street, High Blantyre.

William Adam and his brother, who owned the company, were builders originally from Rutherglen. They came to reside in Blantyre in 1874 to take advantage of the building boom within the town, which resulted from the discovery of coal in the district. One of their largest projects was the construction of Stonefield Parish Church (q.v.). The Provost of Hamilton, John Clark Forrest (q.v.), who was a landowner within the town, donated the site and the church was opened in 1880. The Adam brothers also built many other prominent buildings in the town, including constructions in and around all the local mining collieries.

Adventure School

A small timber school was constructed in the south corner of the Old Kirkyard in 1731 by the Heritors of the parish. This school was later replaced by a new school, which was built at the foot of School Lane (q.v.). It is generally accepted as the first school constructed within the parish. It was situated near the corner of Park Crescent and the present Schoolhouse Lane at Kirkton Park gates. A John Dunlop is recorded at one time as being headmaster. High Blantyre Cross was the site of the original village of Blantyre and it is thought that a school was functioning early in the 17th century and possibly earlier. The old school and houses in School Lane were demolished and the stonework was used in 1863 to repair the Kirkyard wall and construct the wall surrounding Blantyre Old Parish Church (q.v.), which was being built at that time at the corner of Main Street and Craigmuir Road. Recently I discovered a stone in this perimeter wall, directly opposite the door of the boiler house at the rear of the church, with an inscription carved upon it that reads as follows:

JOHN DUNLOP. SCHOOL Mr 1704.

The inscription seems to indicate that an earlier school did in fact exist prior to the construction in 1731 of the Adventure School in the Kirkyard. This school would probably be located somewhere in the neighbourhood of High Blantyre Cross.

Aeroplane 1

In 1860 a flying machine was built at the Smiddy at Broompark Road, 43 years before the first manned flight by the Wright brothers in 1903. Thomas Taylor, a local miller who worked in the Bardyke Mill, was also an inventor of many gadgets that could be used in mills and farms. Thomas built an aeroplane which was powered by a steam engine. Mr Templeton, the blacksmith at the Smiddy, manufactured the parts and assisted Thomas in its construction. The contraption was taken into the field adjoining the Smiddy to attempt its first flight. (High Blantyre Primary School was constructed upon this field.)

The local inhabitants of Larkfield and Barnhill were of course very curious and a large crowd gathered to see the great event. It is not recorded who piloted the plane but we can safely assume that Thomas was the aviator. Numerous attempts were made without success but it was noted that the nose of the aeroplane did in fact lift off the ground. Of course Thomas was not alone in attempting to invent the aeroplane. The principles of flight were known then, the quest being to generate enough speed to get the machine into the air. It was the invention of the petrol engine, 43 years after Thomas' attempts, that enabled the Wright brothers to claim their place in history.

The onlookers watching Thomas' attempts were greatly amused and someone shouted, 'Haw Tam, if God had meant ye tae flee, he would hae gien ye wings.' Tom's reply to this remark was, 'Wha ever lives tae see the day, machines will fly o'er Blantyre.' How right he was.

The Smiddy, seen on the left of the photograph, still stands today.

Aeroplane 2

A local miner, Jimmy Duddy, constructed a mini 'pilot-less' flying machine shortly after the first manned flight

The Smiddy, Broompark Road, c.1920.

made by the Wright brothers in 1903. Jimmy, who lived in Merry's Rows (Elm Street), installed a lathe and machinery in the back part of his room and kitchen, where he manufactured the parts he required for the construction of various devices that he invented. It is claimed that Jimmy's aircraft was a common sight soaring over the rooftops of Stonefield. Having no means of landing, the flying machine would crash land and be brought in pieces by the locals to his workshop to be repaired and reassembled. He contacted the Patents Office about his machine but it is not known if his invention was ever registered.

In those early years of the 20th century, motorbikes were in their infancy and it was to Jimmy that the owners of these new-fangled machines turned when they had problems with their bikes. He was also on standby to carry out repairs to the projector of the Blantyre Electric Cinema, the town's first silent cinema, which was located in the original Masonic Hall (q.v.) above the *Livingstonian* pub at the corner of Forrest Street and Glasgow Road.

Jimmy, who was a 'shanker' at Merry and Cunningham's Colliery at Auchinraith (q.v.), died a tragic death on Fair Saturday 1913, aged 42, when he was summoned to carry out an emergency repair to the cage at the pithead. Whilst carrying out this work, he fell to his death down the shaft. Jimmy Duddy was obviously a man of extraordinary vision and talent, and who knows what achievements he may have had but for his unfortunate death.

Aggie Bain's Cottage

Built in 1536, Aggie Bain's Cottage is the oldest house in Blantyre. Although Crossbasket Tower (constructed in the 13th or 14th century) is older, it was built in part of the parish of East Kilbride. In the 17th century the parish boundary was changed and Crossbasket (q.v.) became part of the parish of Blantyre, but Aggie Bain's Cottage has always been recognised as the oldest surviving house in Blantyre. (It may well be that the Crossbasket Tower was originally a Blantyre property and is the old Blantyre Tower and Fortalice (q.v.) mentioned in ancient Scottish

Aggie Bain's Cottage, c.1890.

documents granting permission to hold a market day once a week. It is possible that the tower was sold within the Stewart families, who held the lands of Blantyre and East Kilbride. No other recorded structure in Blantyre resembled a tower and fortalice.) The cottage is situated on Bardykes Road adjacent to the *Hoolet's Nest* pub (q.v.) on the corner of the lane that links Bardykes Road with Glenfruin Road. The present lane was once the top of the original main dirt track that ran down to the River Clyde to a point thought to be at a crossing directly below Bothwell Castle. Aggie Bain purchased the cottage in the 1890s from the Brownlie family (q.v.), seen here in the photograph.

Agriculture

In the past there were many farms within the parish of Blantyre, the majority of which were located around Auchentibber and Calderside. The following is a list of Blantyre farms: Auchentibber, Auchinraith, Barnhill, Basket, Bellsfield, Blantyreferme, Blantyre Park, Blantyre Works, Broompark, Calderside, Coatshill, Craigknowe, Croftangreen, Crossbasket, Edge, Greenblairs, Hasties, Laighlylock, Lodgehill, Newfield, Newhouse, Park, Priestfield, Shott, Stewartfield, Wheatlandhead (q.v.). Of the above list only four farms remain, Basket, Calderside, Lodgehill and Stewartfield, all of which are beef farms located in the Auchentibber area. Auchentibber farm is occupied but is not farmed. Most of the farms were known locally by the name of the current owner,

Blantyre Works Farm at Farm Road being known latterly as Forrest's Farm.
SEE BRONZE AGE

Aitkenhead Builders

Brothers Robert and James Aitkenhead were prominent builders in the town after 1850 and constructed many of the tenements and private houses in the district. In 1875 Robert built Stonefield Parish School (q.v.) at the corner of Glasgow Road and Victoria Street, now the site of the Clydeview Shopping Precinct (q.v.). Because of overcrowding at the school, an infant school was built in 1892 by James and his son. This building was known as 'the Wee School', and it was situated behind the current Blantyre Library in Calder Street. The site is now occupied by the ASDA supermarket.

The accompanying photograph, taken from Hamilton Drive near the corner with Syde's Brae, shows the site of Aitkenhead's yard.

Site of Aitkenhead's Yard, 1999.

Aitkenhead, Johnny

Johnny Aitkenhead was born in Blantyre in 1923 and lived at 35 Hunthill Road. He began his football career as a schoolboy playing for Calder Street School and was selected to play for the Scottish School Boys International Team. On leaving school he played for the local amateur team, Blantyre Academicals. He was soon signed by Queen's Park FC and then was transferred to Hibernian FC. Unable to claim a regular game because of the Hibs 'Famous Five' forward line of the time, he was transferred again in 1949, this time to Motherwell FC. It was at Motherwell that Johnny made a name for himself and was recognised as an expert at taking penalty kicks. He got the nickname of 'The Penalty King', as he seldom failed to score. His record of scoring 40 consecutive penalties is still impressive. Johnny, who was capped on three occasions by the Scottish League, died in 1987.

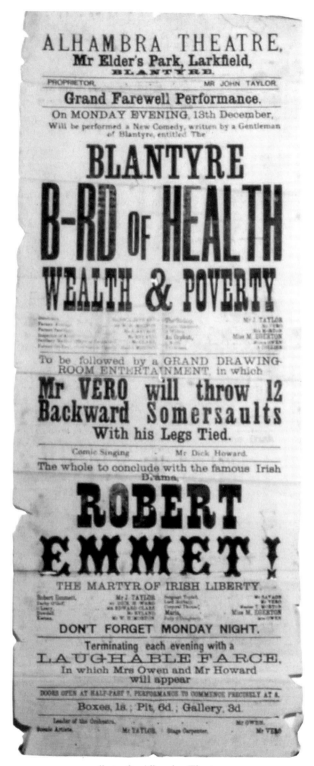

Poster for Alhambra Theatre.

Alhambra Theatre

This theatre stood on the current site of *Finbarr's Pub*, Broompark Road, directly across from Watson Street. It is thought the Alhambra closed sometime in the 1890s. The premises were then used as a boxing booth until 1909, when a Mr Lawson (q.v.) purchased and converted the property into a bakery. He in turn was succeeded by a baker named Ingram. Later the building lay empty for many years until Eddie Collins bought the premises and built a shop at the front and reopened the bakery in the 1960s. The property was then sold and converted into the *Manhattan* public house and subsequently became *Finbarr's*. An old Alhambra Theatre bill, seen here, advertises two plays that were to be performed, and notes that between the plays a 'Mr Vero would throw twelve backward somersaults with his legs tied together'. The price of admission was 1s. 6d. for boxes, the balcony seats cost 9d. and the stalls, 3d. The bill gives the address as 'The Alhambra Theatre, Mr Elder's Park, Larkfield'.

Anderson Church

SEE REV. JAMES ANDERSON (A)

Anderson, Rev. James

Born, Bathgate 1785. Died, Blantyre 1860.
Rev. James Anderson, the first minister of the Free Church in Blantyre, studied at Edinburgh University, and was ordained in 1832 as minister of the parish of Blantyre in the Old Parish Church.

The period between 1833 and 1843 is known within the Church of Scotland as the 'Disruption'. There was a difference of opinion as to how the church should be governed and things came to a head in 1843, when 474 ministers walked out of the General Assembly of the Church of Scotland and declared for a free church in which the congregation would select their minister instead of the 'Patronage' system, under which the local land owner or feu superior had the right to select the minister of his choice, the congregation having no say in the matter. Often the majority of his congregation disagreed with his ecclesiastical politics but gave him unqualified respect.

Having been one of the 474 ministers who 'went out', and having joined the 'Secession' and signed the 'Deed of Dismission', Anderson was declared 'no longer the minister of this church'. Some of the congregation left the Old Parish Church and followed him. In 1844 they built a new church in Stonefield Road and named

Anderson Church, Stonefield Road.

it Blantyre Free Church. The first church burned down in 1871 and was replaced by a more substantial church in 1872, with a fine manse at the rear of the building. It was known as the Blantyre United Free Church but later took the name of its founder and from 1929 was known as the Anderson Church of Scotland until the church closed in 1977. It was later destroyed by fire and eventually demolished. All that remains today is the church hall which is now used as a funeral parlour.

Coincidentally, the minister who succeeded Anderson at the Old Parish Church, the Rev. Paterson, died on the same day as his predecessor and they were also buried on the same day, side by side, in the old Kirkyard.

Mrs Ann Hutton of Calderbank (Calderglen) (q.v.), a heritor of the town, was a keen supporter of Anderson in his opposition to the Patronage system within the Church. She donated £100 to the building of the new church, and it was claimed that without her financial support the project would not have commenced. Besides the money already mentioned, she gave £25 for the slating of the roof and a further £50 to pay off other debts. Mrs Hutton also presented the church with a bell, which after the fire that destroyed the original church, was transferred to the steeple of the replacement church. After all debts were cleared she directed her energies to the construction of a church manse. She contributed another £100 pounds to the project and raised a further £100 from her friends in Glasgow and elsewhere.
SEE JOHN MARSHALL (M)

Andrew's Chip Shop

Johnny Andrew's chip shop was located in McAlpine's Building at 178-180 Glasgow Road directly opposite Logan Street.

Annals of Blantyre

The *Annals of Blantyre* is a book written in 1885 by the Rev. Stewart Wright (q.v.) on the history of Blantyre. It can be read in the Blantyre Reference Library.

Apothecary Hall

SEE BEGGS' BUILDING (B)

Archer's Croft

Archer's Croft was a large field directly across Main Street from the Old Parish Church. It incorporated the land between the current Kirkview Sheltered Housing complex and the first set of gates of Greenhall Park, Stoneymeadow Road and across to the banks of the River Calder on the far side of the Hunthill football pitches. It was here that the youth of the village were instructed in the use of the sword and the practice of archery, which was stated as being 'a great pastime of the lower classes, in which they were bound by Royal Proclamation to practice on Sundays and holidays after divine service'.

A railway line to East Kilbride was built across the middle of Archers Croft in 1885 and is used today as a footpath leading to the columns of the old Blantyre-East Kilbride railway viaduct (q.v.). During construction of the railway line, a Bronze-Age grave was discovered, proving that our community has existed for over 5,000 years. The houses of Afton Gardens, Ellisland Drive, Armour Court and the Hunthill football pitches now occupy the lands of the old croft between Stoneymeadow Road and the River Calder.

Armour, Mary Nicol Neill (née Steel), RSA, RSW

Mary Armour was born in Blantyre on 27 March 1902, and died in the year 2000. She lived with her parents in the Crescents in Victoria Street until she married William Armour, RSA, RSW in 1927. Mary was an artist who painted still life and landscapes in oils and watercolour. She was educated at Auchinraith Primary School and Hamilton Academy and trained at the Glasgow School of Art between 1920 and 1925. In 1927 she received the Guthrie Award, and in 1972 the GI's Cargill Award. Mary taught still life at Glasgow School of Art from 1951 until 1962.

Her works sell for many thousands of pounds and are eagerly collected by art enthusiasts throughout the world. Her paintings hang in many art galleries, including the City of Edinburgh Collection, Aberdeen Art Gallery, Paisley Art Gallery, Dundee Art Gallery, Greenock Art Gallery, Perth Art Gallery and Victoria (Australia) Art Gallery. Glasgow Museums Collections has 16 Mary Armour paintings, the largest collection of her work.

An early example of Mary's work can be seen at the David Livingstone Centre. Livingstone Memorial, as it was formerly known, received the painting as a gift from Mary during the jubilee celebrations to commemorate the opening of the Memorial by the Queen Mother (q.v.) when she was the Duchess of York in 1929.

Asda

Associated Dairies opened their superstore in Blantyre in October 1980 and constructed the Clydeview Shopping Precinct (q.v.) on the redeveloped land on Glasgow Road between Victoria Street and Logan Street, the former site of Low Blantyre Primary School. The opening of ASDA saw the demise of many small shops within the community. Most shopkeepers did not relocate after the demolition of all the properties on both sides of Glasgow Road at the east end of the town, from Victoria Street to Whistleberry Road.

Astricted Mills

An agreement between the landowner and his tenant miller ensured that all the grain belonging to the landowner's tenant farmers was sent to the miller for grinding. By enforcing this agreement, the landowner guaranteed the miller's income, which enabled him to pay his rent to him as feu superior. It also ensured that the farmers had a mill close at hand that could grind the grain which they then sold, giving them funds to pay their rent to the landowner.

The landowner, miller and farmer were in a way interdependent. In some cases the farmer paid the landowner and miller by giving them a percentage of the grain. The mills that worked under these conditions were known as 'Astricted Mills'. There were six known mills and one unnamed mill on the six-mile stretch of the River Calder which forms the south-western boundary of the Barony of Blantyre. The foundations of the unnamed mill can be seen on the bank of the river, south of the General's Bridge (q.v.). The remains of the Bardyke Mill can still be seen under the Spittal Bridge (q.v.) at the 'West End' of Glasgow Road.

SEE MAVIS MILL

SEE PATTONHOLM FORD/MILL

Auchentibber

The name Auchentibber is said to mean, in the Gaelic language, 'the field of the healing waters', which was found near the village. It is said that the sick and disabled came from near and far to 'take the waters' at Auchentibber.

Not much remains of the hamlet of Auchentibber, one of the original Fermetouns of Blantyre (q.v.), located in the south of the parish on the high ground at the top of Sydes Brae (q.v.). The inhabitants were mainly employed in the surrounding farms until the late 1700s, when vast deposits of iron ore were discovered nearby on the banks of the Calderwater. The iron ore was transported to Glasgow where it was put into furnaces and made into pig iron. Later, in 1835, limestone was mined in the vicinity of the village, with production involving the extraction of the iron ore and limestone. This kept the inhabitants in full employment until the early 1900s. A large stone quarry was established at the start of the 20th century, which also provided work until the 1950s.

When the hamlet was established it probably took its name from Auchentibber Farm. Parkneuk was the name of the area above and beyond the war memorial

Quoiting Green, Auchentibber, c.1900.

on Sydes Brae and was clearly marked on early maps of the area. At one time there were over sixty dwellings in the village. Paraffin lamps and dry external toilets were still in use in the 1950s. A decision by the Lanark 5th District Council not to provide electricity or gas supplies to the area led to the demise of the community. Many years would pass before the remnants of Auchentibber finally received gas and electricity.

Auchentibber Inn.

Auchentibber Inn

The proprietor of the *Auchentibber Inn* was Mr J.B. Struthers. The inn was situated on the corner of Auchentibber Road and Sydes Brae, the left gable facing the Sydes Brae. The War Memorial is behind the porch at the left of the photograph, a few metres further up Sydes Brae.

Auchentibber Jaunt

In the mid-1800s, an old woman in her late eighties was taken from her house in Blantyre Mills/Works Village (q.v.) to visit a friend in Auchentibber. On the way home, coming down the Sydes Brae, she was amazed at the wondrous sight of the rooftops of Blantyre and the Clyde Valley laid out like a panorama below her spreading away north to the Campsie Hills, and remarked, 'Weel, I never tho'cht that the world was so large afore.' She had travelled two-and-a-half miles from the village and this was the furthest she had ever been from her house in her life. There are other reports of men and women, some in their nineties, who had barely spent one night away from their home in Blantyre. One old man named William Greig (q.v.) had not ventured out of Blantyre for 88 years. An old lady claimed that when she was a lass she walked to Glasgow one morning and returned that evening. This, she said, was the only time that she had ever been out of the parish of Blantyre.

Auchentibber Quoiting Green

The Quoiting Green was built by the miners of Auchentibber and was known as the model quoiting (q.v.) green of Scotland, such was its splendour (see p.7). J.B. Struthers, the proprietor of the *Auchentibber Inn*, encouraged the locals to construct the quoiting green on top of an old in-filled quarry at the rear of his property. The green was situated in magnificent gardens behind the present War Memorial and surrounded by life-size statues and ornamental walkways. Traces of it can still be seen today behind the War Memorial.

Auchentibber School

The original Auchentibber School was built in 1880 through the efforts of Father Peter Donnelly of St Joseph's RC Church (q.v.), for the education of children whose parents worked in the surrounding stone quarries and farms. Initially 42 pupils enrolled, and by the late 1890s the roll had increased to 108 pupils. At the turn of the century, with the demise of the stone and lime quarries, the population dropped dramatically causing the school to close in April 1902. The Blantyre School Board then purchased the building and it was agreed that the boards of Blantyre and Hamilton would administer the school. Extensions were constructed and the new school was opened on 2 April 1903. The formal opening took place on 4 April. The catchment area for the school was Auchentibber and the Udston district of Burnbank. The school was later transferred to Blantyre Parish School Board in 1910.

Due to the decision of the 5th District Council not to supply electricity to the area the population fell rapidly, with most families moving into council houses in High Blantyre. By 1952 the school had only 18 pupils and it eventually closed on 31 December 1962, with the remaining pupils transferred to High Blantyre Primary School. At the time of writing the old school still stands and at present is being converted into a house.

Auchentibber War Memorial

The inhabitants of Auchentibber erected this memorial to honour the men of the community who lost their lives in the First World War. It was constructed with Italian marble obtained from a fireplace of Hamilton Palace, which was being demolished at that time.

The remains of the Auchentibber Quoiting Green can be found directly behind and to the left of the War Memorial.

Auchinraith

Auchinraith was one of the original six hamlets/fermetouns (q.v.) in the Barony of Blantyre and was located originally at Main Street and Cemetery Road. The Auchinraith area gradually extended east along Main Street and down Auchinraith Road to Whistleberry Road. As Glasgow Road developed in the 1870s to service the new mining community in Stonefield, the Auchinraith district was then generally accepted as the area between Cemetery Road and the top of Craig Street.

Auchinraith Colliery

Messrs Merry and Cunningham, the owners of the colliery, sunk the pit in 1872, and drew the first coal in 1875. The colliery was situated off a cul-de-sac that was located at one time near the bottom of the original Auchinraith Road adjacent to the corner of Craig Street. The bridge and railway line at the top of Craig Street were removed and Auchinraith Road was realigned to eliminate the bend between Craig Street and Logan Street at Auchinraith School. The colliery cul-de-sac was opened up at the end of a small row of miners' houses called Auchinraith Row (q.v.) that was situated in front of the pit, and the road was extended through to the top of Logan Street. The pithead was to the left and behind the Timber Houses as you turned left at the top of Craig Street. The company constructed houses at two separate sites, the one mentioned above and the company's main concentration of houses, Merry's Rows (q.v.), referred to locally as 'Murray's Rows'. At the time of writing the housing project at Victoria Gardens is being constructed on the colliery site.

James Merry, one of the original owners of the company, like many other early proprietors in the mining industry, blatantly broke mining regulations to suit his own ends. As a Member of Parliament, he might have been expected to enforce all mining legislation passed by Parliament in his collieries, but he exploited over 1,000 men whom he employed in his collieries and iron mines throughout Scotland. His employees were paid monthly, but most men were forced to apply weekly,

Auchinraith Colliery Explosion, Funeral Procession.

sometimes daily, for a 'sub' in advance of their wages. These advance payments were granted on the proviso that the money was spent in his company shops. It is said, too, that colliers had to spend half their pay in the company store. Colliery owners operated what can only be described as a racket, which became known as the 'truck system'. The unfortunate miners nearly always found themselves in arrears and therefore never received a full monthly pay, which kept them in a vicious circle of debt. All beverages, including buttermilk, the miners' most popular thirst quencher, could only be purchased at the colliery store as the company had a contract with the farmers in the area to purchase all their milk supplies.

Unlike Monteith & Co., the owners of Blantyre Mills, who provided free medical treatment, a school, a church, a library and many other services to their employees and their families, the mine owners exploited their workmen. They extracted stoppages from their wages at source for all manner of basic services, such as a penny in the pound for the maintenance of the school

(if one was provided) and 2d. a week for the doctor, and money was also taken off for the blacksmith who sharpened their tools. In those early years of the mining industry, the proprietors, by drawing up contracts with the suppliers of the basic necessities of life, such as the one with the local farmers, and by ensuring that the company store was stocked with every item required for day-to-day existence, had a vice-like grip on all their employees. The truck system ensured that the wages paid by the company to their employees were recycled through the company store back into the pocket of the mine owner. Although banned by an Act of Parliament in the mid-1800s, it is claimed that the system continued to be practised illegally by many mine owners until the end of the century.

On reporting to work on 16 August 1931, the miners at Auchinraith Colliery found a notice posted at the pithead advising them to collect and remove their tools as the company was closing down that evening at the end of the day shift. At a stroke, 300 to 400 miners employed at the colliery lost their jobs.

Demolition of Bridge at Whistleberry Road.

Merry's Rows were demolished and renamed Elm Street. The site of the colliery and its coal 'bing' extended from Auchinraith Road to the ground at the rear of Inglis Works, Main Street, opposite Priestfield Industrial Estate.

SEE COLLIERIES (C)

Auchinraith Colliery Explosion

Auchinraith Colliery Explosion occurred at 7.40a.m. on 30 August 1930 and claimed the lives of six miners. The blast occurred 750 yards from the main shaft, in 'Dunsmuir's Section', at the 'Long Wall' in the Blackband Seam. Seven other miners were seriously injured in the explosion. A Government Inquiry into the explosion commenced in Hamilton on Tuesday 11 November 1930, during which 41 witnesses were called to give evidence. The colliery manager was Mr David Gemmell.

Prior to the explosion, considerable gas problems had arisen during the month of May. Firemen had reported gas in Dunsmuir's Section ten days before the blast. No further gas reports were logged in the safety book after 20 August. Fireman Thomas Heggison stated that he found firedamp (gas) in No.1 and No.2 branch roads off 'Jack's Slope' on the day before the explosion, but did not report it as it was not found during his inspection prior to the next shift coming in to work. This discovery of gas should have been reported. It was claimed by some miners that fireman William Sproat did not test for firedamp before he fired the shot that triggered the explosion.

The Inquiry found that all five firemen and all miners neglected their duties that morning. In particular, three firemen had neglected to test for firedamp over a radius of 20 yards from a work place. It was established that a firedamp test was carried out but only in a radius of 20 feet from the coalface. Regulations stated that incombustible stone dust must be spread within an area where coal was being extracted, but miner Robert Clelland claimed in evidence that no incombustible dust was available before firing the shot that morning.

The Inquiry also found that the colliery manager neglected his duty by failing to ensure that the Provisions of the Explosives in Coal Mines Order were enforced in Auchinraith Colliery.

The names of the miners who were killed were:

Richard Dunsmuir, 9 Small Crescent, Blantyre died from his wounds on 31 August 1930
Andrew Kalinsky, 20 Merry's Rows, Blantyre
Richard King, 182 Main Street, High Blantyre
Joseph Regan, 7 Watson Street, Blantyre
George Shorthouse, 10 Russell Street, Burnbank
William Sproat, 2 Auchinraith Terrace, Blantyre

Those injured were:

John Smith, Merry's Rows, Blantyre
William Stoddart, Auchinraith Road, Blantyre
John Wildman, Beckford Street, Hamilton
James Russell, 74 Russell Street, Burnbank
Robert Buchanan, 58 Craig Street, Blantyre
Alex Paterson, 21 Merry's Rows, Blantyre
John Copeland c/o McKerrel, Redmore Place, Blantyre

Auchinraith Junction

A railway spur from Low Blantyre Station (q.v.) to High Blantyre Station (q.v.) was opened in 1882 by the Caledonian Railway to provide a direct train service between Glasgow and Strathaven via High Blantyre and Hamilton (Little Earnock). This section of railway line also had sidings into the pits at Dixon's Collieries at Priestfield. The line branched off the main Glasgow/ Low Blantyre railway and crossed a bridge where the East Kilbride Expressway now spans Glasgow Road. Adjacent and to the east of this bridge, a second bridge brought another branch line from Hamilton West. This was known as the Craighead Junction and approached Blantyre from behind Robertson's Aerated Waters, Springwells and crossed over the bridge at Glasgow Road at the corner of Whistleberry Road. The line from this point became a single track and continued parallel to Auchinraith Road. This section was known as the Auchinraith Junction, and crossed a third bridge over Craig Street (adjacent to Anford Place), then continued around the cemetery wall to cross a fourth bridge over Broompark Road adjacent to Broompark Farm (q.v.) and Dr Jope's residence (q.v.) at Broompark House (now the site of John Ogilvie RC Church). Thereafter it crossed a fifth bridge at the corner of Stonefield Crescent and Hunthill Road, then swung round behind the old High Blantyre Primary School and crossed a sixth bridge over Main Street adjacent to the Old Parish Church and into High Blantyre Station.

The photograph shows the demolition of the bridge in the 1980s at the corner of Whistleberry Road/ Glasgow Road that brought the line from Hamilton West Station up to High Blantyre Station.

SEE RAILWAYS (R)

Auchinraith Primary School, c.1900.

Auchinraith Nursery

Auchinraith Nursery was also known as Campbell's Nursery and was located on the corner of Auchinraith Road and Main Street, High Blantyre. Nurseries such as Auchinraith provided employment for the locals in the summer months. Produce was sold locally but the vast majority went to the Glasgow market. Kirkton House, home for the elderly, now occupies the site.

Auchinraith Primary School

Auchinraith Primary School was situated on the site of Anford Place sheltered housing complex at the corner of Craig Street and the old section of Auchinraith Road towards Logan Street. The school was constructed in 1899-1900 and designed by a Motherwell architect named Alex Cullen, costing £7,500. It had ten classrooms, opened on 13 August 1900 at 3p.m., and enrolled 650 pupils. Two new classrooms were built in 1905. The first headmaster was Mr Joseph McNish, who died in 1903 and was succeeded by Mr John Welsh. Mr James Brown, in turn, succeeded Mr Welsh as headmaster of the school. James Brown was called to serve his country in the First World War, enlisted in the army in 1914 and served as a captain, leading the Blantyre Territorials of the 6th Scottish Rifles. James was killed in action on 16 June 1915 while leading his men at Festubert. A letter to Captain Brown's family from one of his wounded men informs them, 'Our Captain died a hero's death.' Wounded in the shoulder, he got back to his feet and encouraged his men forward shouting, 'Stick it Blantyre.'

He was then shot in the head but still went forward until he was killed at the edge of the enemy trench.

The extreme right of the school in the photograph on p.11, is the side of the school that can be seen in the background of the photograph below.

Auchinraith Row

Built in 1874-5, Auchinraith Row was a single row of tied miners houses situated in a cul-de-sac which sat to the east of the Timber Houses on Auchinraith Road. The original Auchinraith Road turned left down under a railway bridge, then curved right at the top of Craig Street between the railway and Auchinraith School (now the site of Anford Place sheltered housing complex), and past the top of Logan Street. The road was realigned straight through the cul-de-sac and the old section of Auchinraith Road adjacent to the school was blocked off at the top of Logan Street.

The houses consisted of a room and kitchen with a shared outside toilet, a washhouse and a communal well. Messrs Merry and Cunningham owned the row and the colliery situated behind the houses. At the time of writing, the site of the old colliery is being prepared for the construction of new houses, which are to be known as Victoria Gardens. The entrance to the new estate stands on the site of Auchinraith Row. In the photograph, the row, which contained the majority of the houses, ran to the left, on what is now Auchinraith Road, and was parallel to the railway line and Auchinraith School, which can be seen in the background.

Auchinraith Row.

Barnhill.

Baiamund de Vicci

Baiamund de Vicci was an Italian ecclesiastic but was known in Scotland as Bagimund. In the 13th century he was sent to Scotland as an emissary of the Pope to collect the taxes set on Scottish religious benefices to finance the crusades. He would have been familiar with Blantyre Priory (q.v.) as it was on his list which was known as the 'Ragman's Roll'. (q.v.)

Baillie, Joanna

Born 1762. Died 1851.

Joanna Baillie, the famous Bothwell poet, was friendly with Janet Miller, the daughter of Professor John Miller of Millheugh, Blantyre (q.v.). She often stayed with her friend at Millheugh House. Miss Miller practised carpentry among other things, which was considered a very unusual hobby for a genteel young lady of that time. She built herself a heather-thatched stone bower on the banks of the River Calder, in which she pursued her craft. Joanna wrote a poem describing her friend and the Bower of Millheugh, situated near the waterfall:

> *This is no haunt of contemplation*
> *Nor bower in which their dear potation,*
> *Of Easter herbs fair ladies sip*
> *With sparkling eye and glowing lip,*

> *This is a bower of industry.*
> *Yet think not here within to spy*
> *On table laid or wicker seat,*
> *No, here the hammers' active din*
> *Blends with the sound of roaring lin,*
> *Where brawling Calder hastens through*
> *The shady holms of sweet Millheugh*
> *Here from plain'd board the shavings rife*
> *And like sunned mist the sawdust flies,*
> *But scarce a lady of the land*
> *May own a smaller fairer hand,*
> *Than she who neath this roof's cool shade*
> *Plies fitfully her chosen trade,*
> *With skilful slight and eager eye*
> *A female amateur of carpentry.*

The words of this poem were copied from a wooden plaque which was once fixed to the wall of the bower of Millheugh. The plaque was gifted to the Kirk Session of Bothwell Parish Church in 1849.

Baird, William Arthur

William Baird was the grandson of Charles Walter Stewart, the twelfth and last Lord Blantyre (q.v.). He inherited the family seat of Lennoxlove House at Haddington from his mother. She had previously inherited the house on the death of her father on 15 December 1900.

Baird's Rows

Baird's Rows consisted of three rows of tied miners cottages belonging to Craighead Colliery (q.v.). Purdie Builders of Coatbridge commenced construction of the houses in April 1878, in the area at present occupied by Park's bus company, between Forrest Street, Glasgow Road and the East Kilbride Expressway. Water was supplied to the houses from Craighead Pit. The houses were numbered but there were no street names.

Bardykes/Bardykes House

From 25 October 1525 the lands of Bardykes were the possession of the Jackson family, and they remained so for over 400 years. Bardykes House and grounds are located off Callaghan Drive at Bardykes Road at the 'West End' of Glasgow Road. The original agreement on the feu duty for the land of Bardykes stated that,

Bardykes House.

when required, the proprietor must present a red rose to Lord Blantyre.

When the highlanders of Bonnie Prince Charlie's army were returning north after the unsuccessful expedition into England to place the Prince on the British throne, many of the stragglers passed through Blantyre, just as they did when they marched south at the beginning of the ill-fated march. To prevent the highlanders from pillaging his house in search of food, the Laird of Bardykes ensured there was an ample supply of bannocks and whisky at the gates of Bardykes House for the hungry soldiers. The present house was constructed *c.*1900.

Bardyke Mill

Bardyke Mill was also known as the Black Mill. Its remains and lade can still be seen on the River Calder adjacent to

the old Priory Bridge at the West End, Glasgow Road, beyond the housing estate at Callaghan Drive.
SEE ASTRICTED MILLS (A)

Barnhill

Barnhill was one of the original hamlets or fermetouns (q.v.) of the Barony of Blantyre, and was situated at the junction of Broompark Road, Bardykes Road and Hunthill Road. The original road into Blantyre from Glasgow was along Loanend Road from Dalton and turned left, before Malcolmwood farm, down through the field which is the site of 'Queen Mary's Well' (q.v.) to Pattonholm Ford (q.v.). After crossing the river it continued along a field known as 'The Peth', and up the Peth Brae into Bardykes Road. Thatched cottages sat among the trees behind the right-hand wall at the top of the Brae, facing Broompark Road. Some of the foundations of these cottages can still be seen today. The original wall at the top left of the Peth Brae was approximately ten feet high and extended into the middle of the present road. Tucked in behind this wall was Stewart's Cottage, on what now serves as a car park for the *Barnhill Tavern* (*Hoolet's Nest pub*, q.v.). The front door of the house faced the Peth Brae wall and its left gable faced Bardykes Road. The house was also known as 'the Weavers Cottage', as it contained a handloom, as did many of the old original cottages in the barony. Stewart's Cottage was named after the weaver who, at one time, lived and worked there.

Before the construction of the Blantyre Mills in 1785, the only form of industry in the area, other than farming and the six mills on the River Calder, was cottage handloom weaving. Stewart's Cottage was the first of a line of thatched cottages that ran east from the top of the Peth Brae for approximately one hundred yards down Bardykes Road. The last house, known as Jock Stein's Cottage (q.v.), was where Jock bred pigs in his pigsty. The middle section of these houses was demolished, and Dixon's Tenement was constructed sometime in the 1870s directly across from Aggie Bain's Cottage (q.v.) and the *Hoolet's Nest*. The site of the tenement is also part of the *Hoolet's Nest* car park.

The present lane between Aggie Bain's Cottage and the *Hoolet's Nest*, leading to Glenfruin Road, was once the top of the only road down to the River Clyde from Blantyre Village (Kirkton/High Blantyre Cross). It skirted Wheatlandhead Farm and crossed what is now Glasgow Road into the Holmswood Avenue area, and

Barnhill, c.1900.

on down over what was then Blantyre Moor to the Clyde at Blantyre Priory opposite Bothwell Castle, where a ferry once crossed the river.

Adjacent to the *Hoolet's Nest*, directly opposite the top of the Peth Brae, was the 'Back O' The Barns'. Another building, known as 'Barn's End', was situated behind the Back O' The Barns, next to an area of grassland called the 'Dry Well Green' that was used for drying and bleaching cloths. There were also other cottages behind the Back O' The Barns and the *Hoolet's Nest*.

Brown's Nursery was the first cottage in a row of thatched houses that ran along the right-hand side of Broompark Road, away from Barnhill, to the Smiddy, adjacent to the present High Blantyre Primary School. Carved on the walls of Brown's property at the corner of Broompark Road and Hunthill Road were directions to Blantyre Kirk and Hamilton. These two direction stones can still be seen today built into the garden wall at the corner of Broompark Road and Hunthill Road.

Barnhill Nursery

Mr Arthur Brown established Barnhill Nursery in 1834. The nursery, which was founded long before the nurseries of Clydeside, was located in old thatched buildings at the corner of Hunthill Road and Broompark Road. Most of the produce was sold locally and in the surrounding districts, but large quantities were also sold in Glasgow. Mr Brown planted and grew strawberries on the Calder Braes below Barnhill and the Cottage Hospital at Bardykes Road. During the winter months, known as the 'Slack Time', he grew willows on the banks of the River Calder. These were used for making baskets of all sizes.

Barnhill Smiddy

Barnhill Smiddy is situated in Broompark Road adjacent to the present High Blantyre Primary School. The last blacksmith to own and work in the Smiddy was a Mr Templeton who inherited the property from his father. Mr William Morrison, who converted the property into a motor vehicle engineering business, now owns the Smiddy. The date of the construction of the Smiddy is unknown but it is probable that it was built within 50 or 100 years of the construction of Aggie Bain's Cottage, which was built in 1536. These two properties are all that remain of the original hamlet of Barnhill. It was Mr Templeton the elder who assisted the inventor Thomas Taylor in the construction of his 'flying machine', at the Smiddy in 1860.

SEE AEROPLANE I (A)

Barr, Captain George S.

Captain Barr, a veteran of the First World War, was a prominent citizen in the affairs of Blantyre. He resided in a tenement in Hunthill Road near the corner of Stonefield Crescent, and was a member of the High

Bethany Hall, Glasgow Road, c.1910.

Blantyre Ratepayers Association. He also stood for election to the Parish County Council.

Barracks

The Barracks was a tenement complex at Main Street, directly opposite Broompark Road, and was located behind the modern shops and the old Co-op tenement. In 1926 the properties had become run down and deemed unfit for human habitation and most of them were demolished in 1927-8.

Barrack Children

SEE BLANTYRE MILLS/WORKS (B)

Basket Cross

The Basket Cross was an ancient religious monument that once stood adjacent to Stoneymeadow Road opposite Aller's Farm, Stoneymeadow. It is thought that a monastery existed near this spot, as a large ancient circular cemetery can still be seen at Stoneymeadow, among the trees adjacent to the East Kilbride Expressway opposite Dalton Road end. It is believed to contain the graves of the monks of the monastery.

Beadle

In days gone by, one of the important duties of the Beadle of the church was to announce at the 'skailing' of the Kirk, crying out any current or forthcoming events to the worshippers as they were leaving. It was the only means of informing the population of current events from an official source. For example, he would announce what day Lord Blantyre's factor would be in the area to gather the rents, or that certain items were up for sale such as the hind quarter of a 'Mairt' that had to be disposed of, or a hay stack, or field of beans and other unusual items. One such announcement was: 'This is to give notice that there was found on the Sydes an empty sack with a cheese at the bottom of it, whoever has lost the same, by applying to me will get it.'

Beggs' Building

Beggs' tenement stood on Main Street opposite Cemetery Road and was originally known as Lint Butts. It was a small tenement which contained the local chemists shop at its east gable and was known as the 'Apothecary Hall'.

Bethany Hall

The Blantyre Primitive Methodist Church, which originally held its services in Dixon's Hall in Stonefield Road, constructed this building in Glasgow Road in 1905. The church closed during the First World War and was unused until purchased and opened by the Stonefield Independent Co-operative Society in 1925 when it was used for various purposes, such as a dance hall and subsequently as an Unemployment Exchange until approximately 1930. The Christian Brethren then purchased it in 1936 and renamed the premises 'The Bethany Hall'. The Christian Brethren sold the hall to the World of Life Christian Fellowship on 16 December 1996. The Bethany Hall is seen at the left of the photograph and is still extant.

Birdsfield Wagon Works

The company of Messrs Alexander Ingles, located on Main Street directly opposite High Blantyre Industrial Estate, was originally known as Birdsfield Wagon Works, High Blantyre. When the passenger railway line to Glasgow from Hamilton, and Burnbank via Bothwell, closed in September 1952, it was announced that a branch of that line would continue in use as a single track to serve Birdsfield Wagon Works.

Black Agnes, the Lady of Blantyre

SEE THOMAS RANDOLPH, 1ST EARL OF MORAY (R)

Black Mill

SEE BARDYKE MILL (B)

Blantyre

The origin of the name Blantyre is unknown, but various suggestions have been put forward. Bronze-Age remains, dating from 2500 BC, have been found in and around High Blantyre Cross (the original village of Blantyre), indicating that the town may have existed in some form or other since that time. Before explaining my theories as to the definition of the name, it is important to lay out the historical events that occurred in our area between 2500 BC and the first mention of the name Blantyre in 1275 AD, when Blantyre Priory was included in a list of Scottish ecclesiastical establishments which were taxed by Pope Clement IV to finance yet another crusade against the Saracens. There was no consistent spelling of names until early in the 18th century and during that time various spellings of Blantyre appeared. From the Bronze Age until approximately the 9th century AD, ancient British tribes inhabited all of Britain. They spoke an ancient form of the Welsh language, the oldest in Europe. The Romans occupied all of England and southern Scotland but were unable to subdue the tribes north of the Rivers Forth and Clyde. These wild northern people painted their bodies and were called 'Picti' by the Romans, which meant 'painted man'. After the departure of the Romans from Britain after the end of

the fourth century, the country lapsed into a period known as the Dark Ages.

Historians inform us that these ancient people worshipped nature, and that the sun was the father spirit who gave light, heat and life to their world. Their place of worship was the kirk and their standing stones, erected around their sacred sites, were probably an imitation of the sun. The stones were arranged in circular form, and perhaps suggested rays of light and heat emitting from the sun. These circles may well have been the prototype of our kirkyard and Christian churches constructed on these sacred sites.

It is recorded by the Venerable Bede that in 1601 Pope Gregory issued the following Bull:

> All the temples of the idols of that nation ought not to be destroyed; let water be consecrated and sprinkled in the said temples, let altars be erected and relics placed there. For if those temples are well built, it is requisite that they be converted from worship of devils to the service of the true God. They should build themselves huts of the boughs of the trees about those churches which have been turned to that use from being temples and celebrate the solemnity with religious feasting and offer no more animals to the Devil, but kill cattle and glorify God in their feast.

The word 'Kirk' means a circle and comes from the root *circ* (hard c) which in Latin means 'circus'. In old Scots it meant a 'circle of stones' or a round barrow, i.e. a circular burial place. There is a strong probability that Blantyre Kirkyard (q.v.), although altered with the passage of time, was originally a sacred site of the ancient people and was converted for Christian use as instructed by Pope Gregory.

Sign formerly sited at the entrances to Blantyre.

The Blantyre area was part of the kingdom of Cumbria inhabited by the Damnonii tribe whose southern boundary was the River Ribble in Lancashire, England. Their northern boundary was the River Clyde, where they established their northern capital and named it Alcluyd, two Welsh words meaning 'Rock of Clyde'. Most town names are descriptive, as was Alcluyd, which described its location upon Dumbarton Rock. The present-day name for Alcluyd is Dumbarton and was derived from the Gaelic-speaking Scots who, having left Ireland and settled in western Scotland, referred to Alcluyd as Dun-Briton meaning 'Fort of the Britons', a descriptive Gaelic reference to the Welsh citadel.

I believe it is possible that the village of Blantyre was an ancient British settlement around the Old Blantyre Kirkyard at High Blantyre Cross, which may originally have been a druid circle. The kirkyard appears to be a man-made, eight- to ten-foot high circular mound of earth which, if it were a 'druid circle', would have been the centre of the inhabitants' religious activities.

In my opinion it is almost certain that the village of Blantyre (Kirkton) existed before King Alexander II established the Blantyre Priory sometime during his reign (1214-49), the proof being that the King endowed the Priory with the revenues and tithes of Blantyre Parish Church. There is no evidence to suggest that there was any church in Blantyre at that time other than the original one which stood in the Old Kirkyard at High Blantyre.

The inscriptions on the 16th-century communion cups belonging to the Old Parish Church have no letter 'E' in the spelling of Blantyre and it is possible that the old spelling 'Blantyr' inscribed on the cups is a Gaelic corruption of an original Welsh name 'Llantyr', which contains two words, 'llan' meaning consecrated, and 'tyr' meaning ground or land, the consecrated ground being what is now the Old Kirkyard. Blaentir was another old spelling of the name of our town and this could also provide the definition of the town's name: the Welsh word 'blaen' means front, which gives us the interpretation – 'Front-Land'.

The Scots expanded their kingdom of Dalriada in the west of Scotland to include the territories south of the Clyde in the Old Kingdom of Cumbria, better known as the kingdom of the Strathclyde Britons. The Britons were forced further south and, along with other British tribes in conflict with incoming races such as the Gaels

Blantyre Ambulance outside Caldergrove House.

and the Anglo-Saxons, members of west German tribes that had settled on what is now the north-east coast of England, and finally settled the territory that is now Wales. The subjugated Britons who remained in the Blantyre area would be integrated within the society of the victorious Scots and converted to Christianity, and the first Blantyre church would be constructed on their 'llan tyr', the Old Blantyre Kirkyard. The Bishop of Glasgow stated in the 14th century that the barbaric tongue (Welsh) was still being spoken in some sheltered areas of the 'See of Strathclyde'.

Until the discovery of coal and the opening of various collieries within the parish in the 1870s, Blantyre was a typical attractive rural village. It quickly changed as the primitive dirt tracks were unable to cope with the cartloads of coal being transported from the collieries, and were turned into quagmires. The construction of railway sidings into the collieries relieved the congestion and the wear and tear on the old roads, which were later widened and improved.

There was little or no thought given to the design or architecture of most of the tenements that were hastily constructed to service the inhabitants of this new boom-town, and the area gained a reputation as being a rather somber place, probably because of the black smoke emitting from the colliery chimney stacks. There is no doubt that the town's appearance would now be rather bleak when compared to its appearance in the rural days. For many years, Blantyre had been regarded as a fine healthy invigorating district and many visitors came from the cities to recuperate from illness. Hundreds of people from Glasgow and surrounding districts flocked to Auchentibber to 'take the waters', which were thought to have curative properties for many diseases. It was said that the water tasted and smelled of rotten eggs. Access to these healing waters was improved in July 1885 when the Glasgow-Blantyre railway line was extended to East Kilbride from Hunthill Junction, after which travellers could alight at Calderside Halt near Stoneymeadow and make their way from there to Auchentibber and Calderside.

William Miller, the Glasgow poet best known for his nursery rhyme 'Wee Willie Winkie', recuperated in Blantyre in 1871 after a serious illness, and described the town in the following line:

'Fair Blantyre rises beautiful as song.'

David Livingstone also described his birthplace as:

'The sweet and pretty village of Blantyre.'

Coat of arms of the Hamiltons of Blantyreferme.

Blantyre, Mary

SEE BROWNLIE FAMILY (B)

Blantyreferme

Blantyreferme was one of the original 'Fermetouns' (q.v.) of the old parish of Blantyre. A gate now closes off the original road to Blantyreferme, where Blantyrefarm Road turns sharp left a few hundred yards beyond the Priory football pitches opposite Bothwell Castle. At one time this was a favourite walk of the inhabitants of Blantyre.

It is recorded in an ancient document that Thomas Hamilton had purchased the lands of Fremblantyre, around the year 1400, from Dunbar of Enterkin. The names of Hamilton's descendants are recorded until the last member of the family died unmarried in 1773 and was succeeded by his sister's son, James Coats. The spelling of the name of their land in the family documents was 'Blanterferme'. The illustration shows the Coat of Arms of the Hamiltons of Blantyreferme.

Blantyre Ambulance

Caldergrove House, which burned down in 1983, stood adjacent to the Spittal Bridge at the West End of Glasgow Road, and was used as a convalescent home for wounded soldiers during the First World War. The picture, taken at the front entrance of Caldergrove House, shows the ambulance that was purchased by money donated by the people of Blantyre.

Caldergrove was a very substantial house and was last lived in by two elderly sisters. It contained many wonderful antiques and a large collection of stuffed rare tropical birds.

SEE WADDELL FAMILY (W)

Blantyre-Bothwell Railway and Pedestrian Viaduct

This viaduct crossed the River Clyde and carried the London, Northern and Eastern Railway (LNER) line between the stations of Burnbank and Bothwell. The line ran under Whistleberry Road and past the Craighead pit

Blantyre-Bothwell Viaduct.

'bing' to the Blantyre-Bothwell Viaduct which was 120 feet high. The viaduct was the first of many bridges built by the famous Sir William Arrol of Glasgow. Pedestrians crossed the bridge inside an enclosed section directly under the railway track, which was a noisy, nerve-racking experience when a train was crossing above. The wheels of prams and bicycles would slip through the gaps between the timber planks that formed the pedestrian walkway, adding to the apprehension of those who crossed.

The LNER did not have a passenger station in Blantyre, but the London Midland Scottish Railway (LMS) had a large goods station at Whistleberry Road, situated at the entrance to the present Whistleberry Industrial Estate. Racehorses were disembarked at Whistleberry Goods Station and walked down through the woods at the east side of Whistleberry Road to Hamilton Race Course at Bothwell Road.

The railway line over the viaduct closed in 1952 but remained open to pedestrians for some time afterwards.

Blantyre Bowling Club

The original bowling green, established in 1872, was evidently smaller than the present green. The *Hamilton Advertiser* reported that a new green was opened on 10 May 1878 by Dr Grant, which would suggest that the smaller green had simply been enlarged to its present size. Later a tennis court was added on land adjacent to the church manse. The tennis club was disbanded before 1960 and the ground was then used as a car park for the Bowling Club.

Blantyre Burgh

Three referendums were held in an attempt to turn Blantyre into a burgh, but on each occasion the proposition failed.

SEE MAJOR JOHN NESS (N)

Blantyre Castle – Fortalice

It is said that a castle once stood in the old village of Blantyre. It is mentioned in a book by Martin Coventry called *Castles of Scotland*, which states that Blantyre Castle, which had a moat, stood in a district called Old Place, near the Old Parish Church, and was demolished before 1800, with the surrounding area then turned into a farm.

An ancient Scottish charter granted the Tower and Fortalice of Blantyre permission to hold a market day once a week. The Tower and Fortalice mentioned in this document may refer to the Tower of Crossbasket House (q.v), but if the existence of Blantyre Castle can be confirmed it is almost certain that the charter was issued to the structure that stood at Old Place. I have found no evidence for it other than the record in the ancient charter and it may well be that the structure was only a fortified house. It is not recorded on any of the old maps of the town, but Old Place was recorded and was indeed a farm. The following streets, Stonefield Crescent, Stonefield Place, Springfield Crescent, Janefield Place and Greenhall Place now occupy the original fields of the farm.

Access to the farmhouse was along a dirt track that ran parallel to the old railway line, the entrance being close to the railway bridge that carried the line over Hunthill Road. The houses between Nos 27 to 65 Stonefield Crescent now stand on the old railway line which separated the farm track from the area that is now Stonefield Crescent. Houses at Nos 36 and 38 Hunthill Road stand at the original location of the entrance to the old farm track. The address of the present house on the site, still known as 'Old Place House', is 12 Janefield Place. The house was constructed in 1762, and replaced the original farmhouse on the supposed site of Blantyre Castle.

Blantyre Celtic Football Club

Blantyre Celtic Football Club was inaugurated in 1916. They played their home games at Craighead Park, which was located between the Blantyre Greyhound Racing Stadium (adjacent to the East Kilbride Expressway) and Castle Park, the home ground of Blantyre Victoria Football Club in Forrest Street. The area that contained the pitch is adjacent to Park's Bus Depot. The stadium could hold 3,000 people, and the record attendance was in season 1951-2, when a capacity crowd attended a Scottish Junior Cup tie against Johnston Burgh. In their formative years Celtic played in the Lanarkshire Intermediate League before being admitted to the Lanarkshire Junior League, which later amalgamated with the Central Junior League. The club folded when Celtic resigned from the league in 1988 owing to the fact that they could not fulfill their league matches because of financial difficulties.

The player who made the most appearances for Celtic was Danny Malloy, who played in 300 games between 1946 and 1949. Dennis Logie scored the most goals in one season when he netted 30 in 1948-9. Celtic's best run in the Scottish Junior Cup was when they reached the semi-final in seasons 1937-8 and 1946-7.

Two players of distinction who started their careers with the 'Wee Celts' were Dougie Fraser, who signed for Aberdeen, and the legendary Jimmy (Jinky) Johnstone of Glasgow Celtic. In 1963 the great Jock Stein farmed out Jimmy to the Blantyre club when he was manager of Glasgow Celtic. Jimmy was capped by the Scottish Juniors in 1963 before going on to have an illustrious career with the Glasgow giants and playing a significant part when Celtic (the Lisbon Lions) became the first British team to win the European Cup in 1967. Jimmy Johnstone played for Scotland on 22 occasions. He later joined Elgin City for a short spell before being reinstated back to Blantyre Celtic in 1981. He retired due to injury approximately six months later, bringing the career of one of the all-time greats of Scottish football to an end.

A well-known local man, Willie Chassells, who played for six junior teams, had the rare distinction of playing for both Blantyre Celtic and Blantyre Vics. He coached various junior and amateur teams before returning to coach Celtic between 1981 and 1985. Willie ended his football career when he retired after four years as physio with the Scottish Amateur Football Association.

Blantyre Colliery Explosion Dixon's No.1 Pit, 2 July 1879

Barely eighteen months after the explosion in October 1877 (q.v.), disaster struck the community once again, at Dixon's Colliery, High Blantyre, at 9.10pm., on Wednesday 2 July 1879, this time in No. 1 pit. Fortunately the loss of life was not on the same scale as the 'Calamity', but nevertheless it claimed the lives of another 28 miners.

After the day shift had left the pit by 4p.m., the firemen inspected the work places and found no signs of gas. All the victims were 'Brushers', who checked in then descended the pit at approximately 6p.m. to inspect all the workings during the night shift and clear and repair any faults in readiness for the Thursday shift workers.

Since the great explosion of 1877, only safety lamps were used, these being the Clanny and Davy variety. No. 1 Pit was thought to have been clear of gas for some considerable time but, as events turned out, this was not the case. The explosion occurred in the evening in the Ell coal workings as the men were using dynamite to remove an expanse of stonework. A loud report was heard at the pithead, which some men on the surface thought was an explosion within the main shaft.

Firedamp had been reported only once during the three months prior to the accident, when it was detected in the No. 2 heading on 19 May. The owners claimed they had taken every precaution to prevent pipes, tobacco or matches being taken into the workings, or the lamps being tampered with, and several prosecutions had taken place against miners for breach of these rules. The last case was against a miner named John McLean on the day before the explosion, when he was tried at Hamilton Sheriff Court and fined £2 for opening his safety lamp.

James Bennet, the engine-man, and Alexander McMillan were startled by a loud rumbling noise which, according to the engine-man, was like the sharp detonation of a charge of dynamite. The majority of the 161 miners working underground were unaware that an explosion had occurred, and 129 of them reached safety without injury. The first observation of the explosion was by the pithead man of No. 1 pit, who heard a sharp report and saw a little dust coming up the shaft and a slight movement of the cage. He immediately ran for John White, the Oversman, who lived in Priestfield Row, about 150 metres from the pithead. White was at the shaft about 9.30p.m., and he sent the empty cage down the shaft but, finding that it stuck fast at the Ell coal level, proceeded with other volunteers down No. 3 pit shaft to gain access via a communication passage. Shortly afterwards they were joined by Mr Watson, the colliery manager, and steps were taken to ascertain the seat of the explosion and rescue the 31 men known to be in the south side workings.

The first man found was the lamp-trimmer, who was still alive, in the wrecked lamp-station. He was able to explain that the blast came inwards upon him but was so severely injured that he died before he could be taken up to the surface. An attempt was made to push further into the level, and a point about 350 metres from the shaft was reached without seeing any other person. All the brick stoppings on the side of the level road were blown out. The roof was considerably damaged and had fallen at various points. Unable to proceed any further, the volunteers were forced back by the strength of the after-damp.

About 3a.m., when the after-damp had dispersed sufficiently to allow them to continue the rescue attempt, they passed several bodies lying on the level road. When they reached the head of the dook, they found five men who were still alive. One died as he was being taken out, but the other four were got out by about 4a.m. One of the four died later from his injuries. The air was still affected by after-damp but it did not prevent the rescuers from retrieving all but four of the victims. About 11a.m, when no further progress could be made because of the firedamp, it was decided that the search should be abandoned, seeing that there was no likelihood of the four missing being alive, and that efforts should be undertaken to improve the ventilation before continuing the search. About 4a.m. on Friday the last four bodies were finally recovered and sent to the surface. Twelve of the victims were found to be burned, some slightly; the others died from chokedamp.

Owen, one of the survivors, stated that they were knocked over by the blast and all of them thought it proceeded from a shot, although his impression was that it was an explosion. It put all their lights out but, being within shouting distance of each other, they met at the top of the dook where the explorers found them. They discussed the situation and sat there for about twenty minutes until deciding that they should attempt to try to reach the shaft, but after twenty metres they were met with hot after-damp and forced to return to the dook. A second attempt was also unsuccessful, so they returned again to the head of the dook where, one by one, they became unconscious until recovered by the explorers. The three survivors stated that they never heard any sounds from the others.

The explorers searching the clothes of the deceased, especially those victims who were working near to where the gas was found, discovered pipes and tobacco, and by all appearances the men had been smoking. A pipe half-filled with tobacco was found in one hand; on others, lamp keys, matches and pipes proved, according to the proprietors, that they had paid little attention to the special rules which forbade these things being taken into the workings.

The names of the miners who died are as follows:

Peter Berry, aged 58, married, six children, resided Dixon's Rows.

James Bryson, aged 58, married, family, resided Dixon's Rows.

Tague Boyle, aged 22, single, resided Dixon's Rows.

Bernard Cairns, aged 23, single, resided Dixon's Rows. Rescued but died in the engine house.

Henry Duffy, aged 65, single, resided with James Bryson at Dixon's Rows.

Thomas Duffy or McDuff, aged 24, single, resided Dixon's Rows.

John Harvie, aged 44, married, resided Dixon's Rows. Originally from Partick, Glasgow.

Michael Howitt, aged 27, single, resided Dixon's Rows.

Thomas Irvine, aged 60, bottomer, married, grown-up family, resided Dixon's Rows.

Edward Jardine, aged 28, widower, resided Dixon's Rows.

James Lafferty, aged 46, fireman, married, family, resided Dixon's Rows.

Patrick Lynch, aged 30, single, resided Dixon's Rows.

John Malone, aged 38, married, five children, resided Dixon's Rows.

Alexander McArthur, aged 40, married, resided Calder Street, Dixon's Rows.

Patrick McGarvie, aged 55, married, resided Dixon's Rows.

Edward McGarvin, aged 23, single, resided Dixon's Rows.

Patrick McGribben, aged 58, married, grown-up family, resided Parkhead, Glasgow.

John McGuigan, aged 38, married, two children, resided Dixon's Rows.

Robert Mullen, aged 28, single, resided Bowie's Land, Stonefield.

John Murphy, aged 24, single, resided 24 Miller Street, Dixon's Rows.

John Newton, aged 60, single, Dixon's Rows. Rescued but died as he was being carried out.

Bernard O'Brian, aged 28, married, one child, resided Dixon's Rows.

John O'Neill, aged 32, married, three children, resided Dixon's Rows.

Richard Runn, aged 30, married, six children, resided Barnhill.

Alexander Symington, aged 24, single, resided Larkfield.

Edward Thomson, aged 31, married, six children, resided Larkfield.

Patrick Vallelly, aged 21, single, lodged with James Lafferty at Dixon's Rows.

John Wilson, aged ?, single, resided Stonefield.

The three survivors, when found, were unconscious and were brought to the surface by No. 2 pit shaft. Their names were:

Charles Lafferty, aged 18, single, son of James.

Bernard O'Neill, aged 27, single, brother of John.

James Owen, aged 52, married.

Blantyre Colliery Over-Winding Accident at Dixon's No. 3 Pit

On 5 March 1878, less than five months after the terrible events of the Blantyre Explosion in October 1877 (q.v.), six miners were killed at Dixon's Colliery when the cage in which they were returning to the pithead was involved in an accident which resulted in the miners falling down the shaft to their deaths. By comparison with the previous October, the loss was small, but nevertheless it turned three homes into houses of mourning. The cage, carrying seven occupants, was being raised to the surface when an incident known as 'over-winding' occurred. It was drawn over the 'whorles' and wrecked; six of those within were thrown to their deaths down the shaft, which was almost 1,000 feet deep. The sole survivor escaped without a scratch.

The shaft had two divisions, with one double cage in each section. The men finished work whenever they had successfully completed their allotted tasks and the accident occurred at 3.25p.m. when a hundred miners were at work within the labyrinths of No. 3 pit. Thirty-eight had been successfully raised to the pithead just prior to the accident. The cage passed the 'plates', the point where the men ought to have got out, went a

further twenty feet and crashed into the cross beams above the shaft where it was completely wrecked. The unfortunate miners fell to their deaths down the shaft with the exception of Robert Garrity, who managed to cling to the side of the wrecked cage.

At first it was thought there were only three men on board. An eyewitness named John Tracey, who had come up in the previous cage, told how he had seen one man plunge down the shaft and a second man attempt to leap off the cage before the collision but lose his footing and fall down the shaft. Tracy raised the alarm, shouting, 'The cage has gone over the whorles.'

James Paterson, an engineer at the colliery who was inside the Smiddy, rushed to the engine-house and, after noting the state of the cage indicator, ran to rescue Garrity from his position, which was still one of considerable danger. Other than shock, Garrity was found to be unhurt, and was able to walk to his home in Stonefield, Low Blantyre.

Mr Watson, the works manager, who still suffered from the severe burns sustained in the explosion of the previous October, was in his office with his assistant manager Robert Robson and J. T. Robson, the Assistant Government Inspector of Mines. On hearing the alarm, they quickly assessed the situation and established that in fact six men had fallen down the shaft. Robson assembled a rescue party but all knew there was no hope that any survivors would be found. They gained access to the bottom of the shaft via the communication passage between No. 2 and No. 3 pits. Little debris was found and there was no sign of the bodies. It was obvious they were in the sump, which was directly under the shaft and 16 feet deep. Grappling irons were used to drag the water of the sump and recover the unfortunate victims.

When Paterson, the engineer, returned to the engine-house to investigate the readings on the cage indicators, he found they had been altered, as they did not correspond with the readings he had made earlier. He advised the Engine Keeper, Arthur Clelland, who had no duties other than ensuring the safe passage of the cage, to stay at his post. Clelland refused and made his way home by a short cut through the surrounding fields. A lad named Richard Lyon observed that he had 'shifted' and cleaned himself and was making his way towards Glasgow and, on hearing this information, Mr Watson sent the boy to inform the police of what he had seen. Constable Jeffrey went in pursuit of Clelland, and after overtaking him took him into custody. The next day the Sheriff committed him to prison, pending further investigation, on a charge of culpable homicide or culpable neglect of duty. Much sympathy was felt for Clelland, considering his previous good conduct. I found nothing to indicate that he was ever brought to trial.

The names of the unfortunate miners who died were as follows:

Patrick Houghnie, aged 36, who resided at Ann Street, Burnbank.

Martin Houghnie, aged 16, who resided at Ann Street, Burnbank.

Patrick Hopkins, aged 20, a lodger at Ann Street, Burnbank.

Thomas Murdoch, aged 48, who resided at 1 Dixon Street, Blantyre.

Robert Murdoch, aged 20, who resided at 1 Dixon Street, Blantyre.

Michael Currie, aged 38, who resided at Gardener's Place, Auchinraith, Blantyre.

The victims were a group of family and friends who worked together. Thomas Murdoch had lost a son in the Great Disaster in 1877, and now he perished along with another son, Robert. He left a wife and five other children. The Houghnies, and their lodger Patrick Hopkins, had only recently arrived in the district from Durham. They had commenced work in the pit eight days prior to the accident.

Michael Currie, who had also recently moved into Blantyre, left a wife and three children. His daughter was due to be married to Patrick Hopkins.

Blantyre-East Kilbride Railway Viaduct

The Caledonian Railway Company constructed a new section of railway line to link East Kilbride with the Blantyre-Strathavon line. A massive building programme was undertaken to construct the Blantyre-East Kilbride Viaduct to carry the railway across the River Calder. A second bridge was built adjacent to the existing Strathavon Line Bridge, over Hunthill Road at the corner of Stonefield Crescent, to carry the new track to the viaduct. The line was opened in 1885. The railway line at the adjoining bridges was known as Hunthill Junction. The Blantyre-East Kilbride line closed in 1935 and the top of the viaduct was removed soon after.

SEE RAILWAYS (R)

Blantyre Engineering Company

In 1878 a Mr Topping, Iron Founder of Coatbridge, established Blantyre Engineering Company, which was known locally as 'the Foundry'. The company, later owned and managed by Patrick and David Kelly, manufactured machinery mainly for the coalmining industry. Situated at the bottom of Forrest Street, adjacent to the railway, it prospered because of an ideal location in the middle of the Lanarkshire coalfield. The business expanded and was soon receiving orders and contracts from throughout Britain and Europe. When the coalfields were finally worked out, the company, like the collieries, closed in the mid-1960s.

Blantyre Explosion 22 October 1877

Blantyre has made its mark on history as the birthplace of the great missionary and explorer David Livingstone, a fact of which the community is rightly very proud. The town's other claim to fame is the Blantyre Explosion, the worst disaster in Scottish coalmining history. It is a claim to fame that we would willingly do without. Sadly, we cannot change history, but by studying the events of that terrible calamity, we can see the terrible conditions that the miners had to endure to earn their living, and also the consequences such a disaster had on their families and the community.

My initial interest in the event was to try and establish once and for all the exact number of miners killed that terrible day, 22 October 1877. Casualty totals varying between two and over three hundred have been suggested in various books and songs. A group from Blantyre Hertitage Group carried out research into newspaper reports of the day and the proceedings and report of the resultant Government Inquiry. The death certificates at HM Records Office were also examined and an important find by George Hay discovered six additional names. By checking and eliminating names from approximately three hundred and fifty casualties, our research indicated that 216 miners died as a result of the calamity.

This provided a great insight into the circumstances and events surrounding the Blantyre Explosion. A full and comprehensive account, including the detailed supporting evidence for declaring that 216 men and boys died, can be accessed at Hamilton Reference Library and Blantyre Reference Library (*Blantyre Explosion, Dixon's Colliery, Pits 2 and 3, 22 October 1877* by Neil Gordon). Below is a synopsis of the disastrous event.

Dixon's No. 2 Pit, Illustrated London News, *1877.*

It was a dull, wet and miserable day – 'driech' was the term used by the locals to describe the conditions that prevailed that morning. Everything was normal until approximately 8.45a.m., when the inhabitants at High Blantyre Cross and the surrounding areas felt a dull rumbling under their feet. They instinctively looked across Priestfield to Dixon's Collieries that stood on land adjacent to both sides of the present Hillhouse Road and were horrified to see a massive explosion soaring high above No. 3 shaft and smoke pouring from No. 2 shaft. Within minutes, day appeared to turn into night as the flames, debris and plumes of black smoke reaching hundreds of feet into the air blotted out any daylight.

Major Ness, the headmaster of Stonefield Public School, was in his room after supervising the commencement of classes, when a distraught woman rushed into the room crying, 'Maister, Maister, let the weans oot the school. Dixons has blasted and their faithers are awe deid.' An explosion unlike any other in Scottish mining history had occurred at Dixon's No. 2 and No. 3 collieries at High Blantyre.

The Rev. Stewart Wright was dressing in his bedroom in Blantyre Kirk Manse, when through his window, which overlooked the collieries, he saw a sudden flash dart up from No. 3 shaft and heard 'a report not very loud'. Immediately, a dense volume of smoke arose from No. 2 shaft. He described the horrific scene that unfolded before him and 'The blackness of darkness which spread itself like a terrible funeral pall over the surrounding plain.' He was soon at the scene of the disaster, where he waited for hours with hundreds of eager and terrified families and friends awaiting news of the entombed miners. He watched as gallant men

descended the pit, again and again, to rescue, if possible, their buried comrades, but in vain. They merely succeeded in bringing up a few dead bodies from No. 2 pit before they themselves were overcome by the 'chockdam' and had to be brought hurriedly to the surface, where some of the rescuers, more dead than alive, were revived with great difficulty. Still the volunteers came forward, no matter the dangers, demanding to be lowered down until a decision was taken near midnight that no more lives were to be risked. It was then realised by the anxious crowds at the pithead that there was no hope of their loved ones surviving and the magnitude of the calamity became apparent.

A number of hours after the explosion, hopes had been raised when, with great difficulty, 23 miners were rescued after escaping up the partially blocked No. 2 shaft, which was located near the North Level where they had been working. All emerged suffering from the effects of the after-damp. These men were forced to go home to recover but were back at the mine within a few hours to assist in the rescue attempts. Hugh Brown, one of the survivors, did not return home for over a week.

During the long wait for the recovery of the bodies, questions began to be asked. How did it happen? Was there neglect? Did the Oversmen and the Firemen carry out their duties correctly? When they inspected the pits that morning, did they take enough time to carry out a thorough inspection? Before the miners descended the pits, it was the duty of the Oversmen and their Firemen to inspect the entire colliery every working morning and to ascertain there had been no roof falls and that all work places were free of gas or any other hazards that might endanger the miners. On the completion of

Calling for Volunteers, Illustrated London News, *1877.*

their inspections of the workings, they would chalk the date on each coalface where the men would be working that day a proof that the sections had been inspected and that the pits were safe for the commencement of the day's work. It was usually around 6.00a.m. that the miners were 'chapped down', and all the men would be underground by 6.30a.m. The term 'chapped down' referred to the firemen knocking on the metal framework at the bottom of the shaft to indicate that the workplaces were free of gas and that it was safe to descend.

Speculation was rife that the explosion was caused by an accumulation of gas that had been ignited by some means or other, but it was generally agreed that the quantities of gas found previously by miners in the pits would not be sufficient to cause such a catastrophe. The mine owners, the Oversmen and Firemen seemed reluctant to admit there was a history of the presence of gas within the colliery. At the Government Inquiry held in Hamilton from 12 to 22 November 1877, it was proved beyond doubt that the proprietors were well

aware of the existence of gas. The Firemen's books were produced for examination and it was found that no entry had been made by any of the Firemen encountering the existence of gas in the three months prior to the explosion. All Firemen cross-examined at the Inquiry admitted that they found gas regularly, but it was such a trivial amount that it was not worth recording in their reports.

Nine weeks prior to the disaster, this 'trivial' amount was enough to explode and kill a miner named Joseph McAnulty and severely burn his brother, Andrew. The entry in the book relating to that incident did not mention the fact that gas had ignited around the McAnultys, causing Joseph's death within an hour of the blast. Ironically, it was the injuries that Andrew McAnulty received that day that saved his life, as he was still recovering from his wounds at the time of the disaster. It would appear that the owners had deliberately played down the existence of gas in the Blantyre Colliery.

The doctors in attendance at the pithead were Dr Marshall of Dixon's Colliery, Drs Grant and Downie of

Blantyre, Drs Louden and Robertson from Hamilton, and Dr Goff from Bothwell. They dispersed when it was realised that no more survivors would be found. A hearse and carts covered with straw stood by for the removal of the dead. Attempts were made to clean the blackened and blood-stained bodies, before placing them in coffins rather than laying them out for identification on the straw-covered floors of the Smiddy and Joiner Shop. A large wooden hut was hastily constructed as a morgue and it was to this shed that the bodies recovered over the next four weeks were taken for identification. Corpses unfit for viewing were placed in coffins with lids tightly secured and a note attached stating, 'NOT TO BE OPENED'. The personal items placed on the lids of the coffins helped in identifying some of the victims, but, by using this method, mistakes were sometimes made, so contributing to the confusion about how many miners had been killed.

Belts and boots were the most common items displayed on the secured coffins to assist with the identification of miners in the vicinity of the blast. It was obvious that the explosion had been very violent as it had torn the clothing from bodies leaving only their secured belts and boots on their corpses. The most severely mutilated bodies, which had no personal effects on them, were removed immediately and buried in a specially prepared lair in the north-east corner of Blantyre Cemetery. The majority of victims were buried alongside them in the four weeks following the disaster.

There were seven miles of labyrinths and passages within the pits and the distance between No. 2 and No. 3 shafts was half a mile. Roof falls and wreckage obstructed all the causeways and made the removal of bodies extremely difficult. As time passed, unrest grew among the miners at the pithead that not enough was being done to retrieve the bodies of their comrades. Complaints were voiced that the slow explorations and non-recovery of the dead was not acceptable. Over six hundred angry miners gathered to express their anger at the decisions taken during the last few days and raised various accusations against the management. A Cornishman named Robert Coulter was nominated as spokesman for the men and invited to bring a small deputation to meet with the management and Mr Moore, the Mines Inspector. Moore expressed great sympathy with the men, and said he would have been only too glad to bring forward the work of sending the bodies to the surface, without endangering other lives. Eventually the deputation grudgingly agreed in

Reading the List of the Dead, Illustrated London News, *1877.*

the fairness of the decision, but the demonstrations resumed against the decision to close No. 2 pit. A notice then appeared on the wall of the General Office stating that it was not prudent to make any further attempts to recover bodies from No. 3 pit while existing conditions prevailed. The miners became incensed at the decision and gathered on the grassy knoll between the two pitheads and accusations that the management had ignored complaints made to them before the disaster were made and certain individuals were said to be breaking rules and regulations.

As the miners marched towards the pithead to take matters into their own hands, they met Alexander McDonald MP, who had hastened to Blantyre on hearing the news of the disaster. Being respected by the men as a fighter in Parliament for better working conditions for miners, they informed him of the situation and their decision. He counselled them not to go on with their plan, which he felt would only endanger more lives. Mr McDonald informed them that he was deeply sympathetic to their demands and objectives and stated that it had been his lot during the last twenty years to be present at most great mining tragedies that had occurred in the United Kingdom, and he had seen the urgent requests for the recovery of bodies. He sympathised deeply with those who were so anxious to have the bodies removed in the present case, but all assistance to those below was now unavailing. He

Dixon's No. 3 Pit, Illustrated London News, *1877.*

advised them to be patient for a little while longer and not to think of endangering the living, as they would do if they attempted to recover the bodies.

He reassured the gathering that if neglect were found, whether the offender was the Inspector of Mines, the manager or the colliery owner, then that neglect would be told throughout the entire kingdom. This was greeted with great applause and McDonald noted that the greatest neglect on the part of the Inspector of Mines had been exhibited in the district for some time. He implored the miners, however, to leave the present matter in the hands of the authorities, and not persist in making an effort to get into the mine. McDonald concluded by intimating that a letter had been sent to the Secretary of State urging that the relatives of victims should be properly represented at the forthcoming inquiry, and he asked that those who had evidence to give to the committee should do so. The crowd, much calmer after hearing these reassuring words, dispersed and for the rest of the evening the collieries were comparatively deserted. A potentially dangerous situation was diffused.

A committee of four men was appointed who would work with the management team in making future decisions regarding the recovery of the bodies. The group was taken to the bottom of No. 2 pit and shown the extent of the damage and the obstructions that had to be overcome before a clear passage could be made to retrieve the victims. They were also taken as far as possible down No. 3 shaft and encountered the after-damp that was causing the explorers to make hasty retreats from the shaft and the passageways of No. 2 pit. The aggrieved miners on the surface were informed of

the difficulties being encountered by the explorers and told that the committee was satisfied all decisions that had been previously taken were correct, and the threat to enter the pits by force was withdrawn.

No. 3 shaft was finally declared open in the early hours of Saturday 27 October, when a party of specialist miners who had been given lodgings in Priestfield Rows at last cleared the shaft. On hearing the news, gangs of men made themselves available to descend the pit to make further in-roads into the workings. A party of fifty men immediately descended the shaft and it was only when the miners saw the devastation before them that they fully realised the management decisions regarding the rescue attempts had been correct. Wreckage and roof falls completely blocked the passageways from the floors to the roofs for hundreds of yards in every direction. The explosion had spread devastating destruction as well as death throughout the mine. The permanent railway that ran along the main level had been completely destroyed; wagons were smashed to splinters and piled everywhere in great heaps. Debris was intermingled with various types of material including dead horses and human remains.

Funeral carriages became a common sight in Blantyre, as cortège after cortège made its way to the graveyard at Cemetery Road in Blantyre or set off on the long journey to Dalbeth Roman Catholic Cemetery at London Road, Glasgow. Other carriages returned some of the casualties to their home villages throughout Lanarkshire and Glasgow.

The day after the disaster, when it was realised that the death toll would be great, the local clergy responded quickly to the needs of the bereaved families. The Rev.

Stewart Wright administered to the victims of the Established Church, Father Frawley to those of the Roman Catholic persuasion and the Rev. McDonald of the Free Church looked after those belonging to that denomination. Shortly afterwards a committee was established to co-ordinate local relief work. A meeting was held, chaired by the Rev. Wright, which agreed to seek the assistance of competent businessmen in the area, as large donations of money were now arriving from sympathetic people throughout Britain. Accordingly, an invited group of prominent people from the town and surrounding areas met in the manse of the Old Parish Church, High Blantyre and the Provost of Hamilton, John Clark Forrest, was elected chairman, Mr Brown, a Hamilton solicitor, secretary to the fund and Mr McCallum, manager of the Blantyre branch of the City of Glasgow Bank, treasurer. The three local clergymen were also elected onto the committee. Lord Blantyre, Messrs W.S. Dixon and other colliery owners in the surrounding areas were later co-opted. The Lord Provosts of Edinburgh, Glasgow and the other Scottish burghs, various Members of Parliament, and even the Lord Mayor of London and the mayors of the principal towns in England were also co-opted onto the committee.

On Wednesday 24 October, coal and iron masters called a large meeting to consider what could be done with reference to the disaster. These gentlemen also formed a committee and, before leaving the meeting, large sums of money were donated to the Relief Fund. The local Blantyre group decided that it would be in the best interest of the bereaved to amalgamate with this body and circulars were sent to banks throughout the whole of Britain to open subscription lists. It was decided that local efforts should continue to alleviate the suffering being endured by the bereaved, until funds were allocated to them.

Donations large and small poured in from rich and poor alike. The people of South Wales, who had recently had a disaster of their own, donated money from their own fund to fellow sufferers in Blantyre. A telegram was received from Queen Victoria on Wednesday

Priestfield Rows & Dixon's No. 2 Pit chimney shaft with 'Bing'.

Reputed to be Miners at Dixon's No. 2 Pit, c.1900.

24 October, wishing to know the extent of the disaster and requesting to be kept informed of the situation. Inspector Moore informed her that the accident was as bad as had been reported in the newspapers. A second message arrived from the Queen later that evening requesting that her sympathy be extended to the bereaved. The Queen later donated one hundred guineas to the appeal fund.

A concert took place in the Blantyre Works Hall on 16 November which included many well-known theatrical personalities. W. Dixon Ltd, the parent company of the colliery, made the largest single donation of £2,000, a considerable sum in those days. The owner of the company, W.S. Dixon donated a further £1,000. Other large donations were six of £500 and five of £100. Many thousands of donations of sums between £1 and £100 were received from businesses, churches, various organisations and ordinary people throughout Great Britain. Lists of all the donors and their donations were printed every week in the *Hamilton Advertiser*. An unusual donation was received from Lady Emily Hamilton of Dalziel, who furnished each widow with a mourning dress. Although greatly appreciated, many felt that the monetary value of the dresses could have been put to better use.

THE INQUIRY

The Government Inquiry to establish the cause of the disaster opened on 12 November 1877, under the chairmanship of Mr Joseph Dickson, Senior Inspector of Mines, and Mr Robert MacLean, Advocate, Edinburgh. R.V. Strachan represented the deceased.

Mr Alexander McDonald MP and several inspectors of mines also sat at the table. All persons who considered they had information that might assist the Inquiry were invited to come forward. In the end 48 witnesses were listed, with all but one being called to the witness stand. During the first week of the Inquiry the hall was crowded, but attendances dropped away with only the officials and witnesses attending during the final days. There were accusations and counter-accusations and, because of the drawn-out and sometimes long-winded discussions concerning technicalities, the public lost interest.

From the accounts given by the witnesses there can be no doubt that the management was fully aware of the dangerous conditions that prevailed within the mine due to excess gas, and was negligent in that respect. Similarly, the miners, due to recklessness, complacency or ignorance of the dangers that large pockets of gas presented, and their unofficial use of dynamite, must have played a large part in causing the explosion. It was pointed out by chemists and mining experts that all the gas within No. 2 and No. 3 pits could not have been the cause of such a massive explosion. It would be a few years before the cause was established but it is strange to note, today, that the Inquiry was given the cause and failed to recognise it.

One seemingly insignificant statement, among the many hours of evidence and opinions given by the accepted experts of the mining industry, was a suggestion made by William Thomson, the colliery carpenter, a non-technical employee and the last witness to be called. William asked for permission to make a statement and was immediately invited to come forward. He said the following:

> On one occasion Mr Watson the colliery manager told me that the mine being a dry one, like a desert, the coal dust would aggravate an explosion.

This was in fact the answer they had been searching for, but not one person at the Inquiry gave William's testimony a second thought.

The Inquiry concluded on 20 November 1877.

THE CAUSE

When the air is filled with a certain percentage of coal dust, or any other dust of a combustible substance, a flame or spark might start a blaze that will travel through the dust cloud so rapidly it creates a violent and destructive blast. Dixon's collieries were dry pits, whereas most pits in the Scottish minefields were wet. It is now obvious that the ventilation in the pits that morning was poor, possibly due to the furnaces not having reached their maximum temperature after the change over of the cubemen between shifts. We know for certain that a naked flame, a spark or impact, ignited gas and the oxygen reacted with hydrogen and carbon, producing a shock wave that slammed against surrounding surfaces and blasted objects from its path. The explosion itself was over in a few millionths of a second, faster than a man can blink, and the burning which followed began at the seat of the explosion and travelled throughout the mine in a few thousandths of a second.

THE SOLUTION

It was quickly realised that the solution to the problem of the killer coal dust was to introduce non-combustible stone dust into the pits. It was a simple but effective remedy that is still used in collieries today. Shelves were constructed at short regular intervals throughout the workings and piles of stone-dust placed upon them. Nothing could be done to prevent the natural gas within the coal seams accumulating at the workings, or the explosions caused from time to time by naked lights or sparks igniting a pocket of gas. Explosions still occur today but dusting prevents them becoming catastrophes like the Blantyre Explosion. The coal dust within the air cannot reach a critical level, being contaminated with the non-combustible dust, so if a gas explosion does occur, the blast is contained at its source, the flame travelling only as far as the shelves of stone dust. The dust blown ahead of the flames would nullify the explosive dust within the air.

THE EXPLORERS

There were many unsung heroes during the rescue attempts at Dixon's Colliery. The names of miners who risked their lives in desperate efforts to rescue their entombed comrades are unfortunately unrecorded. Some had to be forcibly restrained from attempting to gain entry to the pits for hasty rescue attempts. Eventually they were persuaded to stand by and await instructions as their superiors assessed the best means to overcome the difficulties obstructing the rescue efforts.

The photograph (p.32) shows the 'Blantyre Explorers' receiving bibles from the National Bible Society of Scotland, in recognition of their efforts to save lives and

Bible presentation to the 'Blantyre Explorers'.

recovery of those killed in the Blantyre Explosion. Some of their names are known to us:

> John Pickering, front row, second from the left.
> Hugh Brown, front row, third from the left.
> George Watt, rear row, third from the left.
> John Bowie, rear row, sixth from the left.
> Daniel Hendry, rear row, second from the right.
> Dr William Grant, rear row, extreme right, (q.v.).

CEMETERIES

The following is a list of the cemeteries where the victims were buried:

> Baillieston
> Baillieston Episcopalian Churchyard
> Barrhead Old Catholic Burying Ground
> Bellshill Churchyard
> Blantyre
> Bothwell Churchyard
> Cambuslang Churchyard
> Cambusnethan
> Coatbridge Mount Zion Churchyard
> Dalbeth Catholic Burying Ground
> Glasgow Saint Mary's Churchyard
> Larkhall
> Strathaven Churchyard

EVICTIONS

After the Disaster, the widows of the miners who did not have a family member still working in any of the Dixon's Collieries were given notice to vacate their tied cottages. A few managed to find other accommodation, but the majority could not afford to pay a rent elsewhere. On 16 May 1878, 34 widows received a summons to appear at Hamilton Sheriff Court. It would be natural to surmise that these unfortunate families would have to resort to the Poor House in Hamilton, but the Poor House records at that time do not show any family names involved in the Blantyre Explosion. What became of them?

As I was completing my account, I received a request from a lady for information regarding her family history. I was delighted to discover that her ancestor, Pettigrew (q.v.) of Malcolmwood Farm at Lindsay Hill, Millheugh, had constructed huts for the evicted Blantyre widows, but it is not known where they were located. The Pettigrews can be proud that their ancestor, out of the goodness of his heart, went to the expense of erecting these huts, and thus preserved the widows' dignity and gave them hope.

'THE BLANTYRE EXPLOSION': THE SONG

The tragic event of 22 October 1877 is remembered in a well-known folk song:

By Clyde's bonnie banks where I sadly did wander,
Amang the pit-heaps as evening drew nigh,
I spied a fair maiden all dressed in deep mourning,
A-weeping and wailing with many a sigh.

I stepped up beside her: and thus I addressed her:
'Pray tell me, fair maiden, of your trouble and pain,'
Sobbing and sighing, at last she did answer:
'James Murphy, kind sir, was my true lover's name.

Twenty-one years of age, full of youth and good-
        looking,
To work down the mines at High Blantyre he came.
The wedding was fixed, all the guests were invited,
That wild winters morning my Jamie was slain.'

The explosion was heard, all the women and children,
With pale anxious faces they rushed to the mine.
When the truth was made known,
The streets rang with their moaning
Two hundred and eighteen poor miners were slain.

Now husbands and wives and sweethearts and
        brothers,
That Blantyre explosion they'll never forget.
And all you young miners that hear my sad story,
Shed a tear for the miners who are laid to their rest.

Blantyre Gas Company

This company opened its gas works in Stonefield Road in 1864. The gas provided was more expensive than in surrounding communities and it was taken over by Lanark County Council, Middle Ward Committee, in May 1925. The premises were subsequently used as a garage by Letham's Bus Company. The Gas Work Row, which consisted of approximately six houses, was situated adjacent to the yard gates on Stonefield Road.

Blantyre Kirkyard

In attempting to determine the age of the graveyard in the Old Kirkyard at High Blantyre Cross, we are presented with a few contradictions. In *The Annals of Blantyre* (1885), the Rev. Stewart Wright (q.v.) states that an earlier historian, Professor Wilson, had made reference to 'the sweet Churchyard of Blantyre', where, Wright claimed, 'the daisies that grow on that "Old God's Acre" had not been disturbed for three hundred years'. If this were the case, the churchyard referred to by Wilson could not possibly have been the existing Old Kirkyard at High Blantyre Cross, as that was still receiving the dead during the Rev. Wright's ministry at the Old Parish

Blantyre Explosion Centenary Monument. Designed by Neil Gordon and constructed by Robert Sim.

Church. In the next page of his book, however, Wright refers to the burying ground at Kirkton, which he states had received the dead of Blantyre for centuries. Is this the burying ground referred to by Professor Wilson? The answer would seem to be no and that two different locations are described. On the other hand, it has been suggested that the surface of the original graveyard may have been level with the road and that when no more room was available for graves, the surrounding wall was raised and a top layer of soil laid on top of the earlier graves. This would have created a new graveyard on top of the original site, thus retaining the sacred burying ground adjacent to the church.

The picture shown (p.34) of the second church, dated 1863 prior to its demolition, distinctly shows that this church was constructed on the high level of the Kirkyard above the entrance steps at the front gates. If the decision was taken to lay a deep layer of soil on top of the original site, it must have occurred before the construction of this church in 1793, and after the demolition of the original church the same year. Strangely, no trace has ever been found of the foundations of the first church, which suggests that it may have stood on a lower level or they were completely removed from its site on the upper level to

Blantyre Parish Church, 1863.

provided space for the graves that now occupy the site. The earliest grave in the centre of the Kirkyard is dated 1795 and can be seen close to the tomb of the Barons of Blantyre. It is unlikely that a Christian community would cover the graves of their ancestors and I suggest that the passage of time has simply eroded the oldest gravestones and the ground has been reused.

I was recently involved, with others, in a search for old gravestones within the Kirkyard and we found many lying under a few centimetres of earth and turf. Most of the inscriptions had been eroded but none that were legible was older than the earliest legible gravestone on the surface of the graveyard, which bears the date 1732. There are a few other stones located in the west corner that have dates between 1732 and 1793, which was before the first church was demolished. The existence of these gravestones would suggest that the surface ground of the graveyard was always on the present level, although it is possible they may have been removed from the lower level and simply replaced on the new one to mark the site of the original grave, but this is all

speculation on my part. It may also be that the burial ground referred to by Professor Wilson is at Blantyre Priory, which would in all probability have had a small community adjacent to it.

Before concluding this piece on the Old Kirkyard, I would like to suggest that an inspection of the west wall of the Kirkyard by a qualified archeologist may find evidence that the centre section of the wall, adjacent to the car park of the present church, may have been part of an older building. It may prove to be the lower part of the west gable of the medieval church, and establish the site of the original church once and for all.

Blantyre Mills/Works

Around 1775, David Dale (q.v.) and his partner James Monteith (q.v.) purchased land on the Blantyre Braes adjoining the River Clyde at the foot of what is now Station Road. They also purchased the land on the opposite bank of the Clyde which extended up to the top of Blantyre Mill Road, Bothwell, directly across from the David Livingstone Centre. The old Bothwell Meal Mill stood on the Bothwell bank of the Clyde, between the present David Livingstone Memorial Bridge and the Weir. It was here on the Blantyre Braes that Dale constructed Blantyre Mills, with the assistance and advice of, Richard Arkwright, creator of the world's first successful water-powered spinning mill in Cromford, England. The project placed Blantyre at the centre of a period in history known as the Scottish Enlightenment. The site was selected because the Clyde at this point was wide, deep and fast flowing. Construction commenced around 1778 and considerable expertise must have been required to construct the wells, dams, machinery, and subterranean passages that were essential elements in such a massive undertaking. The Mills were in operation by 1785. In 1792, David Dale sold the Mills to his partner's two sons, James and Henry Monteith (q.v.), who rapidly expanded the Works.

The work in the mill consisted of cotton spinning, steam-room weaving and cotton-yarn dyeing. Blantyre Mill was the first cotton-spinning factory on the River Clyde producing water-twist yarn. A large dam/weir was constructed across the river and sluice gates built to control the water required to drive the machinery. The Works first expanded in 1791, when another mill was erected for the spinning of mule-twist which contained 30,000 spindles. In 1800, when a dye-works was constructed, Blantyre Mills, together with a sister mill in Bridgeton, Glasgow, became the first establishment in Scotland capable of producing Turkey Red cotton yarn. Prior to this, the popular Turkey Red had to be imported from the Far East.

A weaving factory was constructed in 1813 and was extended in 1841 to contain almost 600 looms. By this time there were almost 1,000 employees, of whom almost two-thirds were female. A large self-contained village constructed around the Mills was known as Blantyre Works Village. The Village Gates at the entrance to the complex straddled what is now Station Road, between two tollhouses that stood at the corners of Knightswood Terrace and Rosebank Avenue, as seen in the photograph on p.151. The gates were closed to traffic at 10p.m. every evening. The area beyond Blantyre Station is still known today as the Village.

In 1815 the Waterloo Row (q.v.) was constructed. The population of the Works Village in 1835 was 1,921 and, of that total, 915 worked in the Mills. It was at that time that a second phase in house building for the employees and their families took place, namely the Fore Row (q.v.), Mid Row, and the smaller Cross Row. Also at this time the row was constructed which at present contains the Village Bar. Following further expansion in 1865, the work force increased yet again.

In 1834 the working day from Monday to Friday was 'reduced' to 13¾ hours. It commenced with the ringing of the Works' Bell (q.v.) at 6a.m. and the ringing of the bell at 7.45p.m. brought the working day to an end. Saturday working was nine hours. A forty-five minute break for breakfast was taken at 9a.m. and one hour for lunch at midday. The total hours worked per week was 69 hours, almost double the average working week today. It is hard to believe that even longer hours were worked before 1834.

Wages in the early days of the company were partly paid in bronze coins called 'Store Order for Goods', with values of 5s., 1s., 6d., and a ½d., which could only be spent in shops within the Works Village. The company then reimbursed the shopkeepers in sterling to the value of the bronze coins spent in their premises.

Orphaned children, known as 'Barrack Boys,' were employed at the mills. Some of these children were as young as six years of age, and were bound to the work by their relatives. In 1791 it was recorded that, of the 295 employees at the mills, 60 were Barrack Children. The children were lodged by the proprietor, who employed a schoolmaster for their education in any spare time, which was after work, Monday to Friday, between 8p.m. and 10p.m. A doctor was on hand to look after the children's health, and by the standards of the time, they were considered to be very fortunate.

Henry Monteith and Company went into liquidation in 1904 and the majority of the Works, which had fallen into disrepair, was demolished. The employees' houses were deemed unfit for habitation and condemned in 1913, although some of them continued to be occupied until a fire destroyed a large section of the Fore Row in 1928. The majority of the tenants were rehoused in Knightswood Terrace and Viewfield Avenue that were being constructed at that time by the County Council.

All that remains today of the Blantyre Works Village is the Shuttle Row (q.v.), the birthplace of David Livingstone, the Company Board Room Building, which is now a private house, a section of the Wages Building adjacent to the bridge, and part of the Shuttle Row Washhouse wall which forms the circular stair leading to the playing fields and the African Pavilion.
SEE MILL HOUSES (M)

Bottom Row, 1900.

Blantyre Mills/Works Boardroom

The houses in the photograph above were at the end of a long row situated behind and below the rear of Shuttle Row. The house at the right behind the cart was originally the boardroom of the Blantyre Mills Company, and is the only section of the Bottom Row still standing. The Boardroom today is a beautiful house overlooking the River Clyde adjacent to the David Livingstone Memorial Bridge.

Blantyre Mills/Works Chapel-School

Messrs Henry Monteith & Co. erected a small Chapel-School in 1828 for the dual purpose of worship and education. The chapel, which could seat 400 people, was so arranged that during the week it was used as a schoolhouse. A schoolmaster was appointed with a salary of £20 per year, together with a free house and a garden. Initially the average number of day-scholars was 136, and the average number of children attending evening classes, after work, was 56. The student numbers rose as the number of employees increased following further expansion of the Mills. The premises were also used as a Sunday school and a Community Hall. It was here that a soirée was held in 1856 in honour of David Livingstone when he returned from Africa to his birthplace in Blantyre. After a fire, which destroyed a number of houses in the old rows in 1928, many of the unfortunate families found shelter in the old Chapel-School. Soon after that event it was demolished.

Blantyre Mills/Works Village

SEE BLANTYRE MILLS / WORKS (B)

Blantyre Old Parish Church

The first two parish churches stood in the old Kirkyard at Kirkton, High Blantyre Cross. The construction date of the first, which occupied the centre of the Kirkyard, is unknown. Early churches were traditionally constructed with the altar at the east end of the structure, so it is safe to assume that the east gable of the Old Kirk aligned to Douglas Street, as did the second church which was built to replace it.

When Blantyre Priory was established, which is thought to have been some time during the reign of King Alexander II (1214-49), it was endowed with the revenues of the parish church, which suggests that the original church existed at that time, and it is possible that it was constructed in the 12th century. It was described as a beautiful and substantial structure similar to the original parish church at Bothwell. This is now the chancel of Saint Bride's Church, and a visit there provides us with an idea as to how the original Blantyre Kirk would have appeared.

In 1785 the minister of the old church, the Rev. Stevenson, commented that, 'There is no record of the time when the church was built. It bears evident marks of great antiquity and is in a most deplorable condition.' Seven years later, in 1792, it was condemned as being unsafe and unfit for worship owing to 'decay and rottenness'. It would appear that the second church (see Blantyre Kirkyard), which was constructed in 1793, stood between the original church and the steps at the Kirkyard gates. It had an earthen floor, and in some of the pews a board was laid down to make it more comfortable. This somewhat plain building was demolished when the present church was erected

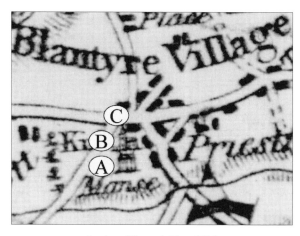

Section of Forrest's Map, 1816.

at the corner of Main Street and Craigmuir Road in 1863. The perimeter wall around the new church was probably constructed with stone obtained from the old church and some houses that were being demolished in School Lane at that time. The Old Burying-ground/Kirkyard wall was also repaired and partially rebuilt with these stones, and in 1885 a commemorative arch with a drinking trough for horses was built into the wall adjacent to the Kirkyard gates by John Wardrop Moore of Greenhall (q.v.).

The section of map shown is an updated version from 1816 of an original map dating from 1790s. It clearly shows three structures in the old Kirkyard: the Manse (A), the original church in the centre (B) and, at the top, a building inside the Kirkyard: the gates (C), which suggests to me that the second church was constructed before the original church was demolished. The existing two houses, in Douglas Street, also appear adjacent to the Kirkyard. The black shape indicating other buildings has been added to an earlier map, to produce a more detailed picture of the town. In early maps, all large houses and churches were depicted with the symbols seen here in the old Kirkyard.

The original Church Manse, built in 1773, was repaired and extended in 1823 by Mr Lockhart, MP for Lanarkshire, who had rented it after selling his home, Whistleberry House (also known as Auchinraith House), while his new house was being constructed at Milton Lockhart, Carluke. The present manse was built in 1972 and the old manse, which stood between the present manse and the church, was demolished in the same year.

The population of the town increased rapidly after the opening of the Blantyre Mills in 1785 and the discovery of rich seams of coal within the parish in 1875. Miners' cottages were constructed at Dixon's Rows, Baird's Rows and Merry's Rows to accommodate the men who flocked to the town for employment in the various pits sunk in and around Blantyre. Other smaller rows were built adjacent to collieries, such as the Priestfield Row and the Priory Row. Many homes were also provided in the tenements above the shops selling all types of wares to the ever-growing community.

It became increasingly evident that the Parish Church at High Blantyre could not provide for the spiritual needs of such a large community and a decision was taken to construct a 'Chapel of Ease' at Glasgow Road in Stonefield. The Parish Church added the word 'Old' to its original name, Blantyre Parish Church, to differentiate it from the new Stonefield Parish Church (q.v.), which opened on 29 June 1880.

The following is a list of ministers of Blantyre Old Parish Church from the first minister in 1567 until the end of the 19th century.

Rev. William Chirnsyde

William Chirnsyde was the last Roman Catholic Prior of Blantyre Priory. Before taking up his duties as Prior of Blantyre on 3 September 1552, he had been Provost of the Collegiate Church of Bothwell. After conforming to the new faith in 1567, he became the first Protestant minister at the church in the Kirkyard at Kirkton (High Blantyre Cross), the centre of the original village of Blantyre. William Chirnsyde preached at Blantyre Kirk until 1572, when he left to take up a new position in Luss.

The Rev. Stewart Wright claimed in 1885 that the ruins of a village that sat adjacent to the old Priory above the River Clyde, directly opposite Bothwell Castle, were still visible. When the Priory was closed after the Reformation, the inhabitants may have followed Chirnsyde to Kirkton.

Chirnsyde purchased two silver communion cups which are still used at Blantyre Old Parish Church. They are over 430 years old and are said to be the second oldest communion cups still in use in Scotland. They were made in Edinburgh, and bear the Dean of Gold and Silversmiths Guild stamp for the period between 1550-70 and are inscribed 'BLANTYR KIRK'.

Rev. John Davidson AM

John Davidson became the second minister at Blantyre Old Parish Church when he succeeded the Rev. William Chirnsyde in 1574, two years after Chirnsyde had left Blantyre to take up a position in Luss. Rev. Davidson also held the benefices of Cambuslang, Dalserf and Hamilton. He died in 1591.

Owing to the lack of ministers so soon after the Reformation, many had to serve more than one parish and so we find that a John Hamilton (q.v.) was 'reader' at Blantyre or assistant to the Rev. Davidson, his stipend being £16 and the 'Kirkland', a portion of land assigned to the parish minister in addition to his stipend for cultivation purposes and commonly known as the Glebe.

Rev. John Brown

The Rev. Brown, formerly of Neilston, became the third minister at the Blantyre Old Parish Church from 1591 to 1593. The reason for his departure from the parish is unknown.

Rev. William Boyd AM

The Rev. Boyd was the fourth minister of Blantyre Old Parish Church. He graduated from Glasgow University in 1587 and was inducted at Blantyre in 1593. After only one year in the post, he accepted a call to serve at the parish church of Glenluce, in the Presbytery of Stranraer.

Rev. John Sangstare AM

The Rev. John Sangstere, inducted November 1594, was minister at the Old Parish Church until he died in November 1609. In *The Annals of Blantyre*, the Rev. Stewart Wright reveals the contents of John Sangstare's will. It is an interesting document that gives an insight into some of the minister's worldly goods.

Items of the Minister's Will 1609.

He bequeathed:

> Ane tydie cow, price £14 Scots; ane quey of three yeir auld, price £l6 13s. 4d.; item, ane stack of aitts in the barn yard extending to 28 threaves, estimate to 8 bolls, price of the boll with the fodder £5, Inde [total] £40; certain pease, estimate to 3 bolls, price of the boll £3 6s. 8d., Inde £10; item, ane feather bed in his Chalmer in Hamilton, price £6 13s. 4d.; item, in Blantyre, ane standard bed of aik, price £6 6s. 8d.; item, ane meal almerie, price £10; item, ane meikle kist, worth £5 6s. 8d.; item, ane lettrom [reading desk], price £2; item, twa chyres [chairs], price of them baith £4 13s. 4d.; item, ane new girdle, price £3 6s. 8d.; item, ane masking fat, in the custody of Robert Hamilton in Priestfield, worth 40s.; item, twa barrells, price 26s. 8d.; item, ane cloak and gown, and the rest of the abuljements of his body, estimate to be worth £40; item, his haill buiks, meikle and little, estimate to be worth other £40 – summa, £190 6s. 8d.

Rev. John Heriot AM

John Heriot was the eldest son of William Heriot, a burgess of Glasgow. In 1609 he was assigned minister of Blantyre Old Parish Church. Due to the enforcement of the Episcopalian form of the Protestant religion on the Presbyterian population by the government of King James VI, ministers were forced to comply or

lose their benefice. It is not known if the Rev. Heriot was forced to conform or if he willingly accepted the government decree. The Episcopal form of worship involved the return of Bishops who were appointed by the King, which gave the crown complete political and ecclesiastical control of the country. The majority of the Presbyterian population in Scotland resented the return of the Bishops, who in their eyes exercised a control similar to that which the Roman Catholic Bishops had enjoyed prior to the Reformation. Presbyterianism was outlawed, but the religion was practiced at conventicle meetings, often held in the open air at remote locations throughout the country. The people who attended these illegal religious meetings were later known as Covenanters and were ready to give their lives for the right to practice their form of Presbyterian worship. These deeply religious people signed the 'National Covenant' in 1638, which resisted the theory of the 'Divine Right of Kings' and the enforcement of an Episcopal system on the Presbyterian Church of Scotland. Covenanters were declared rebels and, without trial, were savagely persecuted, until Presbyterianism was established in Scotland, in 1690, during the reign of William III.

Many Covenanters were executed, but it is claimed that only one parishioner of Blantyre lost his life in the conflict that followed. After the Battle of Bothwell Brig in 1679, the victorious government army published a list known as the 'Fugitive Roll'. One Blantyre man's name appeared in it, that of Andrew Reid, servitor to Robert Smillie at Blantyre Kirk, who was declared an 'Outlaw and a Rebel'. Reid was eventually captured by the notorious Claverhouse and his troops and was executed outside his house at Kirkton, Blantyre, in front of his wife and children. His name also appears in a document called the 'Cloud of Witnesses', a list drawn up by the Covenanters containing the names of martyrs killed during the persecutions. It has been claimed that that another local, a man named Brown, was also executed, but no known evidence proves that he even existed.

It was said that Heriot was the last Episcopalian minister at Blantyre but it is known that three of the four ministers that followed him were Curates. Rev. Heriot was a member of the Glasgow Assemblies of 1638 and 1639, both of which attempted to resolve the problem of Bishops within the Kirk. Owing to failing health in his later years, he had assistants to aid him in his work, and he served the parish of Blantyre for 54 years until he died on 7 December 1665, aged eighty-four. The inscription on his tombstone seems to disagree as to how long he served as minister of Blantyre Parish. It reads as follows:

> Here lies a pastor ten years and four score
> Who taught his flock 55 years and more,
> During his time to his immortal praise
> So blamelessly behaved himself always,
> In holy order, doctrine sweet and sound
> As did become his reverend gospel gown,
> His soul in heaven, his body in the clay
> Wait a reunion at the latter day.

Mr Hew Mitchell was the Rev. Heriot's first assistant and held office from 1636 until 1653. During that time a certain James Hamilton AM was also an assistant to Rev. Heriot and was ordained the year he came to Blantyre.

Rev. James Berrie AM

James Berrie came to Blantyre Old Parish Church before the death of Rev. Heriot in 1665 and was ordained in 1666. His second wife was Anna, the eldest daughter of Sir James Maxwell of Calderwood, and they had a daughter Agnes. On 26 July 1677 Agnes inherited various houses and property in the 'Kirktoun of Blantyr' from her grandfather. One of these properties was probably Crossbasket House (q.v.). Rev. Berrie died in April 1679, aged 59 years.

Rev. George Leslie AM

George Leslie, who was born near Aberdeen, was inducted to Blantyre in either 1678 or 1679. He was the last of the Curates and was 'evicted from his manse, the parish and living' in 1689 when Presbyterianism was established as the form of church government in Scotland.

Rev. Robert Landesse AM

When Presbyterianism was re-established as the national religion the resultant evictions of the Curates from their churches and manses meant there was once again a shortage of Presbyterian ministers. George Leslie's replacement was Robert Landesse of Robroyston, who was born in 1630. He was educated at Glasgow University and was later licensed by the Presbytery of Hamilton, but left soon afterward to preach in Ireland. He is recorded as being minister at Ballymoney, County Antrim and at Garvagh between 1672 and 1686. He returned to Scotland only to be imprisoned in Edinburgh for six weeks owing to the fact that he was a nonconformist. Later, in 1687, he was listed as a member of the Synod of Glasgow and Ayr, having been called to officiate at one of the 'meeting houses' of Glasgow. At his own request he was relieved of this office, and on 12 August 1690 was inducted to Blantyre. A dispute arose between the Presbytery of Hamilton and the Presbytery of Antrim, the latter claiming that Mr Landesse was still bound to the Parish of Ballymoney. After the dispute was resolved, Landesse was permitted to remain at Blantyre where he ministered until his health failed in 1702, when he demitted the charge. It is reputed that when he died, in 1707, he was buried within the High Kirk of Glasgow on 5 August, but there is no record of his interment there in the register of burials.

Rev. Mathew Connell

The Rev. Mathew Connell was called to Blantyre on 23 December 1703, and was ordained and inducted to the parish on 12 April 1704. Because of the apparent High Church mode of his sermons, he was known as 'Mass Connell'. He served the parish for 16 years until he was translated to the Parish of East Kilbride in 1720. One of his sons, the Rt Hon. Arthur Connell, was a prominent West India merchant based in Glasgow during the 18th century, who, along with his sons, helped to lay the foundations of the city as we know it today. Arthur was elected Lord Provost of Glasgow, 1772-3, and was recognised as one of the most respected 'ruling elders' of the city, being unanimously elected, on 7 April 1774, to represent the Town Council at a forthcoming meeting of the General Assembly in Edinburgh.

Rev. Richard Henderson AM

The Rev. Henderson was inducted at Blantyre on 1 August 1722 and served the parish for 48 years until his death on 12 December 1769, aged eighty. Two of his sons, Archibald and Alexander, became prosperous tobacco merchants in Glasgow and Virginia, USA, Archibald becoming the chairman of the Virginia Chamber of Commerce in 1742.

Rev. John Finnie

SEE JOHN FINNIE (F)

Rev. Henry Stevenson MA

Blantyre finally received a new minister when the dispute over the Rev. Finnie ended with his death in 1772. Henry Stevenson was the son of a Dunlop farmer and was born at Stewarton in 1738. He received his MA at the University of Glasgow and, like his predecessor, John Finnie, he was appointed Librarian of the University. He held that post for a year until Lord Blantyre presented him to Blantyre parish, where he was ordained on 6 May 1773.

A short history of Blantyre written by Mr Stevenson was included in the 1835 Statistical Account of the parish, and local historians since that time have been indebted to him for the interesting facts contained within that document. It was Stevenson who in 1785 described the original church as being 'a building of great antiquity but in a most deplorable condition'. After the construction of the new church, the old building was demolished and the extra ground gained was used for new burial lairs.

The Rev. Stevenson was the first minister to preach in the second church. It is thought that the manse, constructed in 1773, was erected due to his efforts as it was built during his charge. In his later years, he had several assistants, one of whom was the Rev. Fergus. Stevenson died on 27 December 1808, aged 70, having given 36 years of service to the parish of Blantyre.

Rev. John Hodgson MD

John Hodgson, born 1781, the son of the minister of Carmunnock, was educated at Glasgow University and in 1804 was licensed by the Presbytery of Jedburgh. He continued his studies at Edinburgh University where, in 1809, he qualified as a Doctor of Medicine, but it was to the Church that he dedicated his life. Rev. Hodgson was presented to our parish by Lord Blantyre and ordained and inducted to Blantyre on 7 September 1809. At the age of 52 years, he died suddenly in Edinburgh on 9 February 1832.

Rev. James Anderson MA

James Anderson, the son of a farmer, was born at Livingston on 29 June 1785. In 1813 he graduated MA at the University of Edinburgh. The Presbytery of Dunblane licensed him in 1816. After being presented on 30 March 1832 to our parish by the tutor of Charles, Lord Blantyre, on his lordship's behalf, he was ordained here on 13 September of that year. During the 'Disruption' of 1843, the Rev. Anderson 'went out', having joined the Free Secession and having signed the 'Deed of Demission,' and was declared to be 'no longer a minister of this church' on 27 June 1843.
SEE REV. JAMES ANDERSON (A)

Rev. Samuel Paterson

The Rev. Paterson, born 11 June 1806, was ordained on 14 September 1843 and served the Church until his death on 2 May 1860, five days before the Rev. James

Anderson, his predecessor, who had left the Old Kirk in 1843 to establish the Free Church at Stonefield Road (Anderson Church). They were buried side by side in the Old Kirkyard at High Blantyre.

Rev. James Paton Gloag DD

The Rev. James Gloag was the last minister to preach in the second Parish Church in the Old Kirkyard at High Blantyre Cross. Born in Perth, he commenced as minister in Blantyre in October 1860 and served the parish for 11 years. It was through his efforts that the present Old Parish Church was constructed in 1863. He was described as 'an able scholar, a gifted preacher, a kindly friend, and one who made himself felt throughout the length and breadth of the parish as a power of good'.

During his charge at Blantyre, Rev. Gloag received the honorary degree of Doctor of Divinity from the University of St Andrews in recognition of his undoubted ability. As one of the most forward theological writers of his time, he published many books on various subjects. On 20 April 1871 Gloag was translated to Galashiels, and was later elected Moderator of the General Assembly of the Church of Scotland.

Rev. Stewart Wright

Inducted on 3 August 1871, the Rev. Stewart Wright will be forever remembered as the author of *The Annals of Blantyre*, a fine book, which has been enjoyed during the last 120 years by anyone with an interest in the history of Blantyre. Many of the references contained within this book are based on the work of Wright. His descriptions of his experiences during the events following the Blantyre Explosion (q.v.) are vivid and dramatic and can be read separately in his book.
SEE REV. STEWART WRIGHT (W)

Rev. C. Scrimgeour Turnbull MA

When the Rev. Scrimgeour Turnbull was ordained on 7 June 1888 to succeed Stewart Wright, he became the last minister to serve at Blantyre Old Parish Church in the 19th century. Turnbull was born 28 February 1860 and was educated at Glasgow High School and the University of Glasgow, where he graduated on 28 April 1882 with the MA degree.

Turnbull was responsible for the construction, in 1892, of Blantyre Old Parish Church Halls (q.v.) that stood on the corner of Main Street and Hunthill Road, the site now occupied by the east end of Kirkview House, home for the elderly. Rev. Turnbull never married and held the charge for 43 years.

Blantyre Old Parish Church Halls

The Blantyre Old Parish Church Halls were constructed in 1892 at a cost of £2,200. Rev. C. Scrimgeour Turnbull, the minister at the Old Parish Church, had the vision of building the property, which contained reading rooms, recreation rooms and a circulating library. The Halls, which stood on the corner of Hunthill Road and Main Street at High Blantyre Cross, opposite the pub, were demolished in January 1989, after which Hunthill Road was realigned at this point.

Blantyre Parish Rifle Corps

SEE MAJOR JOHN NESS (N)

Blantyre Priory

It is thought that the original house that stood on Blantyre Craig, over 100 feet above the River Clyde, was built by Patrick, 2nd Earl of Dunbar, who owned the Barony during the reign of King Alexander I of Scotland (1107-21). The earliest mention of the Priory is in some ancient records stating that the house was gifted to the order of the Augustinian Canons of Jedburgh Abbey. Another record, which may possibly be the same document, written during the reign of King Alexander II and dedicated to the Holy Rood, refers to the Earl of Levenax (Lennox), about 1248, granting a 'carucate terr', which means 'a measurement of land on which a church was founded'. The Priory was endowed with 'the 'tithes and revenues of the local church which stands in a village of the same name'.

The abbot and the monks formed a colony or 'cell' at Blantyre, which could also be used as a retreat from Jedburgh Abbey during the wars that raged for centuries between the English and the Scots. The monks would bring all their valuables and relics to Blantyre. Before the Reformation, the Priory belonged to the Archbishop of Glasgow and during the vacancy of that see, the right was exercised by the crown. Various factions occupied the Priory during sieges of Bothwell Castle when the monks would retreat further north to Restennet Abbey at Forfar.

The first mention that we have of the Priory with a definite date is 1289, as there is a mention made in one of the old Statute Books of Scotland of a Frere William, Priour de Blantir being present at a Parliament which was being held in Brigham near the English border some time during that year. Frere William was a subscriber to Bagimund's Roll, which states that Blantyre Priory was taxed upon a valuation of £66 13s. 4d. (Scots). The same Prior swore fealty to King Edward I of England at Berwick on 28 August 1296.

An earlier tax was levied to finance a crusade against the Saracens. In the year 1254 Pope Innocent IV granted King Henry III of England one-twentieth of the Ecclesiastical Revenues of Scotland, provided he would send an army to join the crusade to the Holy Land. In 1268 Pope Clement IV renewed this grant and increased it to a tenth of the taxes collected. When Henry attempted to levy the tax the Scottish clergy resisted and appealed to Rome, but the appeal was turned down. Henry was promised the money, which he urgently required, as his son was already on his way to the Holy Land with an English army. The Pope then

Ruins of the Blantyre Priory.

sent a special messenger to Scotland to collect the taxes from the Ecclesiastical Benefices whose name was Baiamund de Vicci (q.v.). He was known in Scotland as Bagimund and his list of the properties that were to be taxed was known as 'The Ragman's Roll' (q.v.), owing to the fact that the emblems, seals and coats of arms of the benefices were attached to the list by a strip of fabric.

The Scottish clergy persistently refused to pay these taxes and sent the collector back to Rome empty-handed. The Pope insisted that the tax must be paid, but the levying of it proved difficult, so that the Pope issued Bull after Bull to bring the people to proper obedience. It was the payments made to the English King that caused resentment, Henry III arrogantly claiming that, as representative of the Pope, Scotland should be subservient to him. The Scottish people decided that enough was enough and chose to fight for their liberty under William Wallace (q.v.).

Priors of Blantyre:

Friar William De Cokeburyne (*c*.1296) (q.v.)
Walter Prior De Blantyr (*c*.1380)

William Forfar (*c*.1430)
Dominus William Fresell (Fraser) (*c*.1451)
Dominus William Bassindene (*c*.1457)
Sir Thomas Coittis (Coats)
Sir Robert Coitts (Coats) (*c*.1520)
John Moncrief (*c*.1540)
John Roull (*c*.1547)
John Hamilton (1549)
William Chirnsyde (1552) (q.v.)

Blantyre Rennet

The Blantyre Rennet was a popular cooking apple in the 19th century, grown in various nurseries within Blantyre.

Blantyre Riots

The late Mrs Elizabeth Parry, who was passionate about the history of our town, recorded many of the events she had witnessed and the stories passed on to her by parents and friends. She had a vast knowledge of local events and, after writing about them, simply put what she had written in a drawer and forgot about it. Mrs Parry's writings are invaluable to any researcher of our local history.

The following is a sample of the work that she produced:

WILLIAM SMALL AND THE BLANTYRE
RIOTS, 1887

In the local cemetery is a headstone, inscribed,

WILLIAM SMALL – MINER'S AGENT
DIED 23RD JANUARY 1903
ERECTED BY THE LANARKSHIRE
MINERS
'IN CHANGELESS LOVE TO A NOBLE
FATHER
FOR HIS CHANGELESS DEVOTION TO
GOOD FOR ALL'

Small was an Englishman with a drapery business in Cambuslang. A socialist, he strongly resented the exploitation of the miners and the cruelty of the mines. In the big strike of 1887, when all the Lanarkshire miners were out, he 'shut shop' one afternoon to address a miners' meeting here in Blantyre and thus became deeply involved in their struggle for justice.

On Monday 8 February, a crowd of several hundred strikers, marching back to Glasgow from a meeting in Hamilton, looted a baker's van in Stonefield Road and roused the local strikers to action. They marched down the Main Street (Glasgow Road), pillaging shops as they went. The first was Struthers, Grocer and Wine Merchant. Windows were smashed, goods stolen and premises damaged. This was the pattern of behaviour for two days. Dixon's Store, Baird's Store, Ms Carns, Downs and McFarlanes were but a few of the many looted premises. Order was restored that evening.

Trouble flared afresh early on Tuesday morning. By noon a telegraph was sent to Commander McHardy by the shopkeepers who were alarmed at what was happening. An hour later the Chief Constable, with Sheriff Birnie and a detachment of mounted police, arrived at Stonefield Road as Dixon's Store was being sacked. Sheriff Birnie read the 'Riot Act' (q.v.), whereat the police with drawn swords, and Chief Constable McHardy wielding a heavy stick, charged the crowd, causing them to disperse. However, the looting persisted till very late that night. Several times arrests were made but in each instance the mob, infuriated, attacked the police, compelling them to free the prisoners. At one point the Police Station was attacked and so much damage done that the two prisoners held within were finally released. Many were severely hurt in these incidents, police as well as civilians. Early on Wednesday morning, fifty arrests were made. To maintain law and order, Special Police, a detachment of Hussars and Mounted Police were drafted into the town.

During this turmoil William Small was councillor and guide to the workers, and he continued so till his death, accepting, too, all the secretarial work involved. He strove for union of all the various union branches in the area, and at the formation of the Lanarkshire Miners' County Federation in 1893 was chosen as its first secretary, being paid £2 per week. The miners, as a token of their appreciation and gratitude, had a large, detached cottage, with an extensive front garden, built for him halfway down Forrest Street. On his death, his wife and family moved away and an Irish family called Duffy took over the cottage.

Blantyre Victoria Football Club

The club was originally formed in 1889 but was reconstructed as a junior team in 1900. The home ground is Castle Park, Forrest Street, which has a capacity of 6,000. The record attendance was a full house in 1945 for a Scottish Junior Cup tie against Fauldhouse.

Blantyre Victoria Football Club, 1914.

Vics first won the Scottish Junior Cup (q.v.) in 1950 in their golden jubilee year, in front of a crowd of 44,402 at Hampden Park, when they defeated Cumnock Juniors 3-0. The team was: Warren, Gilmour, McCulloch, Allan, Young (Captain), Wright, Gill, Herbert, Swan, Lennon, Rennicks. Gill, Herbert and Swan scored the goals. The team brought the cup home and was met by a large crowd at the West End. The bus slowly made its way past thousands of supporters to a reception in the Community Hall, Glasgow Road. Guest of honour was the great Jimmy Brownlie (q.v.), who played for Vics before becoming a legendary goalkeeper with Third Lanark and the Scottish international team. After a meal the team toured the town on top of the team bus, proudly displaying the trophy. The journey took longer than expected as huge crowds wearing the team colours lined the streets.

In season 1969/70 Vics won the Scottish Junior Cup for a second time, twenty years after their first success. They defeated Penicuik Juniors 1-0 in a replay at Hampden Park after the first match had ended in a 1-1 draw. Lynn, who played on the left wing, scored the winning goal. The team was: Watson, Thomson, Moore, Brodie, Douglas, Cunningham, McGrain, Gallacher, Lawson, Pickering, Lynn.

At Ibrox Stadium in season 1981-2, Vics won the Scottish Junior Cup for a third time, under manager John Young, when they defeated Baillieston 1-0. The team that day was: Burns, Davenport, McGlinchey, Muldoon, McVie, Grant, McQuade, McGurk, Kennedy, Coggill, Mitchell. Substitutes were Ward and Hamilton. McGurk scored the winning goal.

Over the years Vics have won every tournament open to them. The following is a list of the club's achievements:

Cup Winners
Scottish Junior Cup, 1950, 1970, 1982
West of Scotland Cup, 1944
Central League Cup, 1977
Central Region League Cup, 1996
Lanarkshire Challenge Cup, 1904, 1914, 1916, 1924, 1940, 1943, 1946, 1949, 1968
Lanarkshire Central Cup, 1932, 1944, 1957
Hozier Cup Winners, 1966

League Championships
Lanarkshire League, 1893, 1906, 1911, 1917, 1920, 1927
Central League Championship, 1936, 1980
Central Regional League Division 1, 1981, 1996, 1999
Central Regional League Division 2, 1980
Amongst many famous ex-Vics players are Jock Stein and Billy McNeil (Glasgow Celtic), and Joe Jordan (Manchester United).

Blantyre Weir

The height of Blantyre Weir was increased in the early 1800s as can be clearly seen in the photograph. A

Blantyre Weir.

Blantyre Works Graveyard.

'ladder' was also built into the surface of the weir to allow salmon to return each year to their spawning beds further up the Clyde. This can also be seen in the centre of the photograph. The Village School is at the top right of the picture with the tenement at Ulva Place to the left of the school. Rosebank Avenue can be seen beyond the top of the Clyde Braes.

This view across the Clyde from the site of the old Bothwell Meal Mill shows various other landmarks. The Suspension Bridge can be seen beyond the Weir/Dam. The path leading down to the bridge from the Works School is at top right. The white diagonal path was a shortcut from Ulva Place and Rosebank Avenue.

See Mill Dam Court Case (M)

Blantyre Works Graveyard

The triangular graveyard can be seen in the centre of the above photograph. The tenement at centre right is the Waterloo Row, constructed in 1815, and overlooking the Braes and the River Clyde. The Cross Row (*c*.1880) is in the centre of the picture with a tenement called Mayberry Place at the extreme left. Caskie Drive now occupies the Mayberry Place site and the old graveyard site. Before the construction of the houses in Caskie Drive protesters objected that the graveyard site should not be built upon. The contractors claimed that the old graveyard did not exist, which of course was wrong, but as the last interment was over 100 years earlier, no legal objections existed to prevent the construction of the houses.

Bolton

Bolton is a hamlet and parish near Haddington which was purchased in 1702 by Walter Stewart, 6th Lord Blantyre. The main stained glass window of Bolton church is inscribed with names commemorating Blantyre family members.

Bonnie Prince Charlie

In 1745 Bonnie Prince Charlie, with his army, passed through Blantyre on his march to Carlisle. This year was known by the locals as the 'Hielandman's Year'. An army

Bothwell Castle from the Priory Bing.

in those days fed itself by any means possible, and that included pillaging and stealing livestock, but the Prince issued strict orders that none of his soldiers should molest any person or property in Blantyre, as the parish belonged to a 'Stewart'.

Bothwell Castle

Blantyre Priory was unavoidably involved in the history of Bothwell Castle, as it was situated on top of Blantyre Craig, directly across the River Clyde, with a commanding view of the castle. During the wars between Scotland and England, Bothwell Castle was placed under siege on four occasions. The English laid siege in 1301 and 1336, when the castle was occupied by the Scots. When the English garrisoned the castle, it was placed under siege by the Scots from 1298 until 1299 and again in 1377. It is probable that the opposing armies would have occupied Blantyre Priory during these sieges.

Boundaries

The parish is situated in the north-west of the parliamentary district of Hamilton. The River Clyde in the north and north-west forms the boundary with Glasgow, Uddingston and Bothwell. The River Calder on the west forms the boundary with East Kilbride and Cambuslang. Hamilton and part of Bothwell are to the east of the parish and Glassford flanks its southern boundary. From north to south the length of the parish is six and a quarter miles long. Its breadth is two and a half miles at its widest and a little over a quarter of a mile at its narrowest point.

Bowling Alley

In 1959 the old Picture House Cinema (q.v.) building was converted into a ten pin bowling alley called 'The Blantyre Bowl'. The premises stood on the ground between the entrance doors of the present Blantyre Sports Centre and the pavement of Glasgow Road.

Britannia

At the request of King Charles II, Frances Teresa Stewart (1647-1702) posed as the model for the symbolic figure of Britannia to be cast by the Royal Mint on the new penny and halfpenny coins that he had commissioned. It was claimed that she was one of the King's many mistresses a fact denied by some, but it is generally accepted. There is no doubt that the King was in love with her. Frances was the granddaughter of Walter Stewart, 1st Lord Blantyre, and it is thought that she may have been born in her grandfather's home at Blantyre Priory. Her father, Walter Stewart, the third son of the 1st Lord Blantyre, was a physician at the court of the exiled Queen, Henrietta Maria, wife of Charles I of France. She spent her formative years in France and by the age of 15 she was already famous for her beauty and known throughout Europe as 'La Belle Stewart'. She soon caught the eye of the French King, Louis XIV, and it was thought prudent to send her to London to escape his advances. She was installed at the court of King Charles II and within a short time had become one of the maids of honour to Queen Catherine.

Frances caught the eye of King Charles, who showered her with gifts and offered her titles and even suggested that he would divorce the Queen and marry her. She declined all his offers and eloped with his cousin Charles, Duke of Richmond and Lennox. Charles was furious and sent her husband abroad on diplomatic missions which kept him apart from Frances for long spells. Five years after her marriage, her husband died in suspicious circumstances, falling between his ship and the harbour wall while disembarking and drowning. Some claimed that he was the victim of a conspiracy and fingers of suspicion were pointed at the King.

Broadway Cinema.

Britannia.

Frances became disfigured by an attack of smallpox but remained a member of the royal court for the rest of her life. On her death, in 1702, she left £50,000 in her will to her 'impoverished' cousin's son, Alexander, 5th Lord Blantyre. Her trustees were to buy a house for him on condition that it be named 'Lennox's love to Blantyre'. Lethington Tower in Haddington was purchased and duly named. It was thought by many at the time that the name was out of character for such a noble house and in due course it was changed to Lennoxlove. Lennoxlove is now the home of the Duke of Hamilton, whose family purchased the property in 1948.

The house is open to the public and some of the gifts given to Frances by the King are on display. A fire in the Oak Room (formerly known as the Blantyre-Stewart Room) destroyed eight of 14 paintings of the Lords and Ladies of Blantyre and their families. The surviving six pictures, one of which is the painting of Frances, seen here, were badly affected by smoke damage during the fire but were successfully restored and are now back on public display.

Broadway Cinema

The Broadway cinema was situated on the corner of Glasgow Road and Station Road. The premises opened in 1939 and the first film shown was *Dawn Patrol* starring Errol Flynn and Basil Rathbone. Unlike the old Picture House it was a beautifully appointed cinema, with a large winding marble staircase leading to a lounge level that had thick carpet and comfortable easy chairs. Doors from this area led to a further flight of stairs to the 'balcony'.

Admission prices varied but for many years the price of the balcony was 1s. 3d., the price for the back stalls on the ground level was 9d. and 6d. for the front stalls. It was generally thought that only 'posh' folk and 'winchin couples' could afford the balcony. The 'average' person used the back stalls and the 'not so well off' used the front stalls. A Saturday afternoon matinée was screened for children.

Posters similar to the one shown here, advertising the first films ever shown in the cinema, were displayed throughout the town. Each bill was shown twice nightly

The Broadway's Opening Programme in 1939.

The Bronze-Age urn found at 11 Belairs Place.

and ran for two consecutive nights, Monday to Saturday. A typical 'night at the pictures' consisted of the main feature, a 'B' film, the newsreel and, if you were lucky, occasionally a cartoon.

When all the seats were taken, queues formed around the cinema. As people left and seats emptied, the number available was called by the commissionaire. For example, 'First four for the back stalls, and the first two for the balcony.' There was a separate queue for each section. The posh folk queuing for the balcony stood on the inside of the pavement on Glasgow Road, against the wall of the building, towards Birrell's, the sweet shop. The queue for the back stalls stood on the outside, adjacent to the road. Pedestrians had to squeeze through a narrow gap in the middle. The people queuing for the front stalls stood behind a metal rail that ran the length of the cinema down Station Road. When seats became available, people would take them even if it was in the middle, or near the end, of the film. They would subsequently leave the cinema where the film reached the point in the story line where they had entered. The last films shown, on 30 August 1969, were *Shalako*, the main feature, *Thunder of the Guns* the supporting film.

The empty building was destroyed by fire and demolished. A supermarket was constructed on the site, which was later used by the Housing Department of South Lanarkshire Council until they moved in 1999 to the newly constructed David Dale House in John Street.

Bronze Age (2000-700 BC)

Ancient graves with urns dating back to the Bronze Age have been discovered in various districts of Blantyre. In April 1939, while ploughing one of his fields at Coatshill Farm, a farmer named Jackson damaged his plough when it struck a large stone, which on removal revealed four upright slabs of a stone cist. Within the cist sat a small urn, which was broken when it was removed. Bones were also found but turned to dust on being touched. The inside of the chamber was 76 cm. long and the width tapered from 61 cm. to 53 cm. The depth was approximately 51 cm. The contents of the grave are seen in the photograph. The location of the site was the rear garden at 11 Bellairs Place. The urn was completely restored by staff at Kelvingrove Art Galleries, Glasgow.

Around 1832, a similar cist was found at Shott Farm near the Old Parish Church, and fragments of six larger urns were found in other parts of the same field. During the construction of the railway across Archer's Croft (q.v.) (Armour Court and Ellisland Drive) to the Blantyre-East Kilbride railway viaduct (q.v.), a fine example of a Bronze-Age grave was found.

The site of Camp Knowe, a Bronze-Age hill fort, can be seen on a rise in the field opposite the house of what was, until recently, Marshall's farm at Calderside, Auchentibber. Anciently this field contained water between the fort site and the road, a map belonging to the Marshall family clearly stating that it flooded in winter. Farmers cut a section through the banking at the east of the site to allow the water to drain into the stream below. Camp Knowe was 200 metres in circumference and stood in a very strong defensive position, surrounded by water and with a sheer drop to the stream. Near the site, a subterranean structure made of flag stones was discovered around 1880 but its location has now been lost.

Broompark Farm

Broompark Road took its name from Broompark Farm, the farmhouse situated directly across the road from where the gates of John Ogilvie RC Church are now located. The last owner of this farm was Tam Watson. Broompark Railway Bridge crossed the road at this point, adjacent to the farmhouse, taking the line up to the double bridges at Hunthill Junction (q.v), at the corner of Stonefield Crescent and Hunthill Road. After the removal of the high banking which carried the railway line, the houses at the top left of Stonefield Crescent were constructed on the site.

Brown, Daisy (School of Dance)

Daisy Brown was the proprietor of a dance studio in Glasgow Road, located in a shop adjacent to the Picture House Cinema (q.v.). Daisy and her husband Jack, who was the manager of the cinema, were involved in show business for many years. They lived with their family in nearby Alpine Street. Daisy's 'School of Dance' produced many talented dancers who went on to perform professionally in theatres throughout the country. Her students presented an annual show which was usually staged in the hall of the Miners Welfare Institute at Calder Street. Their two children, Joyce and Bobby, also became involved in the theatre. Bobby was known as 'Scotland's Boy Comedian' and dressed in the style of Harry Lauder.

Brown, James

In 1900 James Brown was appointed as the first headmaster of Auchinraith Primary School (q.v.).

Brown, Thomas G.

Tom Brown was a Painter and Decorator whose yard was situated on Glasgow Road directly opposite Victoria Street. The business was the oldest establishment of its kind in Scotland. Brown was elected a member of the first Blantyre School Board in 1873.

Brownlie Family

In 1979 three American sisters from Arizona, who were in Blantyre to trace their family tree, visited me seeking any information to assist them with their research. They informed me that Aggie Bain's Cottage (q.v.), Barnhill, was previously known as Brownlie's Cottage. Their ancestor, Robert Brownlie, sold his cottage to Aggie Bain when he emigrated to America in 1868. They also told me a story passed down through the family concerning their great, great grandfather, John Brownlie (born 1744, died 26 July 1831). Early one morning, when John was leaving the cottage, he found an abandoned new born baby in a basket, which was sitting on his doorstep in the lane which now leads to Glenfruin Road. A note was pinned to a shawl, asking them to take the child in and raise her as their own and requesting that she be called Mary. A week before this incident Mrs Brownlie had given birth to a baby girl and, by coincidence, had named her Mary.

Nevertheless she took the baby in and raised the child as her own. She was keen to grant the request regarding the child's Christian name but she could not possibly raise two girls named Mary Brownlie so had the abandoned baby christened Mary Blantyre. Mary married a Robert Gray, and had a family, a record of which can be seen in the International Genealogy Index (Mormon Database) in most public libraries.

Brownlie, Jimmy

Blantyre man Jimmy Brownlie is still recognised today as one of the all-time greats of Scottish football. Jimmy, who was born in 1885, claimed he learned his goalkeeping skills between the posts of the sheds of the old High Blantyre Primary School. He was playing for Blantyre Victoria (q.v.) when he was asked to sign for Glasgow Celtic but was informed that he would only be an understudy to their current goalkeeper. Confident of his own abilities, he refused their offer and in 1906 signed for the now defunct Third Lanark FC and became a legend within the game. Third Lanark was one of the top teams in the Scottish First Division, and Jimmy was first team goalkeeper for 17 years until 1923. Jimmy was 5 feet 11 inches tall, weighed 13 stones, and was known within the game as 'The Man with the Iron Clutch'. When Jimmy, who was a bricklayer by trade, was due to play in a home game at Cathkin Park, he worked until midday and, after a quick change, caught a tramcar to Glasgow. He proceeded to a pub called the *Horse-Shoe Bar*, where he had a half pint of beer and a slice of toasted cheese, the pub's specialty, then caught another tramcar to Mount Florida to join his teammates at Cathkin Park, which was close to Hampden Park Stadium.

Jimmy was capped by Scotland on 16 occasions and only conceded 11 goals in those matches. He also gained 14 caps with the Scottish League and played in four 'Victory Internationals' after the First World War. In 1912 he was awarded the equivalent of the present Player of the Year Award, when he received the Silver Cup as the most popular player in Scotland. In 1912 he was earning £11 a week, which was a remarkable wage at that time. In season 1923/24 Jimmie was appointed player-manager of Dundee Hibs, the forerunner of Dundee United. He held the position until 1931 when he was appointed secretary manager, and was manager between 1934 and 1936. In 1938 he was appointed joint managing director of the club.

Jimmy Brownlie died in 1973.

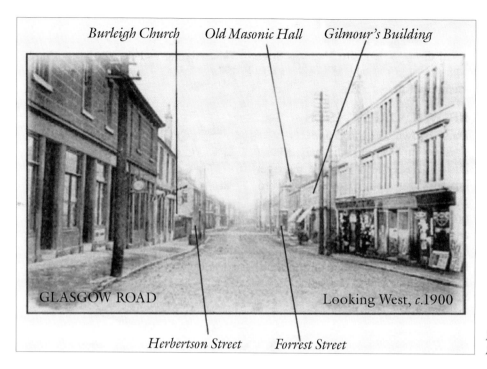

Burleigh Church   Old Masonic Hall   Gilmour's Building

GLASGOW ROAD   Looking West, *c.*1900

Herbertson Street   Forrest Street

Location of Burleigh Memorial Church.

Bryce, James

James Bryce, of Scottish ancestry, was born in Belfast in 1838. He was a noted historian and wrote two major books, *The Holy Roman Empire* and *The American Commonwealth*. He was a Professor of Civil Law at Oxford University in 1870. As Liberal MP for the Parish of Blantyre, he held various important posts within the government, which included Chancellor of the Duchy of Lancaster in 1891, President of the Board of Trade in 1894 and Secretary of State for Ireland in 1896. Later Bryce was appointed UK Ambassador to America and resided at the British Embassy in Washington. His father was a lecturer at Glasgow University and lived in Thornhill Avenue, where he had constructed a large house. James inherited the house and resided there when escaping from his governmental duties.

'Buggy Building'

The 'Buggy Building', a three-storey building, was part of a row of tenements that stood on Auchinraith Road directly opposite Elm Street. It was constructed by Guy Semple, who named it Melbourne Place. It is said that the nickname 'Buggy Building' was given to it because the timbers used for its rafters and flooring joists were obtained from buildings that were lying derelict at Blantyre Mills. It was suggested by some at the time that the old timbers, because of their age, must surely have been infected by bugs (woodworm). The two-storeyed section to the right of the 'Buggy Building' was known as James's Building.

Burleigh Memorial Church

The Burleigh Church, originally known as the East Church, was constructed in 1880 on the corner of Glasgow Road and Herbertson Street, and was demolished in 1978. The western section of Reid the Printers now occupies the site. The church was named after its first minister, John Burleigh, who died 28 October 1922. For the first year of its existence the church members rented Dall's Shop in Gilmour's Building (q.v.), Glasgow Road, for £25 per annum. The church moved during its second year into a larger shop in Henderson's Building for seven months, then to the Masonic Hall above the Livingstonian Bar on the corner of Glasgow Road and Forrest Street. These premises were later occupied by the Blantyre Electric Picture House Company.

Calaterium

A story of our ancient ancestors is handed down to us by Geoffrey of Monmouth in his book *British History*. It tells of a battle having been fought between the Britons and foreign invaders at 'the wood Calaterium'. The historian Glennie says that 'Calderwood', on the banks of the River Calder opposite Blantyre, would appear to be the site of 'Calaterium Nemus' of Geoffrey of Monmouth. The proximity of the Bronze-Age fort of Camp Knowe at Calderside may support this claim.

Calderbank House

The earliest record available of the house is from 1816, when Calderbank appears on Forrest's Map of Lanarkshire. The occupant of the house between 1816 and 1835 was a Mr Struthers, of whom nothing is known. The estate then passed to John Hutton (q.v.) and his wife Ann Elizabeth Yuille. The 1841 census records that Hutton's widow, Ann, and her sister were resident in the house. Ann died in 1864 and it is not known who owned Calderbank from that time, but it may well be that it was still owned by the Hutton family until 1878 when the owner was John Richard Cochrane (q.v.), a power-loom cloth manufacturer, whose offices were in Waddell Street, Glasgow. An original Calderbank House was possib;y situated adjacent to the new railway line, abandoned due to the noise created by the passing trains and the present Calderglen House(q.v.) constructed to replace it.

Calder Braes

The Calder Braes stretched north from the Peth Brae at Barnhill, along the banks of the River Calder directly below Bardykes Road. Apples, pears, plums, strawberries and vegetables were grown in these fields and sold in Hamilton and Glasgow, long before the orchards of Clydeside and Lanark were established.

Calderglen House

It was recorded in 1878 that the owner of Calderbank House was John Richard Cochrane (q.v.), a power-loom cloth manufacturer. The estate originally stretched from the present main entrance on Blantyrefarm Road to Newton Road end near Fin-me-oot. John Hutton (q.v.) or his wife Ann, previous owners of the house, sold a section of the estate to the Caledonian Railway Company to allow them to construct the Newton/Blantyre-Hamilton line as a branch from the main Glasgow-London line. The Newton/Hamilton branch line was opened on 17 September 1849. There is a line of thought that the noise caused by the passing trains created intolerable living conditions within the house, or structural damage was caused by the heavy trains passing nearby, and the decision was taken to construct a new house some 200 yards away from the railway.

The map is the only one I have seen that shows the supposed out-houses of Calderglen House, and by any standards they are of considerable size. The large

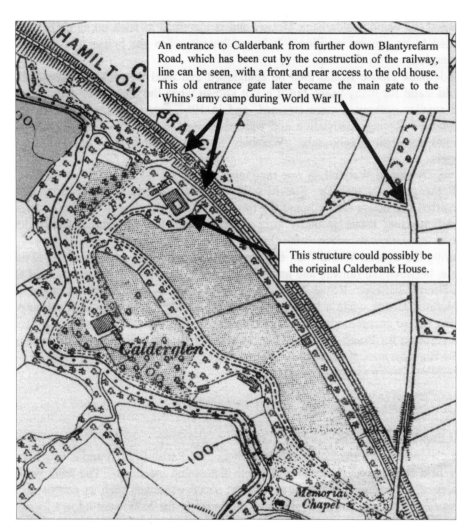

An entrance to Calderbank from further down Blantyrefarm Road, which has been cut by the construction of the railway, line can be seen, with a front and rear access to the old house. This old entrance gate later became the main gate to the 'Whins' army camp during World War II.

This structure could possibly be the original Calderbank House.

Site of Calderglen House.

building with the enclosed courtyard may be the original Calderbank House, as it was surely too large to be an out-house. If it was the earlier Calderbank House, it was at least as large as the new house, which retained the name and is identified as such on all early maps showing it in its present position. It is not known when the house was renamed Calderglen. Calderbank House would stand for many years, but it is not known when the house was demolished. The smaller out-houses were retained, and in 1952 purchased by the Greyhound Racing Association to be used by the Shawfield Stadium as kennels for their greyhounds. Wembley Stadium Limited later purchased the kennels.

At one time a family named Waddell owned the house but it was a Dr Suckle who sold the property to a company which converted it into a home for the elderly. At the time of writing, a large private housing estate is under construction within the grounds of Calderglen House. During the Second World War the government confiscated a large section of the estate between the railway line and Blantyrefarm Road for the construction of an anti-aircraft battery. Royal Artillery personnel were billeted in the basement of Calderglen House while a large army camp, called the 'Whins', was constructed on the site to accommodate them and the guns. The Whins Camp was also used as a barracks for Polish troops. After the war, owing to the lack of available housing in the Blantyre area, families of squatters lived in the timber huts.

Calderview Building

Calderview once stood on Hunthill Road at the corner of Stonefield Crescent. In the early 1900s a Captain Barr, who at one time was a county councillor for the district and well-known within the community, lived in a house in this tenement.

Caldwell Halls

The Caldwell Halls were owned by the Stonefield Parish Church and it was here that they held their Sunday school and youth fellowship meetings. The halls were also used for badminton and hired out for social occasions, such as dances. Because of the long irregular shape of the building, it was known as the 'Coffin Halls'. It stood on the corner of Glasgow Road and Auchinraith Road, where the East Kilbride Expressway now crosses Glasgow Road, and was demolished in the early 1960s.

Camp Knowe

Camp Knowe is the site of an ancient British fort at Calderside, Auchentibber.
SEE BRONZE AGE (B)

Campbell's Nursery

SEE AUCHINRAITH NURSERY (A)

Carabine, Jimmy

Jimmy Carabine was a famous Scottish footballer born in Baird's Rows, Blantyre. Between 1934 and 1945 he played over 400 games at right back for the now defunct Third Lanark FC, and also played for Scotland on 14 occasions. During the Second World War he guested for Heart of Midlothian FC. As a youth, Jimmy played with Blantyre Saint Joseph's Boy's Guild, and then junior football with Larkhall Thistle before signing for Third Lanark. After his playing days were over, he was appointed manager of his beloved Third Lanark from 1946 until 1949. Jimmy later became a respected sports journalist with a Glasgow newspaper.

Jimmy told a story of being married on a Saturday morning and then dashing to Cathkin Park to play in a match. He took his bride with him and she sat in the stand. Just after half time Jimmy was ordered off, and about twenty minutes later his wife, who knew nothing about football, indignantly enquired, 'When is Jimmy coming back on?'

Causeystanes

A tollbooth was once located at Causeystanes, on Main Street at the corner of Broompark Road, to collect money from travellers with carts, etc. on the 'Turnpike Road'(q.v.). By law, proprietors of businesses had to upgrade the road at the front of their properties to a standard known as 'Turnpike'. They were then entitled to collect a toll from anyone who drove carriages or carts along the road.

Cemeteries

The old Kirkyard of Blantyre received the dead of the parish for many centuries until it was handed back to the care of the Kirk Session of the Old Parish Church in May 1875 and the new Parochial Cemetery was opened at Cemetery Road. The new cemetery was extended in April 1900. The Blantyre Mills Works village had its own graveyard (q.v.) located in Caskie Drive which was used until the opening of the parochial cemetery in 1875. The new Priestfield Cemetery at Hillhouse Road was opened in May 1981 on the site of Dixon's Colliery No. 1 Pit.

Central Co-op

The Central Co-operative (Co-op) building contained several Co-op shops, with the Head Office above those at the corner of Glasgow Road and Herbertson

Central Co-op, c.1925.

Street (opposite Forrest Street). The first Co-operative in Blantyre was registered in 1883 and the section of the building on the right of this photograph was built at that time. The section in the foreground, on the corner of the building as it turned into Herbertson Street, was constructed in 1885. The Co-operative

Chieftain bus at Stoneymeadow, c.1955.

Society movement expanded rapidly throughout the community. In those early years a dividend was paid annually to its members, but later it was paid quarterly.
SEE CO-OP BAKERY (C)
SEE CO-OP HALL (C)

Chapper Upper

The Chapper Upper was a man paid 6d. a week by miners to knock on the door or shutters of their house and waken them in the early hours of the morning in order to go to work.

Chieftain Bus

Laurie of Hamilton, the proprietors of the 'Chieftain Buses', ran a service from Hamilton, along High Blantyre Road, Burnbank, Main Street, High Blantyre, and up Stoneymeadow Road, and across the General's Bridge to East Kilbride Village and Hairmyres Hospital.

Church of the Nazarene

The Church of the Nazarene was established around 1900 by a group of like-minded people who met to worship in each other's houses. These services were known as 'Cottage' or 'Kitchen Meetings'. Later, in 1909, under the guidance of Brother John Drysdale, they held their services in the Caldwell Halls (q.v.), Glasgow Road, which was situated on the corner of Auchinraith Road adjacent to the Rosendale Tenement (q.v.) (almost directly across Glasgow Road from the present east-

bound access ramp to the East Kilbride Expressway), and called their group 'The Blantyre Holiness Mission'. In 1910 they purchased a large Nissen hut to be used as a church and erected it in Jackson Street. The inauguration service of the Blantyre Pentecostal Church of Scotland took place on 10 March 1910. It was conducted by the Rev. George Sharpe DD, the first minister of the church who also served as minister of a sister church at Parkhead, Glasgow. In those early years of the church, members had to take a vow to abstain from smoking cigarettes and drinking alcohol.

The first resident pastor was the Rev. George Dempsie, appointed on 31 August 1910. Since 1907, 24 ministers have served as pastors, the best known of whom was the much respected Rev. William Mackie, who served

Church of the Nazarene.

from 1969 until 1987. Rev. Mackie was a butcher in the Central Co-op at Glasgow Road and occasionally at the High Blantyre branch.

When the local council was constructing the flats in Elm Street in 1952, Bill Clayden, a member of the congregation, asked the council to lay a path to the rear of the church to provide the congregation with access to the premises from Elm Street. The authorities agreed to this request and, after the new entrance was completed, Mr Clayden suggested that the layout of the interior of the church be completely reversed. With the agreement of the congregation, he carried out the work virtually single-handedly.

Time eventually caught up with the old Nissen hut and the present church was constructed directly opposite. The old structure was later demolished. Mrs Janet Mackie officially opened the new church when the first service and dedication took place on 24 October 1982.

Clay Road

The Clay Road was a path that linked Glasgow Road and Main Street, High Blantyre. Victoria Street was constructed over it. A section of the original Clay Road can still be seen today at the top of Victoria Street leading to Main Street.

Clinic

The Public Health Institute and Children's Welfare Centre in Victoria Street was opened in 12 October 1928 and was known locally as the 'Clinic'. A new Health Centre, in which all local doctors, with one exception, had a surgery, was constructed adjacent to the Clinic. It opened in August 1983 and was severely damaged by

fire and replaced by the present building, which, at the time of writing, has been partly demolished and is being expanded and redesigned. To accommodate the new structure, part of the original Clinic building has been demolished. When the construction of the new Health Centre is completed, the remainder of the Institute will be demolished and a car park for the new premises constructed on the site.

The Social Works Department, which occupied the Clinic after it was vacated in 1983, moved to David Dale House in John Street when it was officially opened on 26 June 2000.

Clyde Row

Clyde Row was a long row of miners' cottages situated on the left of Sydes Brae approaching Auchentibber from High Blantyre.

Clydesdale Oil Works

The Clydesdale Oil Works were located in Blantyre Works Village on the site of the flats built beyond Anderson Gardens, at the foot of Station Road. The Works regularly caught fire and it seemed the fire brigade attended an outbreak there at least once every month. The company closed in the late 1950s.

Another oil works, owned by William Sommerville & Sons, was located at the bottom of Forrest Street adjacent to the Blantyre Engineering Company (q.v.). This company also closed in the 1950s.

Clydeview Shopping Centre

Clydeview Shopping Centre, Glasgow Road, was opened in October 1980 on the land between Logan Street and

Clinic, Victoria Street/Calder Street, 1938.

Glasgow Road/Victoria Street, site of Clydeview Shopping Centre.

Victoria Street. The following properties previously occupied the site: running west from Logan Street to Craig Street, was the Post Office, then a long tenement called the Central Building in which was located the Co-op Chemist. Harpers Garage was situated on the other corner of Craig Street, then a small tenement containing two shops with four houses above. Adjacent to this was a three-storeyed building known as Whifflet Place and, finally, Low Blantyre Primary School (q.v.), which was located on the corner of Victoria Street.

Coats of Blantyre

The earliest mention of the Coats family is Sir Thomas Coattis who, according to the Coats' family history, is recorded as being the Prior of Blantyre *c.*1500. This is the only mention that I could find that he held that position. His son Sir Robert Coatts was Prior of Blantyre *c.*1520. Their descendants are recorded in various old documents as landowners within the community for hundreds of years.

Cochrane of Calderglen

John Richard Cochrane purchased Calderbank/Calderglen House in 1878. Cochrane was a power-loom cloth manufacturer, whose head office was in Waddell Street, Glasgow. He also owned the Birdsfield Brick Works at High Blantyre, and worked until he was 90 years old. In the 1880s Cochrane was appointed Justice of the Peace for Lanarkshire. He was a member of the Royal Society of Arts, London and died in March 1921, aged 94 years.

Cochrane suffered a tragic loss when his 23-year-old son Pelham Maitland Cochrane was killed by a train as he walked along the railway line to Calderglen House. As the house was approximately half-way between Blantyre Station and Newton Station, the family found it quicker to leave the train at Newton and walk along the line to their house at Calderglen Estate. On 14 July 1883 Pelham, an army officer, alighted at Newton Station, accompanied by a fellow officer. Fifty metres from the platform of the station they observed a ballast train coming towards them. Pelham's friend stepped to the right of the track but Pelham stepped to his left onto the down line and into the path of the Hamilton express, which cut him to pieces. His father built a beautiful private chapel within the grounds of Calderglen Estate (near Dura Drive) and interred his body there. Four other family members were buried within it. In 1925 the mosaics, seen here, that adorned the walls of the chapel were gifted, along with other ornaments, to the Burgh of Hamilton and now hang on the walls of the main staircase of Hamilton Town Hall. The chapel was stripped of its remaining fitments when the Cochranes sold the estate in the 1950s. The doors and the stained glass windows were gifted to the Burleigh Church, Glasgow Road.

Mosaic from the Chapel at Calderglen Estate.

Mosaic from the Chapel at Calderglen Estate.

After the death of Pelham Cochrane, the Caledonian Railway Company erected a timber platform adjacent to Calderglen Estate for the use of the Cochrane family which was known locally as 'Cochrane's Halt'.

Cokeburyne, William de

William de Cokeburyne was Prior of Blantyre about 1296. It is recorded in an old English document that Edward I of England issued a writ in Wemyss, Fife, dated 5 March 1303/4, commanding Robert de Barde (Baird), the Sheriff of Lanark, to desist from distraining the pledges for the ransom of Friar William de Cokeburyne, Warden of Blantyre Priory (q.v.), as this was in violation of the conditions on which John Comyn, the Regent, and his adherents had surrendered to the King. It would that appear that the Friar was an adherent of Comyn at the Battle of Falkirk. He was then held as hostage by Barde (Robert the Bruce) on the King's behalf until his ransom was paid.

Collieries

It was fortunate for the inhabitants of Blantyre that coal deposits were discovered in 1868 at a time when the cotton mills at Blantyre Works were in decline. The Works finally closed in 1904 and many of the redundant employees obtained jobs in the collieries sunk in and around the town. Before the 1870s, coal was carted in from Cambuslang and Hamilton. Early test borings in the 1860s seemed to indicate there were no coal seams in the strata under Blantyre or the Quarter district of Hamilton, which geologists found puzzling, but further test borings in 1868 discovered a slip or fault in the coal belt formations under Hamilton. Subsequent test borings in Blantyre found rich seams at 100 fathoms, far deeper than the other collieries in the Lanarkshire coal belt. The geological fault, which caused the coal belt suddenly to drop below Hamilton, reappeared at Dechmont, and was known as the 'Lanarkshire Fault'.

Eight pits were sunk within the parish of Blantyre. Dixon's Collieries Limited, the largest owners in the area, commenced test borings in 1867 and large deposits were found throughout the district. Dixon's No. 1 and No. 2 were sunk in 1871 and were in production by 1873. Dixon's No. 3 pit was sunk in 1873-4 and was on line by 1876. The three pits were situated on what is now Hillhouse Road, between the Sydes Brae and the roundabout at East Avenue between the Priestfield Industrial Estate and the Hamilton International Business Park, and occupied the ground on either side of the road to the foot of the Sydes Brae. No. 1 pit stood on the land now occupied by Priestfield Cemetery and the adjoining slip road from the East Kilbride Expressway. Part of Hamilton International Business Park stands on the site of No. 2 pit.

Bothwell Castle Colliery (Priory Pit).

No.3 pit was situated on the site of the Priestfield Industrial Estate adjacent to Hillhouse Road. The premises of the Raeburn Brick Company now stand on the site of No. 3 pithead, but the site of the shaft was never built upon. It stood on the vacant ground between the brickyard and the Hillhouse Road, at the corner of East Avenue. Dixon sunk a fourth pit at Larkfield, the site of which is now occupied by the football pitch at Stonefield Road, directly across from Burnbrae Road.

Merry and Cunningham were the proprietors of Auchinraith Colliery which was sunk in 1872 and was in production by 1875. It was located on the open ground at Auchinraith Road adjacent to the timber houses which, at the time of writing, is being prepared for the construction of new houses that will be called Victoria Gardens. Before construction could start, considerable time was taken to infill the two old pit shafts.

Baird and Co. was the proprietor of Craighead Colliery (q.v.), which was situated beyond the railway bridge on the left of Whistleberry Road adjacent to the railway line. The pit opened in 1876 and was immediately followed by Bothwell Castle pits, Nos. 3 & 4, known locally as the 'Priory Pit' because of the nearby ruins of the old Blantyre Priory. The pithead was adjacent to the railway line close to Blantyrefarm Road. Most miners made their way to the colliery by a timber staircase at the railway bridge at Station Road, which led to a path that ran parallel to the railway line, a distance of about one mile. All that remains of this colliery is the building that contained the pit baths, still used today by a small engineering company.

Russell & Summerlea Iron Company was the proprietor of the Spittal Pit, which was outside the Blantyre boundary at the West End but was always considered a Blantyre colliery where many Blantyre miners were employed.

Two small drift mines were located within the parish. Craigmuir Colliery, of which nothing remains, was owned by Dunlop & Company and was situated near Hamilton Drive to the south of Blantyre Old Parish Church. The other, Dykehead Colliery, was owned by Dunn & Ure. The exact location of this small mine is unknown but it is safe to assume it was situated at Dykehead, a field at the top left of Sydes Brae flanked by Parkneuk Road and the parish boundary with Hamilton at Earnock Road. Access was from Earnock Road a few metres from the corner of Parkneuk Road. Two rows of cottages once stood at this corner and may have been constructed for the miners of a limestone pit which was also located in this field. The Dykehead area, the limestone pit, and the miners' cottages can be seen on the second edition Ordnance Survey Map, 1898.

Congregational Church

The Congregational Church in Craig Street, which was formed on 8 March 1877 by the Rev. H. Liddell and originally known as the Evangelical Union Church, consisted of 56 members. In 1878 the Rev. William Wylie was accepted as minister and was inducted on 5 May of that year. The construction of the church, seen here, commenced on 10 April 1878, and the foundation stone was laid by William Wilson Esq. of Glasgow. A parchment with the above information, found behind the foundation stone when the church was demolished in 1954, was headed, 'Craig's Hall', High Blantyre. The exact location of Craig's Hall is unknown but is generally thought that it belonged to John Craig, a local landowner. The church was constructed on the newly laid road called Craig Street that replaced the old Slag Road connecting Glasgow Road and Main Street, and I think it safe to assume that John Craig owned the land upon which Craig Street was constructed, and that it was named after him. It is probable that John Craig was a benefactor of the early church, when you consider that his property was used as a temporary church in 1877.

A group was formed with members of other churches which, from time to time, trudged up the Sydes Brae to Auchentibber carrying a small box containing a portable organ to hold meetings in the school hall. Before 1900 the church also had a silver band, which was seated in the choir area and played during services. One of the ministers, the Rev. D.W. Thomson, was the first to draw to the attention of the Rev. J.I. McNair the state of David Livingstone's birthplace in the Shuttle Row, which had become run down. He pointed out its possibilities to McNair, who was at that time President of the Congregational Union

Congregational Church, c.1880.

of Scotland and was largely instrumental in bringing the David Livingstone National Memorial to pass.

The church was demolished in 1954 when it was discovered that underground workings had made the building unsafe. In 1920, when the structural faults became apparent, a special fundraising effort commenced to finance the reinforcement of the church and re-slate the roof, which was in need of repair. The present church was constructed and opened for worship in 1958. In 1993 the church left the Congregational Union and joined the Congregational Federation in Scotland.

Co-op Bakery

The Co-op Bakery was located on the original route of Auchinraith Road (now the top of Craig Street). The houses in Carrick Gardens now occupy this site.

Co-op Hall

The large Blantyre Cooperative Hall at Herbertson Street was used for many functions, such as weddings, concerts and dancing every Saturday night. Prior to the opening of the Picture House Cinema (q.v.) in 1913, the hall was used as a cinema, showing silent movies at 6p.m. and 8.30p.m. The entrance fee was 4d.

Cosy Corner Pub

The *Cosy Corner Pub* was situated at the end of a tenement on the corner of Greenside Street and Glasgow Road. The year '1876' was engraved on a chimney, and the year '1875' inscribed on the lintel above the close that gave access to the rear of the building. Greenside Street was located alongside the west wall of the present Sports Centre. The site of the present floral gardens, from the west side of the Sports Centre to directly opposite Victoria Street, was originally known as Hart's Land.

Cottage Hospital

It was felt by local doctors that there was an urgent need for a general hospital within the parish. In

Co-op Bakery, c.1930.

February 1906 a public meeting in Blantyre to elect a committee and discuss the possibility of raising funds to construct a Cottage Hospital took place. Mr Andrew Miller Bannatyne of Millheugh was elected as chairman and Mr George Campbell, manager of the Clydesdale Bank, appointed honorary secretary and treasurer of the group. After receiving donations from throughout the community, a sum of £4,162 was raised. The hospital was constructed in Bardykes Road overlooking the River Calder at a cost of £3,000. In the male ward there were four beds for adults and two cots for children, whilst in the female ward there were two beds for adults and two cots for children. The hospital received its first patients in February 1910 and was officially opened by Mrs Miller Bannatyne of Millheugh House on 25 June 1910. It was the first local general hospital to be constructed in Lanarkshire and was still in use in the early 1930s. The hospital is now a private house located at 63 Bardykes Road.

Before the construction of the Cottage Hospital, a Fever Hospital known as the 'Hospital for Infectious Diseases' had been constructed in 1880 to treat inhabitants who had contracted contagious diseases. They were treated and kept in strict isolation in the hospital which was situated at the top of what is now Victoria Street. Its front gates were where the houses between Nos 110 and 118 Victoria Street now stand at

Cottage Hospital.

the corner of Burnbrae Road. This hospital also became a private house and its last residents were a family named McShannon.

Craig, Robert

In 1967 Robert Craig recorded a remarkable victory when he became the first Scottish Nationalist Party candidate in the Blantyre district to be elected as a councillor in the Lanarkshire County Local Elections.

Craighead Colliery

Craighead Colliery, owned by Messrs William Baird & Company, was situated on the left side of Whistleberry Road adjacent to the present Hamilton Circle railway line, between the railway bridge and the premises of Ireland Alloys. The colliery and its refuse 'bings' occupied the land from Whistleberry Road to the Clyde Braes at the old Blantyre-Bothwell Railway Viaduct (q.v.).

Craighead House

Craighead House was situated on the left side of Whistleberry Road between Irelands Alloy Company and Bothwell Bridge. The mansion, which had been lying empty for three years, was destroyed by fire on 18 February 2002 and demolished a few weeks later. The property had latterly belonged to the Jesuit Fathers of the Roman Catholic Church and was used as a religious retreat. Sir Walter Scott was a regular visitor to the house and it is claimed that he wrote a large part of *Old Mortality*, which was based on the Battle of Bothwell Bridge, here, and that the mansion of 'Fairyknowe', in the book is based on Craighead House.

Craigneith Castle, Auchentibber

The ruins of Craigneith Castle stand on a high cliff near Calderside, above the River Calder, directly opposite the site of Calderwood Castle. The last building to stand on the cliff was a 'folly' constructed by the owners of Calderwood Castle to enhance the view from the castle and provide a panoramic view of the castle and its estate. There is no evidence that a castle ever stood on the cliffs of Craigneith, but, if it did, the castle could be one of a few buildings within the parish that may have been the Tower and

Robert Craig being congratulated by Winnie Ewing MP, 1967.

Fortalice of Blantyre mentioned in an ancient Scottish document of 1360 which states that King David II granted a charter for a market to be held once a week within the Parish of Blantyre.

Croftfoot House

Croftfoot House is located behind the site where the former police station at Main Street, High Blantyre once stood. The house has three dates on different sections of the premises. Above the main door is the year 1731, under which is the face of a demon-gargoyle, and above this is a carving of what appears to be a cherub. The year 1730 is carved above the door of the old stable, which would indicate that an older house once stood here, and above the old barn, which is now part of the house, is the year 1732. An old well in the rear garden between the house and Kirkton Public Park is covered over. In the 1880s Colonel Jackson, a well-known public figure, owned the house.

Crossbasket House

Crossbasket House is situated on the Stoneymeadow Road adjacent to the General's Bridge. The original building was the 'Keep' or 'Tower' at the west gable of the house. It is thought this was constructed in the 13th century and extended over the centuries to give us the structure we have today. At one time the tower was a tied-jointure house belonging to the Laird of Mains, East Kilbride and may be the Tower and Fortalice of Blantyre mentioned in ancient Scottish documents which granted the Parish of Blantyre the right to hold a market once a week. There are no indications as to where this Tower and Fortalice was

Crossbasket House, c.1890.

situated, but Crossbasket would have been in existence at the time the proclamation was decreed. The 'Lords Commissioners of Surrenders and Tiends' issued a decree, dated 1634, disjoining the lands of Crossbasket from East Kilbride and incorporating them within the Parish of Blantyre. It is said that Mary Queen of Scots slept in Crossbasket House the night before her defeat at the Battle of Langside while her army camped on the Calder Braes below Bardykes Road.

The earliest record of the Tower can be found in documents from the 13th century relating to the history of East Kilbride. Alexander Lindsay, an illegitimate son of Lindsay of Mains, East Kilbride, obtained the lands of Crossbasket in 1494, but the estate soon passed back to the legitimate branch of the family. In 1532 Robert of Crossbasket, belonging to the illegitimate branch of the family, acquired the estate and the lands of East Kilbride. His son Robert inherited the Tower of Crossbasket, and in 1560 he became the Provost of Glasgow. In the years from 1579 to 1581 he also sat in Parliament representing Rutherglen. In 1579, the year that he became an MP, he was also 'Bailie of the Priory of Blantyre'. The Lindsays owned the estate until 1690 when it was sold to Archibald Stewart of Blackhill. Around 1661 a lawyer called John Kincaid purchased the property. He, in turn, sold it to Thomas Peter sometime between 1700 and 1709. Thomas Peter was a merchant and Dean of Guild of Glasgow who was later elected Bailie of Glasgow. His son General Peter inherited the estate, and some say it was he who constructed the General's Bridge (q.v.) on Stoneymeadow Road. (Another opinion, which I favour, is that General Stewart of Torrance, East Kilbride built the Bridge.) Thomas Peter's other son emigrated to America and married President George Washington's daughter and a memorial commemorates that branch of the Peter family to this day.

Crossbasket Tower, therefore, is the oldest structure in Blantyre. It probably took its name from the 'Basket Cross', an ancient stone cross thought to have stood a small distance from the Tower on the lands of Basket. Near this monument there was also a sacred font with a long inscription, but this was so old and worn that even in the year 1740 it could not be read. In that year, both the cross and the font were vandalised and demolished by a religious fanatic who saw them as Romanist symbols, an act which was loudly condemned from the pulpit of the Old Parish Church. The Basket Cross stood at the foot of a wooded slope beyond the wall and the Lees Burn, directly across Stoneymeadow Road from Allers Farm. Along with an ancient grave-yard adjacent to Allers Farm and the East Kilbride Expressway, it would seem to substantiate claims that a religious house of some kind was located near here. The circular graveyard is reputed to be the burial place of monks from a monastery that once stood close to this site.

It is thought the name Basket is derived from the words 'Bas-Gait', meaning 'low road'. Another suggestion is that the cross might have been 'Cros Pascaid', named after Pacent, a Welsh saint whose cross is said to have stood near Crossbasket Tower. The final suggestion is that the name was derived from the words 'Pas Cet', meaning 'cross at the exit of the woods', which certainly describes the area where the cross is thought to have stood.

The construction of the Turnpike Road (Stoney-meadow Road) to East Kilbride replaced the old 'Pack Road' that ran through the trees along the ridge of high

ground, 100 yards to the north of the present road. It is thought this old track, which can still be seen, was part of a network of roads that crossed Scotland, linking the east coast with Ayr on the west coast. The track came down the slope, passed the Basket Cross and Font, crossed the ford at Lees Burn and continued up the present access road to Allers Farm and continued south-west to the coast. The East Kilbride Expressway runs directly across this old Pack Road.

During the 19th century various families occupied Crossbasket House, the best known being the distinguished chemist Charles McIntosh, the inventor of waterproof cloth used in the manufacture of raincoats. Many of his experiments involved dyes and, as the mill on the River Calder at the rear of the house was originally constructed as a dye mill, it is safe to assume it was McIntosh who built it.

One other interesting occupant of the house was James Clark, a well-known and respected merchant in Glasgow who it would appear added the final part of the house as his initials appear on a plaque on the east gable. Eight of the Clark family lived in Crossbasket, along with 11 household staff. In all there were 15 staff employed on the estate. James Clark died in September 1873.

Various families owned the property after Clark's death, including Thomas Dunlop Findlay, an East India Merchant. It is said that the decision was taken to sell Crossbasket in 1932 because female members of the family disliked the sight of the 'dirty coal miners' at High Blantyre making their way to and from Dixon's Collieries. The family purchased Baturich Castle on the banks of Loch Lomond near Balloch and received offers for the estate from the Roman Catholic Church, hoping to establishing a religious retreat, and from the world-famous Scottish music hall star, Sir Harry Lauder, but both bids were unsuccessful.

The estate was purchased by James Little in 1932, and by 1935 he had sold the three estate cottages. Little installed electricity in Crossbasket House many years before anyone else in Blantyre had an electricity supply. In 1976 the house was donated to the 'Roosevelt Memorial Trust', who established in Crossbasket the 'James Little Polio Trust' to treat suffers of that terrible disease. During a visit to Scotland, President Roosevelt's widow stayed as a guest at Crossbasket House.

The house was purchased in 1981 by the Pentecostal Church and administered by Pastor P.D. Cochrane as a Christian Centre. At present it is being used in a similar fashion by Latter Rain Ministries.

Curling at Blantyre, c.1912.

Cross Guns Tenement

Cloudhowe Terrace at the West End now occupies the site of the Cross Guns Tenement. The original name of the pub in the tenement was the *Cross Guns Public House*.

Cross Row

The Cross Row was one of four rows of buildings constructed at the bottom of Station Road by the Blantyre Works mill owners to provide housing for their employees. Cross Row was demolished in 1928.

Cuddie Burn

The 'Cuddie Burn' is the boundary between Blantyre and Burnbank. The water rises at Shott, High Blantyre and runs mainly underground to join the River Clyde near Bothwell Bridge. A section of the burn, still above ground, can be seen in the glen adjacent to the High Blantyre Industrial Estate and Ballantrae Road.

Curling Pond

The curling pond was located on a piece of land south of the Blantyre-East Kilbride Viaduct that crossed the River Calder between Millheugh House and Greenhall House. The land was flooded in winter by the Rotten Burn that flows into the Calder near this point.

Livingstone Memorial Centre.

Dale, David (1739-1806)

Some maintain that David Dale was a herd boy in Stewarton, others that he was the son of an Ayrshire grocer. By the age of 24 he had become a prosperous cloth merchant. At one time he was an agent for the

David Dale.

Royal Bank of Scotland. Later he constructed and owned the first cotton mill in Scotland. He commissioned the famous inventor Richard Arkwright to come to Scotland to find suitable sites for the construction of cotton-mills and two were found on the River Clyde at Blantyre and at the Falls of Clyde, New Lanark. Construction of Blantyre Mills (q.v.) commenced around 1778 and production began in 1785.

Daly, Edward

Edward Daly was born in 1886. His father was a victim of the Udston Pit disaster in 1889. At the age of 11 he left school and worked in collieries in the Hamilton area. Later he emigrated to America and worked in the mining industry for five years before returning to live in Blantyre. He joined the Independent Labour Party

and was influenced by Keir Hardie, the founder of the Labour Party. In 1923 he was elected as a member of the Blantyre Council and in 1927 he became a County Councillor. He lost his seat in 1929 but was elected County Councillor again in 1935 for the Stonefield Division of Blantyre, a post he held until his retirement in 1964.

Edward Daly.

Daly was elected Convener of Lanark County Council in 1958 and awarded the CBE in 1963 for his services to the community, which included encouraging companies to locate to the new industrial estate at High Blantyre after the Second World War. As Housing Convener he was responsible for the demolition of slums in the district and the construction of new council houses. He died on 28 June 1970.

Danskins

At one time the Danskin family were the proprietors of the shop at the corner of Stonefield Road and Broompark Road which is presently occupied by Margaret McGregor. The building was constructed and owned by a family called Cranston. The proprietor of the shop before Margaret was Eddie Collins, who also owned the bakery and shop at Broompark Road which stood on the site of *Finbarr's Public House.*

David Dale House

David Dale House, located in John Street, was constructed in 1999-2000. The first staff entered the premises in February 2000 and the building was officially opened on 26 June 2000.

David Livingstone Centre

Prior to the opening of the David Livingstone Memorial by the Duchess of York on 5 October 1929, the only indication that the great explorer was born in Blantyre was a plaque inserted into the gable wall of Shuttle Row in 1897. Livingstone Memorial changed its name to the David Livingstone Centre in 1990 and renovations were undertaken. On 1 April 1999 the Scottish National Trust became joint administrators of the David Livingstone Centre with a view to becoming the sole owners of the property in 2002, since when extensive modernisation and renovation has taken place.

David Livingstone Memorial Bridge

The first David Livingstone Memorial Bridge was constructed in 1952 to replace the old Suspension Bridge (q.v.) which closed in 1949. The photograph shows the demolition of the first Livingstone Bridge on 28 May 1999. It was replaced by the present David Livingstone Memorial Bridge (q.v.) that was officially opened in October 1999.

Queen Elizabeth, The Queen Mother, opening the David Livingstone Memorial.

Demolition of the old David Livingstone Bridge.

Davidson the Drapers

The address of Davidson Drapers and Clothiers shop was 166 Glasgow Road, opposite Logan Street, where the roundabout is now sited.

Devlin Grove

Devlin Grove home for the elderly, seen here under construction in 1983, was officially opened in February 1984. The present warden of the establishment is June Stone, a position she has held since the opening of the premises. The view above is looking east along Glasgow Road from the roof of Clydeview Shopping Centre. The Post Office (its roof is in the right foreground) was demolished in 1999.

Devlin, Michael

Michael Devlin, a Blantyre man, was the author of a book entitled *Foundation Chains*, a story based on the coalmines of Blantyre. A copy is available in the Mitchell Library, Glasgow.

Dixons's Rows

Dixon's Rows was a large concentration of tied cottages constructed to provide homes for miners employed by Messrs Dixon and Company, the owners of four collieries within the parish of Blantyre. The majority of the streets were in the area between Calder Street, Stonefield Road, Camelon Crescent and Boswell Drive. Each block contained four single-storied houses consisting of two rooms. The main living room was usually called 'the kitchen', and the bedroom was simply known as

Construction of Devlin Grove Home for the Elderly, 1983.

'the room'. Both rooms contained two 'set in beds', also known as 'hole in the wall beds'. The floors were made of uneven flagstones and the main room had facilities for cooking over the fire. Originally there was no sink or plumbing of any kind within the houses. Around 1930 a sink was provided in the main living room but there was no water supply. Water for cooking and washing had to be drawn from a communal well located in the street. The four families of each block shared an external toilet and a large washhouse, which was located at the rear of the row.

Streets of various lengths consisted of long rows of these blocks with a large 'pend' between each block. The four longest streets, which ran parallel to each other, extended from Stonefield Road to what is now Boswell Drive. The present Calder Street extended further up Stonefield Road to the top of Dixon Street, Hall Street, and finally to Park Street overlooking the Gas Works, the buildings of which were occupied by Letham's Bus Company. The smaller rows at Carfin Street, Govan Street and Miller Street ran parallel to Stonefield Road from Dixon Street, across Calder Street, to the dividing fences of the backcourts of the tenements on Glasgow Road. When the houses in Miller Street were demolished, the road was renamed Priory Street. The smallest row was Burnside Street, located off Calder Street, which ran parallel to the east side of Priory Street.

Dixon's Sports Day

An annual sports day was held for the employees of Dixon's Collieries in a field located between Victoria Street and Boswell Drive. The Health Centre and Blantyre High School now occupy the site.

Drowning Tragedy

In 1962 a tragic event shocked the community and the entire country. The winter of that year was one of the coldest in living memory and for the first time in many years the River Clyde had frozen over. Four children all aged four, David Law, James Pollock, Peter Cairney, who lived in Knightswood Terrace, and Martin Mitchell of Viewfield Avenue, made their way to Tommy Morgan's shop to buy sweets. The shop was a wooden hut situated on Station Road, directly opposite Viewfield Avenue at the bottom gable of the tenement at Ulva Place. After spending their 'pennies' they left the shop and wandered down the dirt path that ran diagonally across the Braes from behind Tommy's shop to the Old Suspension Bridge. The children's parents became aware that they were missing and a search party was hastily organised. Tracks were soon found, and the small footprints in the snow led the searchers across the Braes to the edge of the river, then continued onto the ice of the frozen river between the bridge and the weir. The footprints terminated at a spot where the ice had broken and it became obvious that the toddlers had fallen through the ice and perished. The surrounding ice was so thick that it hampered the search for their bodies. When the thaw set in some days later, the bodies of three of the children were recovered in the lade beyond the sluice gates adjacent to the weir. Unfortunately the body of little James Pollock was never found.

Dry Well Green

See Barnhill (B)

Duddy, James

See Aeroplane 2 (A)

Dunallon Loop

In 1903 the Hamilton, Motherwell & Wishaw Tramways Company constructed a single-line tram network that ran from the Livingstone Memorial Church at Glasgow Road to Hamilton and Larkhall. The line also branched left at Hamilton Cross and continued to Motherwell and Wishaw. In 1907 the Glasgow Tram Company extended the track from their terminus at Cambuslang to link up with the Lanarkshire system at the Priory Bridge. Passengers on a Lanarkshire tram intending to travel to Cambuslang or Glasgow had to alight at a section of track known as Dunallon Loop at the west end of Glasgow Road and board a Glasgow tram to continue their journey. Dunallon Loop was situated on Glasgow Road at the corner of Coatshill Avenue. A loop in the track at this point later became the terminus for both companies and allowed the trams to turn and begin their return journeys. Various loops were constructed throughout the network and were used as passing points when trams travelling in opposite directions met.

A house named Dunallon, constructed on the site of a demolished house of the same name, stands close to the original terminus.

SEE TRAMCARS (T)

Dunbars of Blantyre

The Earls of Dunbar were at one time the owners of the lands of Blantyre. Ancient charters reveal that in 1368 King David II of Scotland granted the Barony of Blantyre, along with other lands, to his cousin George Dunbar, the nephew of Thomas Randolph (q.v.), the 1st Earl of Moray. These lands had been resigned by George's father, the Earl of March. George became the 10th Earl of March when he succeeded his father in 1369 and was known as one of the most ambitious nobles of his time. He was regarded as a traitor to his country when, for various reasons, he deserted the Scottish cause and embraced that of England, ravaging the Scottish borders with fire and sword and fighting on behalf of the English king at the defeat of the Scottish army at the Battle of Homildon. He was later reconciled with his country and returned to Scotland where he died in 1420 but was certainly the most treacherous noble ever to own the lands of Blantyre.

Like his parents before him George disposed of the lands of Blantyre. The parish was sold to a kinsman, David de Dunbar of Enterkin, whose descendants owned the parish for the next two centuries until the Barony was sold to Walter Stewart, the Commendator of Blantyre Priory who later became the first Lord Blantyre (q.v.) in 1606.

'Reddendos' (q.v.) were levied annually on landowners as a token of their fealty to the crown, and by these the lord of the manor was bound, with his retainers, to join the king's army in times of war. The sovereign would determine these reddendos, some of which were very unusual. That levied by the king on the Barony of Blantyre when it was in the possession of John Dunbar was a gold necklace or neck chain, increased to two gold chains when his son Patrick inherited in 1455. Much later it was recorded that one eighth of a necklace of gold of the weight of a 'Harry noble' was paid for the lands of Birdsfield and Bellsfield in the Barony of Blantyre.

Dunlop, David

In 1875 David Dunlop was appointed by the new Blantyre School Board to be the first Headmaster of High Blantyre Public School at Hunthill Road near High Blantyre Cross. He was previously a teacher at Greenock Highland Academy.

Dunrobin Castle

Dunrobin Castle in Golspie, the seat of the Duke of Sutherland, was built between 1845 and 1851. This magnificent castle was initially arranged in suites named after different branches of the Stewart family, such as the Duke of Argyle. The Stewarts of Blantyre were one of these family groups and had a suite named after them known as the 'Blantyre Suite'. Each comprised a complete set of sitting rooms and bedrooms decorated in a style of their own and furnished in a most costly and elegant manner. All had a magnificent view of the North Sea and were separated from the other suites by a wide gallery or passage. Dunrobin Castle was set aside in 1851 by the Duke of Sutherland for the use of Queen Victoria. Today it is one of the major tourist attractions in the north of Scotland.

Dux Awards

In 1910 two Blantyre students won the Hamilton Academy Dux Awards. Dux boy was Selbie MacNeill Campbell, son of Mr George Campbell, manager of the Clydesdale Bank at Glasgow Road, Blantyre. Dux girl was Miss Jane Fleming, who resided at the Blantyre Works Rows at the bottom of Station Road. The house in which she was brought up overlooked the old Works' School in which David Livingstone received his early education. Her father worked as a pointsman with the Caledonian Railway Company at Blantyre Station.

Dysholm Mill

Dysholm Mill was one of five mills that once stood on the River Calder. It was situated adjacent to Pattonholm Ford (q.v.) directly below the old Cottage Hospital on Bardykes Road and took its name from Dysholm field, on the opposite side of the river, which contains the site of 'Queen Mary's Well' (q.v.).

Elm Street with Stonefield Parish Church, 1978.

East Church
SEE BURLEIGH MEMORIAL CHURCH

East Kilbride Expressway

In 1975, during the redevelopment of Blantyre, the pit 'bings' of Auchinraith and Priestfield Collieries were removed and an extension added to the first phase of the East Kilbride Expressway which ran from the Crossbasket House entrance to the Whirlies roundabout at East Kilbride. The new section, which opened in 1978, extended the expressway from the present east-bound Blantyre slip road at Stoneymeadow Road, adjacent to the General's Bridge at Crossbasket, to the Raith roundabout at Bothwell Bridge.

Education

The earliest record of a school in Blantyre is a minute of a general meeting of the heritors of Blantyre dated 18 May 1731. It reads as follows:

> The Heritors taking to their consideration that notwithstanding and by the 9th Act of the session of the fifth Parliament of King William, it is expressly stated and ordained that the heritors of the parish meet and provide a commodious house for a school, yet they have never had any such school, and in order to supply that defect they have agreed to build a house 22 feet long and 18 feet wide on the south-side corner of the Church-yard, at a cost of one hundred pounds Scots.

The school was erected in the corner of the Kirkyard adjacent to the old Parish Church car park at the entrance gate to the present manse.

Later a Parochial School to replace the old timber school in the Kirkyard was constructed at the bottom of an old street called School Lane (q.v.) and was situated close to the present site of Kirkton Public Park gates. It is recorded in 1860 that 50 was the total number of scholars attending the Parochial School at that time, when, over one hundred scholars attended the Blantyre Works School in Low Blantyre. Records indicate that the school roll never exceeded fifty.

The top of School Lane can still be seen adjacent to *Carrigan's Pub* at High Blantyre Cross.

SEE ALSO ADVENTURE SCHOOL (A)

Education Act 1872

Prior to the Education Act of 1872 schools provided by the landowner, heritors, or proprietors of large industrial businesses such as Blantyre Mills. Not all children were provided with an education but the Act made education compulsory and established School Boards in every district whose remit was to construct schools in every parish in the country.

Erskine House.

Erskine House

Alexander Stewart, 5th Lord Blantyre, purchased the barony of Erskine in 1703. Robert Walter Stewart, 11th Lord Blantyre, demolished the old mansion on Erskine Estate and constructed the present Erskine House in 1828. Today it is a hospital for injured and disabled soldiers. An obelisk, 20 metres high, was erected in memory of Robert Walter Stewart by the people of Erskine, which can still be seen today on land adjacent to Erskine House.

Obelisk at Erskine House.

Stonefield Road from Glasgow Road.

Fermetouns

A 'fermetoun' was a small group of houses that formed a hamlet and was mainly occupied by farm workers. There were six fermetouns within the Parish of Blantyre: Blantyreferme, Barnhill, Hunthill, Auchinraith, Auchentibber and Kirkton at the centre of the town at High Blantyre Cross. Springwells may well have been a seventh fermetoun as it was on the route of the Glasgow-London stage-coach that made its way from Blantyre via Auchentibber to the next staging post at *Hamilton Inn*, now the Hamilton Museum.

Finnie, Rev. John

The Rev. John Finnie, son of a Glasgow tailor, attained his MA degree at the University of Glasgow in 1749 and, licensed by the Presbytery of Glasgow in 1759, became Librarian at the University. He was presented to Blantyre Old Parish Church (q.v.) by Lord Blantyre on 8 May 1770. The local parishioners objected to his appointment because of his 'body weakness and infirmity', claiming that he was more infirm than their previous minister, who died of old age. Mr Finnie was therefore minister of Blantyre, in name only, for two years. The parishioners' views were obviously well founded as he died two years later on 2 November 1772.

John Finnie was employed at one time as tutor to the family of Mathew Orr, a merchant of Stobcross, Glasgow. He suggested to his employer, who was a wealthy landowner in the city, that he should build a village on his land on the banks of the River Clyde close to the village of Anderston, to take advantage of the shipping industry that was based on the river at that point. Mr Orr acted on his advice and honoured Mr Finnie by naming the village 'Finnieston'. The village grew, prospered, and eventually became part of Greater Glasgow. The name is still used today for an area of the Broomielaw at Clyde Street, Glasgow.

Fore Row

The Fore Row, which was originally named the Glasgow Row, was a long row of houses at Blantyre Mills that extended up Station Road from what is now Anderson Gardens to Caskie Drive. Another row was located directly behind. With two other lines of tenements, the parallel rows of houses formed three sides of a quadrangle that sat directly above the Clyde Braes, the Works' School which stood on the site of Anderson Gardens completing the quadrangle seen at the right

Model of Blantyre Works.

Weaver's Cottage, c.1925.

in this photograph of the model of Blantyre Mills/ Works and Village. All the employees' houses were demolished in 1928 after a fire seriously damaged a large proportion of the rows. The Shuttle Row, the end of the Wages Building and a section of the Bottom Row are all that remain today.

Forrest, Colonel John Clark

John Clark Forrest was one of the most influential men who ever lived in Blantyre. He held the military rank of colonel, was a banker in Hamilton, a Justice of the Peace, and served as Provost of Hamilton for six years. He was elected to the Blantyre School Board in 1873 and gave a large donation towards the construction of the Cottage Hospital (q.v.), which opened in Bardykes Road in 1910. Forrest was one of the largest landowners within the parish of Blantyre and sold large areas to the local authorities at the east end of Glasgow Road for the construction of shops and houses. John Street, Clark Street and Forrest Street were named after

Colonel John Clark Forrest.

him. A bust was erected by public subscription and can be seen today in Hamilton Town Hall.

Forrest also gifted the land that is now Stonefield Public Park to the people of Blantyre, and stipulated that it must only be used as a public park and for recreational purposes, which makes one wonder why his clause was not observed when the decision was taken to construct the sheltered housing at Stonefield Park Gardens within the Public Park.

SEE BARNHILL (B)

Forrest, Jock

Jock Forrest was a handloom weaver who lived and worked in a cottage that stood at the top of the Peth Brae, Bardykes Road, on what is now the car park of the *Hoolets Nest pub* (q.v.). The property was known at different times as Stewart's Cottage and the Weaver's Cottage.

Frame, Janet Fulton

Janet Fulton was one of the few people in the world who lived in three different centuries. Aged 29, she emigrated to New Zealand in 1926 under the domestic service emigration scheme and is one of only five inhabitants in that country to hold the distinction of having been born in the 19th century. She was born on 30 August 1897 in the three-storied building that once stood at Braedale, Hunthill Road, adjacent to the entrance to Millheugh opposite Watson Street. She was the fourth in a family of seven. Her father was a miner and worked in one of the local collieries.

Janet never married and spent most of her working life in service to wealthy families and in this capacity travelled the world. Her recollections were remarkable, especially the childhood memories of Blantyre. Her mother became almost blind in her later years and it fell to Janet to attend to her needs. She stated, 'Ma Faither was a coal miner but was well educated. Even the working people in those days were well educated in Scotland. I think that was what stood by me, having an education and having knowledge of lots of things'.

Frawley, Father John

Father Frawley was born in Buttevant, County Cork, Ireland and was ordained at the Irish College, Paris in 1875, then served for one year at St Margaret's, Kinning Park, Glasgow. Because of ill health he was moved to 'the country,' to serve at St Margaret's in the parish of Airdrie. When he was transferred from Airdrie on 16 September 1877 to establish a church in Blantyre, he became the first Roman Catholic priest to serve in the parish since the time of the Reformation. His house was situated on Glasgow Road, directly across from Mayberry Place.

He was instrumental in the construction of Saint Joseph's School-Chapel (q.v.), which opened on 24 October 1878 and is seen here in Glasgow Road, at the bottom of Stonefield Road, where the present St Joseph's Parish Hall now stands. The school was

Father John Frawley.

on the ground floor and the chapel, with over 600 seatings, was in the upper floor. Within five weeks of commencing his appointment in his new parish, Father Frawley was confronted with the human tragedies caused by the Blantyre Explosion at Dixon's Colliery on 22 October 1877 (q.v.). The Rev. Stewart Wright of Blantyre Old Parish Church spoke very highly of the actions of Father Frawley during and after the 'Calamity'.

Father Frawley's health once again deteriorated and he had to resign his post after serving the parish for three years. He emigrated to Australia in June 1880, where he died at Inglewood, Victoria on 28 April 1881, while only 30 years of age. The Roman Catholic community holds the memory of Father Frawley and his remarkable achievements in the three short years he served the parish of Blantyre in high esteem.

Fulling Mill
SEE MILL DAM COURT CASE (M)

St Joseph's School-Chapel at the bottom of Stonefield Road, c.1890.

Glasgow Road.

Galbraith, William

William Galbraith started work at Blantyre Mills in 1798 and worked there for 72 years until his death in 1870. Old Willie claimed that he remembered the day that Emperor Alexander III of Prussia visited Blantyre Mills. The Emperor did in fact visit Glasgow when Henry Monteith (q.v.), the proprietor of Blantyre Mills, was the Provost of Glasgow and presided over the reception held in the city to honour the Emperor. The Emperor expressed a desire to visit a manufacturing town and it is probable that Provost Monteith invited him to inspect his works at Blantyre Mills.

Gallacher, Billy

Billy Gallacher can be described as one of the better known personalities of present-day Blantyre. He was born

Blantyre Works, c.1880.

in Auchentibber and educated at Auchinraith Primary School and Calder Street Junior Secondary School. It was obvious, even at primary school, that he was destined to play football at senior level, such was the skill he displayed at an early age. He signed with Motherwell FC and, after his career ended there, played junior football with Blantyre Victoria (q.v.) and Rutherglen Glencairn. In 1970 he was a prominent member of the Blantyre Vics team that defeated Penicuik to win the Scottish Junior Cup in front of 30,000 fans at Hampden Park.

Billy started his working life in the administration office of the Blantyre Co-op in Herbertson Street. Later he moved to Whitbread Brewers, and from there to Bells Whisky. As he advanced within the company he witnessed many mergers within the licensed trade. As Trade Relations Manager with United Distillers, and latterly United Distillers & Vintners, his job appeared to be one long social whirl of trade, charity and sports sponsorship events and Billy is known throughout the country within the licensed trade and sporting circles. The highlight of his career was in 1999 when he received the Scottish Licensed Trade News Award for Lifetime Achievement. Hazel Irvine, the BBC Television sports presenter, presented him with it at the Hilton Hotel, Glasgow.

Recently Billy retired after thirty years service to the licensed trade, during which time he raised hundreds of thousands of pounds for charities throughout Scotland. At one remarkable event that he organized, £26,000 was raised in one day. As well as fronting events throughout Scotland, he is always willing to give his undoubted talents and charm to any local event and was heavily involved in the centenary celebration events to raise funds for Blantyre Victoria Football Club's new pavilion.

Gallagher, Father Daniel

Daniel Gallagher was born in Ireland in 1811 and educated there before coming to Blantyre where he gained employment at the Blantyre Mills. He was a close friend of David Livingstone and assisted him in his Latin studies. Daniel later went to Rome to study for the priesthood and, after his studies were completed, returned to Scotland to become the first priest to serve at St Margaret's Airdrie, the first post-reformation Catholic Church in Lanarkshire. Later he established St Peter's Church in the parish of Partick in Glasgow. Father Gallagher died in Partick on 8 March 1883.

Gardiner's Place

Gardiner's Place was a tenement that stood on Main Street opposite Broompark Road.

Gazette *Newspaper Office (to left) on Glasgow Road*, c.1925.

General's Bridge.

Gazette Newspaper

John Clifford was the proprietor and publisher of the *Gazette* newspaper. Founded on 27 November 1925, the first edition appeared in December 1925. The original telephone number was 'Blantyre 321'. All local news was reported and notification of forthcoming events given. The newspaper, where all the births, deaths and marriages were listed, was essential reading in every home in Blantyre. The office and the printing press were at Hastie's Farm, Glasgow Road (see p.75), on the site now occupied by the gardens directly across from the Clydeview Shopping Centre at the corner of Victoria Street. The last edition of the *Gazette* was printed on 31 January 1964.

General's Bridge

It is not known when the bridge was built and there are several opinions as to who constructed it. The present bridge may well have been built during the construction of the Turnpike Road in the late 1800s, replacing an earlier bridge. In my opinion it is probable that General Stewart of Torrance, East Kilbride constructed the General's Bridge to give easier access to his property at Crossbasket House (q.v.), Stoneymeadow Road. The lands of Crossbasket were at one time part of the parish of East Kilbride.

Gilmour's Building

Gilmour's Building, seen on the left of the picture, stood on the corner of Forrest Street and Glasgow Road, and extended east to the taller Grant's building seen at the right of the photograph. Between the two buildings was a rough track that led down to Baird's Rows (q.v.) miners' cottages. Gilmour, who owned the building, had a draper's shop and a grocer's shop at the east end of the tenement. The white front of the Victoria Café, seen in the centre of Gilmour's Building, was better known as 'Angie's Ice-Cream Shop'. Richardson's butcher's shop can also be seen at the extreme left.

Glasgow Tigers

The first meeting of the Tigers was at the White City Sports Ground in Glasgow on 29 June 1928. They

Gilmour's Building, Glasgow Road, c.1965.

continued to race there until 1969 when, following the closure of the stadium, they moved to Hampden Park. The club was also based at various times at Celtic Park, Shawfield Stadium and Cliftonhill Stadium, Coatbridge. Glasgow Speedway Promotions took a decision to move to a new venue in 1977 and, fittingly, the town of Blantyre was chosen because of its strong links with speedway in the west of Scotland and local riders recognised by speedway enthusiasts as some of the greatest participants ever to grace the sport. A track was constructed on the inside of the rails at Blantyre Greyhound Stadium.

Tigers were not alone in using the Blantyre track as a home base. In 1981 Berwick Bandits competed there for a short time. Blantyre also staged a Junior International in August 1981 when Young Scotland narrowly defeated Young England. Tigers had to 'flit' once again when it was announced that Blantyre Greyhound Stadium would be demolished as it stood on the line of a proposed new road, the East Kilbride Expressway, which now runs directly over the stadium site.

When the merits of the greatest speedway riders are discussed, the names of the great Blantyre riders, Tommy Miller (q.v.) and Ken McKinlay (q.v.), immediately spring to mind. The exploits of Tommy and Kenny can be read elsewhere in this book. This particular piece is about the three amazing Beaton Brothers and their achievements with Glasgow Tigers and other clubs.

From an early age, Jim Beaton (snr), well-known in the community as the proprietor of Beaton's Coaches, was always interested in motorbikes, and as a teenager competed in sand racing on beaches around Scotland. Jim became involved in the promotions of Glasgow Tigers when he became a partner in Glasgow Speedway Promotions Limited. George, the eldest son of Jim and Betty, was a member of the Glasgow Tigers junior team but in 1972 he was killed in a car crash near the entrance to the Spittal pit.

Bobby Beaton became one of the greatest and most spectacular riders in the history of the Glasgow Tigers. He joined the club in 1968 at the age of 16 and, after a quick learning period, established himself in the first team by the end of that season. In 1970 Bobby went with a party of other British riders to compete in the Rhodesian Open Championship where he gained valuable experience. He was recognised as one of the top British riders when he gained second place in the 1972 National League Averages, scoring 315 points. He repeated that result in 1973 with a total of 276 points. Bobby was then transferred in 1974 to Hull where he continued to produce spectacular results. He also rode for Newcastle and Edinburgh before returning to the Tigers in 1985. In 1980, Bobby Beaton was ranked at No. 7 in the best all-time performances in the history of the Glasgow Tigers, with a total of 1,019 points gained in only four years with the club.

Jim Beaton (jnr), younger brother of Bobby, made his debut for the Tigers in 1971 as a 16-year-old before moving to Berwick to gain experience. During his time there, on 10 June 1972, he was involved in an horrific accident and his right arm all but severed. Doctors fought for over six hours to save his arm, which they

Bobby Beaton.

Jim Beaton Jnr.

did, but declared it would be of little use to him and that he would never ride again. Jim was made of stern stuff and for almost a year went through 27 operations and countless hours of physiotherapy to try and improve the use of the limb. He never regained full use of his arm but perseverance and the desire to ride again enabled him to make a comeback in 1975. Unfortunately, the administrators of the sport felt that Jim was a danger not only to himself but also to other riders. He set his sights on proving everyone wrong, overcame all the problems that confronted him and made his second comeback for the Tigers in 1978 and then became a regular team member.

Jim rode a modified bike with a specially adapted clutch and a thumb-controlled throttle on one side which made it virtually impossible to gate. So successful was his control of the new bike that he won maximum points for the first time in his career in 1979. One can only speculate how good a rider Jim would have been but for his accident, but there are those who said he was a better rider than his brother Bobby at the same age. If that were the case, he must have been some prospect when one considers the heights that Bobby reached in

the sport. There can be no doubt that Jim and Betty Beaton and their three 'Beaton Boys' were the backbone of Glasgow Tigers during the 1970s and 1980s.

The latest addition to the Tiger team is young Gary Hamilton who signed in March 2003. Gary, the nephew of the Beaton Boys, has decided to ride under his mother's famous name and will be known professionally as Gary Beaton. There are high hopes that he will reach the heights in the sport achieved by his famous uncles.

In 1980 Dick Barrie, a man who had followed Glasgow Tigers since 1949 and was respected for his speedway knowledge, was asked his opinion as to what would be the greatest Tigers side of all time. It was no surprise that three of his team of seven riders were Blantyre men, Tommy Miller, Bobby Beaton and Ken McKinlay whom he named as captain.

Govan, Alexander

Alexander Govan was born in Blantyre in 1869, a weaver's son who served his apprenticeship as a mechanic in a weaving factory in Bridgeton, Glasgow. He attended evening classes at the Glasgow and West of Scotland Technical College, where he won a medal for engineering design. It was claimed that Alexander might have been Scotland's answer to the famous American automobile magnate, Henry Ford, but for his unfortunate death in 1907 at the age of 38 years.

As a young man he went into business with his brother-in-law, John Worton, in Bain Street, Bridgeton, making a bicycle which they called the 'Worvan', derived from a combination of their names. Unfortunately the venture failed, and Govan went to England to seek more experience in the cycle industry. When he returned to Glasgow, he involved himself in the excitement over the motor car, which was about to go into commercial production in Scotland through the enterprise of another pioneer, George Johnstone. Govan sought and gained the financial backing of William Alexander Smith, a prosperous Glasgow merchant involved in a variety of business enterprises. Smith owned a failed cycle factory in Hosier Street, Bridgeton and it was there they launched the venture called the Argyle Car Company which led to car assembly.

In 1899 Govan produced a car, which he called the 'Argyle Voiturette' modelled on the Renault. Such was the success of the enterprise he had to find larger premises and subsequently moved to a palatial new building at Alexandria, in the Vale of Leven, where the firm became so successful that at one time they were producing more cars than any other manufacturer in Europe. Only Henry Ford's company in America was bigger than Govan's and it was to America that he went to see what intelligence he could gather. But the prospect of a Scot competing at the highest level in the world car market was shattered when the young visionary collapsed in the Grosvenor Restaurant in Glasgow. His death, soon after, was at first put down to food poisoning but later evidence indicated it may have been due to a cerebral haemorrhage. The early death of Alexander Govan in 1907 had serious consequences for the whole Argyle project. Govan was described as a striking although private person, and was highly respected in industrial circles in the West of Scotland.

Grant's Building

The three-storied Grant's Building stood at the east end of Glasgow Road beyond Forrest Street, directly across from where Reid Printers are now located. It was also known as Henderson's Building. The old dirt track leading to Baird's Rows ran down its west gable.

Grant's Building.

Grant, Dr William

For many years in the latter part of the 1800s and early 1900s, William Grant was a well-respected doctor in the Parish of Blantyre. He was appointed Chairman of the School Board in 1906 but is best remembered for his fearless and dedicated efforts during the attempts to find survivors after the explosion at Dixon's Collieries in 1877. Time and again he ventured into the gas-filled pits with the Explorers in the hope that he could administer medical aid to any survivor. Sadly, the few that were found died later in hospital. Dr Grant lived in Broompark House, on the site of John Ogilvie RC Church at Broompark Road. He can be seen in the photograph of 'The Explorers' on p.32.

Gray, John (The Blantyre Hero)

John Gray was a miner who, in 1913, lived in the Shuttle Row. While sitting in his home, John heard a

Alexander Govan.

Clyde Braes and Blantyre/Bothwell Viaduct.

commotion outside, a boy named John Morvan, aged 12, having slipped off the lade wall and fallen into the River Clyde. John rushed to the lade wall and dived into the river in an attempt to save the boy. He managed to reach the lad, but as he was struggling to get him to the riverbank he took cramp and, sadly, both drowned.

Greenhall Brick Works

The proprietors of the Greenhall Brick Works were the Moore family of Greenhall. They constructed a large kiln on their land near Calderside. Access to the brickworks was by a track known as the 'Chain Link Road', the entrance to which was adjacent to the General's Bridge. The track ran up through the woods and along the top of the high bank above the River Calder to a large open field. The extensive remains of the brickwork kiln can still be seen.

Greig, William

William Greig, who died late in the 19th century, had never been outwith the Parish of Blantyre during the last 80 years of his life; he was one of many who could say the same. Late in the 1800s another old lady claimed she had never been out of Blantyre except once, when she walked into Glasgow one morning and returned the same night.

One old woman in her eighties visited Auchentibber and claimed that the jaunt was the farthest she had ever been from her home at Blantyre Works.

Hunthill Road.

Hamilton, John

In 1574 John Hamilton was a 'Reader' at the original Blantyre Parish Church (q.v.) in the Old Kirkyard at High Blantyre Cross. Owing to the lack of ministers after the Reformation, preachers had to serve as many as six different churches. When the Rev. John Davidson was busy elsewhere, John Hamilton carried out his duties and preached the sermon at the Kirk. His stipend was £16 per annum plus the Kirkland (Manse).

He was born near Lesmahagow and had strong Presbyterian convictions during the time when 'Prelatism' (the Episcopalian Church) was rife. Because of his refusal to acknowledge the rule of Bishops, he was deprived of his living by Parliament on 11 June 1662. The Privy Council ratified the Act in October 1662 but the Rev. Hamilton continued over the following seven years to preach illegally in Blantyre at open-air Conventicles and in the homes of like-minded Presbyterian families. In 1669, he was arrested and imprisoned in Edinburgh for 'preaching in his own house to his family and friends who had gathered there'. During his internment his health suffered and he was released in 1672 upon the application of his brother, Sir Robert Hamilton of Silvertonhill, who paid 1,000 marks for his 'compearance'.

After Rev. Hamilton's expulsion in 1662, a Mr Richard Brown AM came to Blantyre in 1664 as a colleague and assistant to the Rev. Heriot. After Heriot's death in 1665, Brown moved to the parish of Bigger.

Handlooms

In 1835 it was recorded that there were 128 handloom weavers in the Parish of Blantyre, most of whom had looms in their houses.

Harper's Garage

Gilbert Harper was the proprietor of Harper's Garage on the corner of Glasgow Road and Craig Street, the site now occupied by the access pavement from the pedestrian lights on Glasgow Road to the main Clydeview Shopping Centre (q.v.).

Hendry, R.W.

R.W. Hendry had chemists shops in Glasgow Road and Main Street in the late 1800s and early 1900s.

Heritors

In 1791 there was a total of 37 heritors within the parish that paid Feu to the Lord of Blantyre, ten of whom did not reside within the parish. The landed property, which was mostly only a few acres, had belonged to the same families for centuries, but by the end of the 19th century only a few of the proprietors could trace descent from the original heritors. A Mrs Scott owned Blantyreferme, that once belonged to the Hamilton family, John Clark Forrest (q.v.) owned the lands of Auchinraith (q.v.), which anciently belonged to the Clark family and the Jackson

The Post Office, Main Street, c.1900.

family owned the lands of Barnhill and Bardykes that were once owned by another family of the same name, who gained the property when it was granted to them in a Charter dated 25 October 1525.

The Millar family of Millheugh obtained the grant of their land in the 15th century from Dunbar of Enterkin (q.v.), then the owner of the parish. Later, in 1603, a new deed for the lands of Millheugh was obtained by the family from Walter Stewart, the 1st Lord Blantyre. 'John Myller of Mylnehugh', in the year 1564, also purchased a ground rent from the 'Laird of Calderwoode'. Myller bound himself to restore this possession upon receiving payment of 'one hundred pundis Scotts, any day, betwixt the sun rising and going down, within the parish Kirk of Blantyre'. I would suggest that the property he had gained was the Tower of Crossbasket (q.v.) and its adjoining estate, which at that time was owned by the Laird of Calderwood, East Kilbride.

High Blantyre Post Office

The Post Office, which was adjacent to the bank, was located in the tenement building situated on Main Street at the corner of Cemetery Road.

High Blantyre Station

High Blantyre Station, owned by the Caledonian Railway Company, opened in 1863 and was situated on the Glasgow-Strathaven line adjacent to the Old Parish Church at the corner of Craigmuir Road. The passenger service was withdrawn in 1945 and the company then used the line solely for freight for the next eight years before this service was also withdrawn. The track continued to be used by Dixon's Collieries at Priestfield to transport their coal until the closure of the last colliery in the 1950s.

SEE RAILWAYS (R)

Hill's 'Laun'

Hill's Pawn Shop was located in a small tenement named Hill's 'Laun' (Land) in Glasgow Road adjacent to Low Blantyre Primary School, midway between Victoria Street and Craig Street. The Post Office in the Clydeview Shopping Centre now stands where Hill's tenement stood. The front of the tenement was closer to Glasgow Road than the current frontage of the shopping complex. Haddow, the dentist, had a surgery in this tenement for many years, having previously occupied premises in Hart's Land, which was directly opposite on the north side of Glasgow Road.

Hoolet's Nest

The *Barnhill Tavern* is better known as the *Hoolet's Nest*. The present building was constructed in 1900. The old Hoolet's was originally a small low building that stood on the present site of the *Barnhill Tavern*. In this photograph of Barnhill (q.v.), *c.*1890, the original *Hoolet's Nest* can be seen above the head of the man on the right and below the sign on the gable of Aggie Bain's Cottage. An early proprietor of the *Hoolet's Nest* was Nelly Moir. A more recent one, the late Peter MacDonald, was married to Margo MacDonald (q.v.) who won the Govan constituency seat for the Scottish National Party in a by-election in 1973.

Hope Hall

Hope Hall was located adjacent and to the rear of the *Gazette* Newspaper Office (q.v.), off Glasgow Road, and situated on a path leading down to Brown

Brothers' Painters and Decorators workshop which was directly opposite Victoria Street. The front of this small tenement faced Stonefield Public Park. Roman Catholics from Ireland, who had come to the district to work in the surrounding collieries, used the hall as a chapel until the first St Joseph's Church-School (q.v) was constructed in 1878.

Hospital Road

Hospital Road was located on the site of the present Catherine's Walk off Main Street. A row containing four houses stood on the east side of this old road, that probably took its name from the fact that it led to the Hospital for Infectious Diseases, which originally stood in a field that is now the corner of Victoria Street and Burnbrae Road.

Hunter, David

David Hunter, the grandfather of David Livingstone (q.v.), was a tailor who had a shop in the wages building at Blantyre Works. Livingstone's father, Neil, was

Barnhill, c.1890.

apprenticed to Hunter but was never an employee of the Blantyre Mills Company. He married Hunter's daughter Agnes in 1810.

Hunthill Junction

Hunthill Railway Junction was created when a separate bridge was built adjacent to the one which crossed over Hunthill Road at the corner of Springfield Crescent and carried the 'Auchinraith Spur' from Low Blantyre to Strathaven via High Blantyre Station and Hamilton. The new bridge took a branch line to East Kilbride via the Blantyre-East Kilbride Viaduct (q.v.) which was constructed to take the new line across the River Calder. The Glasgow-East Kilbride line via Blantyre opened on 1 March 1885. The huge support columns of the viaduct can still be seen.
SEE RAILWAYS (R)

Hurley Park

Irish miners who worked in the local collieries laid out a hurley park in a field between Park Street, Dixon's Rows and the Gas Works. The site is that used by Letham's Bus Company.

Hutton, John, of Calderbank

During a search of the old Kirkyard, an old gravestone was discovered after clearing away moss that covered a pile of stones. It was collapsed and bore a weather-worn coat of arms but the main panel containing the names and dates of those interred had been removed, leaving no clue as to who they were. A chalk rubbing was taken of the coat of arms in an attempt to acquire further information. Firstly, a number of us from the Blantyre Heritage Group visited the Mitchell Library in Glasgow to try to solve the mystery owner of the coat of arms. The Head Librarian suggested to George Hay

Impaled coat of arms.

that we contact the Lord Lyon in Edinburgh. A copy of the rubbing was sent to the Lord Lyon, which resulted in his secretary, Mrs Roads, sending a description of the arms.

The rubbing was of a matrimonial 'Impaled' coat of arms (uniting two families). The original arms belonged to John Hutton, 1692, and John Yule of Darleith, 1676. The Lord Lyon's description of the two coats of arms is as follows:

John Hutton MD, Royal Physician

ARMS: A Lion Rampant between three arrows, two in chief and one in base, and on a chief Guiles three Bezants.
CREST: A Serpent catching at a finger of a man's hand which issues from a cloud.
MOTTO: 'Si Deus Quis Contra'. Translation: 'If God is with us who shall be against us'.

John Yule of Darleith

ARMS: Argent on a fess betwixt three crescents sable a garb branded Guiles.
MOTTO: 'Numine et Virtute'. Translation: 'By God's will and strength'.
(Various interpretations can be given to the above Latin mottos but it is thought that the translations presented here are acceptable.)

The impaled coat of arms in the Kirkyard belonged to John Hutton of Calderbank, great great grandson of the Royal Physician, John Hutton MD, and to his wife Ann Elizabeth Yuille, great great granddaughter of Yule of Darleith. They were married on 11 January 1812 at Bonhill, Dunbartonshire.

John Hutton MD was born in Caerlaverock, Dumfriesshire. Knowing this, some excellent investigative work by George Hay resulted from a visit there. He was looking for information which might explain the presence of the coat of arms in High Blantyre. On this trip he came across a manse at Bankend where he made enquiries. Fortuitously this resulted in Mr Neale Lawson explaining the history of the manse and Hutton Hall. Hutton led an extremely interesting life. He began as a herd-boy to the Episcopalian Minister of Caerlaverock and was given a good education from his master. He became a physician, graduating MD at Padua. He left Scotland for Holland, and happened to be the nearest doctor at hand when Princess Mary of Orange met with a fall from her horse near the village where

Hutton had set up a practice. The attention he gave to the Princess was greatly appreciated by her husband, Prince William of Orange, who appointed him his First Physician. Hutton accompanied the Prince to England in 1688 when William and Mary were invited to redress the grievances that existed in Great Britain at that time. He landed at Torbay with an English and Dutch army and forced James II to flee. William and Mary were proclaimed rulers the following year.

Hutton was admitted a Fellow of the College of Physicians on 30 October 1690, when he presented the College with a large sum of money, a feat he later hoped to repeat. He was incorporated MD at Oxford and elected Fellow of the Royal Society on 30 November 1697. He was appointed in 1692 to the position of Chief Physician to King William III and Queen Mary, and to the Sovereign's Forces and Hospitals within the Dominions, and was at the King's side during the Battle of the Boyne and the siege of Limerick. After the death of King William he served as Member of Parliament for Dumfries Burghs between 1710 and his death in 1712, and was buried in the Chapel of Somerset House, London. In 1708 he bequeathed around £1,000 to provide funds for pious and educational purposes in Caerlaverock.

George Hay continued the hunt locally by looking at the censuses from 1841. He discovered that a Mrs Hutton lived at Calderglen House (q.v.) in 1861 and her death certificate showed that she was married to James Hutton.

At the time of the research into the coat of arms, no-one seemed to be aware of the Hutton family of Calderbank (Calderglen), Blantyre. It was some time later that a friend, Bill Galloway, stated that a Mrs. Hutton of Calderbank was mentioned in a booklet, printed in 1893, to celebrate the jubilee of the Anderson Church. Mrs. Hutton was born in 1783, and died at Calderbank, Blantyre, on 26 September 1864, aged 81 years.

Note : Further research revealed that Ann Yuille was the daughter of George Yuille of Darleith, Dunbartonshire. According to a Statistical Account for Bonhill, Dumbarton, Ann's father possessed a mansion at the south end of Loch Lomond.

Hydepark House

Hydepark House once stood on Broompark Road across the entrance to what is now Springfield Crescent.

I

Glasgow Road from Burleigh Church.

Industrial Estates

The Blantyre Industrial Estate, Main Street, High Blantyre was constructed in 1948 after the Second World War, and many prominent engineering companies rented premises there, including Rolls Royce (q.v.), Honeywell and Reyrolle Belmos. Too many to mention occupied factory units throughout the years but two of the most prominent that gave employment to many of the inhabitants of Blantyre were Simplicity Patterns, clothing manufacturers, and the E.K. Jig and Tool Company. The Industrial Estate still flourishes today and expanded with the construction of a group of small factory units at the top of East Avenue, adjacent to the Hillhouse Road, called Priestfield Industrial Estate.

Hamilton International Business Park to the south of Hillhouse Road has been added recently to this industrial area. Construction commenced in 1999 on the adjacent land at the Rab's Score Road and now many international companies occupy this impressive estate. At the time of writing, more buildings are under construction. The name of the estate is a strange one as it is only a few hundred metres from the heart of Blantyre. As it is mostly located in Blantyre, popular opinion is that its name should be Blantyre International Business Park!

Two small industrial estates were also constructed in Low Blantyre. Auchinraith Industrial Estate is situated off old Herbertson Street in Rosendale Way, adjacent to Glasgow Road, and another is located on the site of the old Slaughter House at the bottom of John Street.

Ironstone and Limestone Mines

From the 1700s until the early 1900s ironstone and limestone were mined in great quantities in the upper and southern areas of the parish, namely at Auchentibber and Calderside, where numerous deposits were found. The principal proprietor in the ironstone industry was Messrs Colin Dunlop and Company at Blackcraig near Calderwood. This firm wrought huge quantities of limestone in Auchentibber and the surrounding areas, and it was here that the young David Livingstone would search for fossils in the limestone refuse tips and along the banks of the River Calder. Later he would tell of his delight when he found shells in the carboniferous limestone, long before geology became a popular pastime. Ironstone and limestone were also wrought at the Lady Nancy Pit (q.v.) directly across the East Kilbride Expressway from Crossbasket.

Glasgow Road and Joanna Terrace.

Jackson, William

William Jackson was one of the thirty heritors of the town that paid Feu to the Lord of Blantyre. The Feu on Jackson's property at Croftfoot House, located behind High Blantyre Police Station, was a single rose which was to be given annually to the Lord of Blantyre as a 'Reddendo' (q.v.) signifying his loyalty to him. Jackson was elected as a member of the first Blantyre School Board in 1875.

Jacksons of Bardykes

The Jacksons of Bardykes held lands and a prominent position in Blantyre for over four hundred years, John Jackson receiving the lands of Bardykes in 1502. The family had valuable mineral estates in Hallside and Spittalhill and were joint proprietors of Messrs Jackson, Buchanan & Company, one of the largest wholesale tea dealers in Scotland. A John Jackson was elected as county councillor for the Stonefield Division in 1890 and it was thanks to him that the dirt track at Station Road, which was described as a 'quagmire', was resurfaced. It was claimed that people often missed their train because their feet had become stuck in the mud, such was the condition of the original road.

It is probable that John Jackson sold the land at the east end of Glasgow Road to the local authority, just as John Clark Forrest did with the land on the other side of Glasgow Road. Jackson Street was named after John and Logan Street was probably named after his wife,

Janet Logan. It is also likely that Herbertson Street was named after another line of this family.

John Street

When John Street was constructed, it provided the inhabitants who resided at the east end of the town with an alternative route to Low Blantyre Station and was originally called New Station Road. A pedestrian lane at the bottom of John Street, which is still extant, linked the new road to the station.

Jope, Doctors

The Jopes were a husband and wife team of doctors who had a practice in Glasgow Road near Forrest Street and served the community for many years. Prior to the opening of their surgery in Low Blantyre, they had

Broompark House.

Dr Jope's Surgery, Broompark Road.

premises at Causeystanes (q.v.) in Broompark Road, adjacent to where the dentist's surgery is at present located. In the photograph, the surgery is in the two-storey building on the left, adjoining the pub. After they closed this surgery, Mr and Mrs Jope held the High Blantyre practice in their home at Broompark House. They were the last owners of Broompark House and sold it to the Roman Catholic Church, who demolished the house and constructed John Ogilvie RC Church on the site.

K

Ruins of the Blantyre Priory.

Kelly, Sir Robert

Sir Robert Kelly was born in Blantyre in 1903, one of ten children of James Kelly, who played for and captained Glasgow Celtic FC and later became chairman of the club. Sir Robert was educated at St Aloysius and St Josephs, Dumfries and was a stockbroker by profession. Like his father, he became a director of Glasgow Celtic FC, and was chairman of the club between 1947 and 1971. He later became Celtic's first president. In 1969 he was knighted for services to Scottish football. He died on 20 April 1971.

Kerr, Hugh B.

Hugh B. Kerr was a builder who had a large yard and garage for his lorries and equipment behind No. 53 Station Road, extending up to the top of Kerr Street. Access to the garage area was by an entrance adjacent to No. 55 Station Road. The yard extended to the present site of St Joseph's School (at the rear of the houses on Station Road) and most of the houses of Park Lane stand on the site.

Kerr constructed the houses in Kerr Street and gave the street its name. It is thought he also built the houses between the corner of Kerr Street and the corner of Farm Road, from Farm Road to No. 59 Station Road, and possibly more.

Kerr, Robert

Robert Kerr of Auchinraith purchased some of the cotton factory units at Blantyre Works in 1816 from Henry Monteith (q.v.) & Company. He also purchased a house called 'Woodhouse' at Station Road from the Coats family. The east wing of St Joseph's School was constructed on the site of the old house, the entrance gates of which were located directly opposite No. 50 Station Road. Beyond the gates, a one hundred metre long avenue, flanked on both sides by trees, led to the house. Woodhouse, which faced Station Road, was demolished in the mid-1950s.

Kidd's Building

See Sproat's 'Laun'

Kirk Players

At a meeting of the Ways & Means Committee of the Old Parish Church, a suggestion by Russell Smith was adopted that a pantomime be performed to raise funds for the church. The Kirk Players Amateur Dramatics was established in 1983, the group's primary aim being to raise funds for the church. A Christmas pantomime has been staged every year since the group was established and has been very popular due to the lavish costumes, the stage settings and the enthusiasm of all those participating.

Kirkton, c.1880.

Kirkton

Kirkton, one of the original hamlets of the Parish of
Blantyre, was situated at High Blantyre Cross and is
probably the original village of Blantyre. In the picture,
the old houses of Kirkton, which were originally
thatched, can be seen at the right on the corner of
Douglas Street. The dangerous angle of the Old Kirkyard
wall can also be seen on the right beyond the little girl
in the foreground.

David Livingstone Memorial Bridge before demolition.

Ladysmith Bus

During the 1920s and 1930s the Blantyre-based Ladysmith Bus served the route between Low Blantyre, High Blantyre and Burnbank. The proprietor was a Mr Pate, who operated from his home at 'Ladysmith Cottage', Auchinraith Road.

Lady Nancy Pit

The 'Lady Nancy Pit' was situated in the field directly opposite the entrance to Greenhall Public Park at Stoneymeadow Road. The gorse covered 'bing' of the Lady Nancy can be seen from this point at Greenhall, on the opposite side of the East Kilbride Expressway and High Blantyre slip road, adjacent to the bridge over the dual carriageway. The pit was worked out before the end of the 19th century.

It is thought the ironstone pit was owned by the Moores of Greenhall and named after Lady Nancy Moore, an ancestor of Lieutenant Colonel Wardrop Moore (q.v.). A family member was at one time the British High Commissioner to New Zealand and received a knighthood, but the gentleman's Christian name, or the date of his appointment, is unknown. It is known that Wardrop Moore of Greenhall visited New Zealand with his family on six occasions in the latter part of the 19th century, each visit entailing a long and arduous journey by sail ship. Taking this into account, it is obvious that the family had strong ties with New Zealand.

To confirm the story, I contacted the British High Commissioner to New Zealand who put me in touch with the British High Commission in London. I was informed that the position of British High Commissioner did not exist during the 19th century, that the first Governor of New Zealand was appointed in 1840 and that this office existed until the late 19th century. No British Governor named Moore ever held the position, but it is possible that a member of the Moore family was connected with the British Civil Service and served in some capacity in the British Governor's administration and was knighted for his services.

Ian Liddell, a well-known Blantyre-born businessman related to the Littles of Crossbasket, spent much of his time as a child in and around Crossbasket Estate. He and his wife resided in Crossbasket House for the first four years of their marriage. He told me of a story

Lady Nancy Pit and bing.

Lawson's Bakery, Broompark Road, c.1910.

handed down by the many owners of Crossbasket. The pit was named after a Lady Nancy who was a daughter of one of the earlier occupiers of Crossbasket Estate, a sickly child who, on sunny days, was taken to the field opposite the house where the servants of the household would attend her. At meal times a white flag was hoisted above Crossbasket Tower to indicate to the party that it was time to return to the house, and thereafter the field was known locally as the 'Lady Nancy'. When ironstone was discovered under this field, the proprietors of the mine retained the name.

Larkfield

Larkfield is the area around the junction of Stonefield Road, Stonefield Crescent and Broompark Road.

Lawson's Bakery

Lawson's Bakery was located in Broompark Road, opposite Watson Street. *Finbarrs' public house* now stands on the site.

Lennoxlove

Lennoxlove House in Haddington, anciently called Lethington, was at one time the seat of the Lords of Blantyre. The original tower belonged to the Maitland family from 1345 and was the birthplace of John Maitland, Duke of Lauderdale (1616-82). The property was purchased in 1702 for Alexander, 5th Lord Blantyre, and was named Lennoxlove in honour of his aunt, the Duchess of Richmond and Lennox, who gave him the means of purchasing it by leaving him £50,000 in her will, a huge fortune at that time. The Duchess, whose family line was the Stewarts of Lennox, instructed her trustees to find a house for her impoverished nephew and name it 'Lennox's love to Blantyre'. This was soon abbreviated to its present name, Lennoxlove. The tower is of great antiquity, with walls 25 metres high and three to four metres thick, and is unsurpassed in strength and height by any similar structure in Scotland. When Charles Walter Stewart, the 12th and last Lord Blantyre, died in 1900, he left no male heir and the property passed to his second daughter, Ellen, and her husband, Sir David Baird of Newbyth. The Duke of Hamilton purchased Lennoxlove in 1948 and it is now his family home.

Lindsay Hill

Lindsay Hill is the road leading from the Millheugh Bridge up to Malcolmwood Farm, where it joins Loanend Road. Before the construction of Loanend Road, the route to Glasgow from Blantyre was a dirt track that extended from the bottom of the Peth Brae straight down to the Calder. The river was crossed at 'Pattenholm Ford' (q.v.) (below the *Hoolet's Nest pub* (q.v.) and Cottage Hospital (q.v.)), and one continued up through Dysholm field in which 'Queen Mary's Well' (q.v.) was located. It is thought that the road continued across the high ground to the south-west of Dechmont Hill.

Lint Butts

The small tenement named Lint Butts stood on Main Street almost directly across from Cemetery Road. The chemist's shop in High Blantyre was located in this property and was known as the Apothecary Hall.

Livingstone, David (1813-73)

Blantyre will forever be associated with David Livingstone. Born in the Shuttle Row at Blantyre Mills on 19 March 1813, he was one of seven children, five sons and two daughters, of Neil Livingstone, a tea-peddler, and his wife Agnes Hunter, who married in 1800.

Lennoxlove.

Dr David Livingstone.

They lived for a time in a house in Rose Street, on the south side of Glasgow, but returned to Blantyre to live with Agnes's parents in the Shuttle Row where all the Livingstone children were born. They were a very religious Presbyterian couple who encouraged their children to read and educate themselves as best they could. David's sister, Janet, later stated that her parents originally lived in the Fore Row that stood on Station Road where Anderson Gardens and Caskie Drive now are.

Prior to commencing work at the age of ten as a piercer at a loom in Blantyre Mills, Livingstone received his early education in the schoolroom in the ground floor of Shuttle Row. Each evening, at the end of a 14 hour working day, he attended school between 8p.m. and 10p.m. His thirst for knowledge was so great that, at work, he would prop a book on the edge of the spinning jenny and read it as the machine went back and forward. His work entailed the tying of broken threads and tending the loom. David claimed that he walked 20 miles a day whilst carrying out his duties. After a number of years as a piercer he became a spinner and the increase in his earnings made him determined to save enough money to further his education.

When he was 23 years of age, he began medical studies at Anderson College, Glasgow. He obtained lodgings in Rotten Row, and walked home to Blantyre

at weekends. After a breakfast of porridge, he would set off for Glasgow at 5a.m. every Monday morning. During his two years of study he became aware of an appeal by British and American churches for medical missionaries to go to China and decided to apply for entry to the London Missionary Society in Essex. He was accepted and commenced his studies there in 1838. After two years at Chipping Ongar, Essex, he returned to Glasgow in 1840 where he was ordained, after which he successfully took his medical degree.

His departure for China was delayed by the Opium War at that time and he was persuaded by Robert Moffat, the famous missionary to South Africa, that he could achieve more by taking up his work in Africa. Convinced that this was indeed his calling, he sailed for Africa and arrived in Angola Bay, near Cape Town, on 14 March 1841. Livingstone married Mary, the daughter of Robert Moffat, on 2 January 1845, and she accompanied him on all his expeditions until 1852 when her failing health and the safety of their four children, Robert, Agnes, Thomas and William Oswell (a fifth child had previously died), persuaded him to send them to Scotland to live with his parents at their house at Peacock Cross, Hamilton. Mary only lived at Hamilton for six months before moving to London.

By July 1842, he had travelled farther into the Kalahari region than any European. He became the first white man to set eyes on Lake Ngami in August 1849, for which he received a gold medal and was awarded 25 guineas from the British Royal Geographical Society. Determined to bring Christianity to the vast continent, to eliminate the slave trade and to open up its interior to commerce, Livingstone made three major expeditions between 1853 and 1873. He traced long stretches of the Zambezi River and it was during his Trans-African expedition (1853-6) that he discovered Victoria Falls on 17 November 1855. He travelled extensively between the equator and Cape Town and from the Atlantic coast to the Indian Ocean coast in the east.

When news reached 'civilization' of his adventures within the 'Dark Continent', he became a great hero and awakened the interest of the outside word in the largely unknown continent of Africa. He received a hero's welcome when he returned to Britain in December 1856, and spent many months touring the country attending receptions and speaking of his adventures. He received the freedom of the cities of Glasgow, Edinburgh and London. On 31 December 1856 he attended a soirée in his honour given by his 'ain folk' in the old school hall at Blantyre Mills.

On 13 February Livingstone had tea with Queen Victoria at Buckingham Palace and on 12 December 1857 he had lunch with the Prime Minister, Lord Palmerston, the day after it was announced in the House of Commons that he had been commissioned to lead a government-sponsored expedition to the Zambezi. His book, *Missionary Travels and Researches in South Africa*, was published in 1857 and seventy thousand copies were sold; with the £9,000 he received, a considerable sum in those days, he set up a trust fund for his children.

Livingstone returned to South Africa in 1858 to continue his work there, taking his wife Mary and son William Oswell with him. The three other children were left with his mother in Hamilton. Mary had been brought up in Africa, found the wet and cold climate of Britain disagreeable, and longed to return to the only country she had ever known. She discovered that she was pregnant again and had a daughter at her parents' home in Kuruman whom she named Anna Mary. She made the decision to take her children to Hamilton and left them there with the rest of her family before returning to Africa to rejoin her husband, but died in April 1862 in Shupanga, during Livingstone's explorations along the Zambezi River.

In July 1864 Livingstone returned to Britain via Bombay for the second and final time. He was not received with the same enthusiasm that his first return had aroused as some of his recent expeditions had not achieved their objectives , but he was in great demand to make public speeches throughout the country although he only addressed the British Association of the Advancement of Science. Livingstone then returned to Hamilton as he desperately wanted to see his children. He had never seen his youngest child Anna Mary, who was now aged five, and his eldest son, Robert, aged 18, had emigrated to America. His father, Neil, had died and his mother was now 80 years old. After spending a considerable period with his family, he prepared his journals for publication and *Narrative of an Expedition to the Zambezi* was produced in 1865.

After returning to Africa in 1865 Livingstone's main aim was to find the source of the River Nile, and with this in mind he undertook an unsuccessful expedition from 1866 until 1873. This venture presented him with many hardships that caused his health to deteriorate, and nothing was heard of him for three years. A cry went round the world, 'Find Livingstone.' The *New York Herald* took up the challenge and sent journalist Henry Morton Stanley to find him. After a long and difficult search Stanley found Livingstone in the village

Ten pound note, Clydesdale Bank (front).

Ten pound note, Clydesdale Bank (rear).

of Ujiji, on 23 October 1871, and memorably uttered 'Dr Livingstone, I presume?'

Livingstone's health improved after receiving supplies and medicine from Stanley and together they explored north-east of Lake Tanganyika. In March 1872 Stanley returned to Britain but Livingstone, preferring to stay in his beloved Africa, refused Stanley's offer to accompany him. He died on 1 May 1873, in Chitambos village. One of his servants found his body by his bedside, kneeling in the act of prayer. After burying his heart under a large tree, a party led by his three faithful servants, Susi, Chambo and Jacob Wainwright, carried his body overland to the Atlantic coast. The journey took ten

'Dr Livingstone, I presume?'

months and ended at Zanzibar in February 1874, where the body was put aboard a ship to London. Livingstone was buried with great ceremony in Westminster Abbey on 18 April 1874.

Within ten years of Livingstone's death, missionaries who followed in his footsteps had established a mission station on the south shore of Lake Nyasa and named the village Blantyre, after the birthplace of the great man. An amusing story is told regarding Livingstone's naming of Lake Nyasa; seeing the huge expanse of water for the first time, he asked an inhabitant in a nearby village what it was called. The native informed him that it was 'Nyasa', which in his language meant 'lake'. David used the local names in his notebooks, and duly recorded this as Lake Nyasa, little knowing that he had named it 'Lake Lake'.

LIVINGSTONE ANCESTRY

Neil Livingstone was born in September 1789 at his father's croft on the Island of Ulva. David's grandfather, because of extreme poverty and famine caused by the failure of the kelp and potato crop on the island in the latter part of the 1700s, moved with his family to Blantyre where he gained employment as company cashier at Blantyre Works. According to his daughter, Janet, Neil, was apprenticed, against his will, to the tailor, David Hunter. A father's word was law within the family in those days and, as Janet recalled, 'My grandfather exercised in his own family all the authority of a Highland Chief.'

Neil was in daily contact with his master's daughter, Agnes, and soon fell in love with her. They were married in 1810 and had seven children. Livingstone's parents were poor but his father, like his father before him, was a very religious and highly principled man who had a great fondness of books. No alcohol was allowed into the house and the only books that he permitted to be read were works on religion, travel and missionary journals. Neil at some point left the tailoring trade and became a tea-peddler.

After David Livingstone's death, his sister Janet gave an insight into her family. She recalled that two of her brothers, Charles and Neil, died when they were barely three years old and were buried in the Old Kirkyard at High Blantyre beside their maternal grandfather, David Hunter, after whom Livingstone was named.

David Hunter (q.v.) was born, the son of a crofter, in the parish of Shotts. Janet stated that her great grandmother spun yarn and that her great grandfather was a tailor who earned 4d. per day plus his food. According to

family tales told around the fireplace in the Shuttle Row her great grandfather was the only person in the parish of Shotts who could write. David Hunter, who learned his father's trade, married Janet Moffat and they owned a cottage and a croft in the parish of Airdrie. He fell on bad times after his wife's death, when, in Janet's words, 'a great dearth happened within the parish and my grandfather, who was of a gentle nature, trusted meal and corn to many who failed to pay him'.

Hunter's 15-year-old daughter, Agnes, nursed her mother throughout her illness until her death. After the failure of her father's business, she moved with him to Blantyre Works. Hunter started a tailoring enterprise and opened a shop that was located in the Wages Building, part of which still stands adjacent to the David Livingstone Memorial Bridge and is now a listed building. Agnes kept house for her father and assisted him by embroidering the garments that he produced. She died on 18 June 1865, just ten days after her son David had returned to Africa after his last visit home. David Hunter, who like his father was a very religious man, had died in 1834, and, as stated previously, had been buried in the Kirkyard of Blantyre Old Parish Church.

Livingstone Folk Four

The Livingstone Folk Four, who performed throughout Scotland in the 1960s, were a popular local folk group whose members were John Dempsey, born in Craig Street, Dave McCabe, born in the 'Buggy' Building (q.v.), and brothers, Ken and Dave McKay, who were born in Mayberry Place.

The Livingstone Four.

Livingstone Memorial Bridges

The old Suspension Toll Bridge (q.v.), which had been condemned and closed in 1949, was replaced by the

Suspension Bridge viewed from the Blantyre Bank, c.1950.

The first David Livingstone Memorial Bridge.

Construction of the new David Livingstone Memorial Bridge.

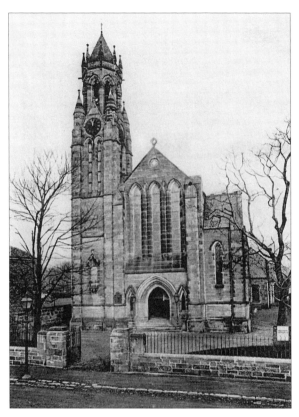

Livingstone Memorial Church.

first David Livingstone Memorial Bridge in 1952, one hundred metres downstream from the site of the old Bridge. This bridge was in turn demolished in May 1999 and replaced by the present David Livingstone Memorial Bridge, which opened on 18 October of the same year and stands on the same site.

The first Livingstone Bridge fell into disrepair, after years of neglect, which was caused by a dispute between Hamilton District Council and Strathclyde Regional Council as to who should maintain and paint it. The bridge was declared unsafe due to deterioration caused by rust. When the day of the demolition arrived, it was found after cutting the main supports of the bridge, that they could not pull it down. The attempt was abandoned and the next day further acetylene burning took place to weaken the bridge sufficiently for two heavy machines, one on either side of the river, pulling simultaneously on heavy cables attached to the main supports, to get the bridge down.

I was honoured to be the first pedestrian to cross the new David Livingstone Bridge while I was filming its construction. There were no side rails and I suppose it was quite dangerous, but I found it an exhilarating experience.

Livingstone Memorial Church

Livingstone Memorial Church traces its roots back to 1876 when a group of like-minded people gathered together in their homes to worship as they saw fit. These early Christian meetings were known as Kitchen Gospel Meetings. During the following year, Sabbath services took place in a shop in Stonefield. In 1878 arrangements were made for the selection of a suitable site and erection of a church. A timber church was constructed and the name 'Livingstone Memorial United Presbyterian Church' adopted. The first Interim Moderator was appointed and an Evangelist engaged who held the first communion later that year. The church was raised to congregation status in 1878, and in 1880 the Rev. Robert Mackenzie MA was ordained as minister and an architect appointed to design a permanent building.

An organ was presented to the church in 1881, and in the following year the present church was opened. The service was conducted by Rev. Professor Blaikie, author of *The Personal Life of Livingstone*. Funds were raised by various means and in 1886 a clock and bell were placed in the spire. After the Rev. MacKenzie left in 1888, the Rev. Thomas A. Hugh MA was ordained as minister in 1889. A bazaar held in Glasgow in 1890 raised £1,000, which helped to fund the construction of the church hall in 1894. After the Union of Churches in 1900, the church changed its name to Livingstone Memorial United Free Church. A manse fund was started in 1901 and the communion table was presented in 1905, followed by the Pipe Organ in 1907. Mrs Livingstone Wilson, the daughter of David Livingstone, unveiled a statue of her father in 1913 which had been placed in a niche in the wall adjacent to the front doors of the church. In 1920 a War Memorial was placed at each side of the pulpit, commemorating the 25 church members killed in the First World War.

After many delays, a manse was eventually constructed in 1929.

Livingstone Toilet Saloon

This odd name belonged to John Anderson's hairdresser's shop at 148 Glasgow Road in the early 1900s.

Loanfoot

Loanfoot was an area of land with a group of houses at the bottom left side of the Sydes Brae as you approached from Douglas Street. The coal 'bing' of Dixon's Colliery No. 2 pit later covered the fields behind the houses. This small group, with their back gardens, stood on the site of the roundabout where the bridge carries the East Kilbride Expressway across Douglas Street.

Loaning

The Loaning was the lane between Aggie Bain's Cottage (q.v.) and the *Barnhill Tavern* (*Hoolet's Nest*) (q.v.) that led to an old dirt track that passed Wheatlandhead Farm (q.v.) (now located in Highland Avenue) and continued down to the River Clyde to a point opposite Bothwell Castle. The open land that lay between the village of Blantyre at Kirkton (now High Blantyre Cross) and the 'Dandy' (the woods along the banks of the River Clyde) was known as Blantyre Moor.

Logan's Pub

This public house sat on the corner of Main Street, Hunthill Road and School Lane, and is at present known as *Carrigans*.

Lords of Blantyre

Walter Stewart, 1st Lord Blantyre

Walter Stewart was the only son of the second marriage of Sir John Stewart of Minto, Provost of Glasgow and commandant of the castle of that town. He was a cousin of King James VI of Scotland/James I of England and was educated with him by the celebrated George Buchanan. He later had the Priory of Blantyre bestowed on him by the King and was designated Commendator of Blantyre in 1580 when he was nominated one of the Gentlemen of the Bedchamber. He first appears as a Privy Councillor on 15 November 1582. When the esteemed Buchanan died in September of the same year, Stewart succeeded him as Lord Privy Seal. He was then appointed to the office of Assessor to the Treasurer on 26 April 1583 and was tutor to the Duke of Lennox.

The King was notorious for appointing his favourites rather than men of ability to positions of power, and when Chancellor Maitland, the King's closest adviser, who had been protected by him during many scandals, was forced to resign in 1592, Walter Stewart was promoted to take his place and became, along with the Earls of Mar and Morton, one of the King's chief advisers. Strangely, when he took on the highest office in the country next to that of the King himself, Walter Stewart, as Commendator of Blantyre Priory, was termed the 'Prior of Blantyre'. It was he who then attended to the administration of the Priory on behalf of the King.

On 6 March 1595 he had bestowed on him the office of Treasurer, including the abolished post of Treasure-depute, a position he held for one year. Stewart fell out of the King's favour when he was involved in a case raised against the monarch by Mr Robert Bruce, who was one of the most popular of the Presbyterian clergy in Edinburgh. It was known that Walter was in favour of Bruce, so it was thought expedient by the other judges that he should not take part in the judgment, but the King was furious when the complaint was upheld against him and held his old friend responsible for the outcome. He was interned in Edinburgh Castle and compelled to resign his office as Treasurer on 17 April 1599. However on 11 March 1600 an Act was passed acknowledging his long and faithful service to the King and on 10 July 1606 Walter was raised to the peerage under the title of Lord Blantyre. The proclamation reads as follows: 'Walter Stewart, Prayour of Blantyre ves maid knight of Cardonald and thairafter barone, baronet and lord of our Sovereign Lord's Parliament and ordained in all tyme thereafter to be called Lord of Blantyre.'

Lord Blantyre held many high level posts and was involved in all the important legislation passed by Parliament and other historical events during his peerage. In 1604 he was one of the Scottish nobles who signed the aborted Treaty of Union of the Scottish and English Parliaments, which came into effect a century later. It is said that his wife left the Priory with her children to live in Cardonald because of 'ghostly images and noises', so leaving Lord Blantyre to live there alone. 'The good old Prior of Blantyre', as he was known, died on 8 March 1617. His wife was the fourth daughter of John Somerville of Cambusnethan and by her he had three sons and one daughter.

William, 2nd Lord Blantyre

William succeeded his father on 12 June 1621. He was created a Knight of the Bath on 2 June 1610. On the resignation of his parents, he and his future wife, Helen Scott, were granted on 20 June 1620 the barony of Blantyre and other lands and the mansion of Blantyre Craig. Helen was the daughter of Sir William Scott of Ardros and had eight children, two of whom would inherit the title Lord Blantyre. William was a Justice of the Peace in Edinburgh in 1620. He died on 29 November 1638.

Walter, 3rd Lord Blantyre

Walter succeeded his father and inherited the title on 11 May 1639. He married Margaret, daughter of Sir William Mure of Rowallan, and died without issue in October 1641. His brother Alexander succeeded him.

Alexander, 4th Lord Blanyre

Alexander inherited the title in 1641. He married Margaret, daughter of John Shaw of Greenock, and had two children by her. He was one of the 'Engagers', a group of noblemen who offered the army of Scotland to the disposal of Charles I. The Scottish Parliament put the Engagers on trial and Lord Blantyre was fortunate to escape punishment; a special Act was passed in June 1649 stating that, although he had acted as the route-master of a troop, yet he was 'drawin thairinto throw perswasioune of counsall and out of ane vaine and childish desyr to see the ordour and fashione of arms' and was pardoned on giving satisfaction to the General Assembly. The date of his death is unknown and he was succeeded by his only son.

Alexander Stewart, 5th Lord Blantyre.

Alexander, 5th Lord Blantyre

Alexander inherited the title from his father in 1690. He swore an oath of allegiance to the Prince of Orange after the Revolution and sent a letter of congratulations to King William. He further demonstrated his loyalty by raising a Regiment of Foot, and was commissioned as its Colonel. In a letter to Lord Melville in July 1689 he declared, 'I have levied one regiment for his Majesty's service and I hope it shall be found inferior to none of the other regiments; and this week I have advanced near eight hundred lib. Sterling for clothing them, and shall have them readie at a call when ever the King shall command them; and if his Majesty think fit to honour me with his commands ... I shall desire to possess life and fortune no longer than my willingness continues to venture them for my religion and King.'

On the 9 June 1702, at the meeting of Convention in Edinburgh to join the Scottish and English Parliaments, Alexander, as one of the seceding members, protested as to its legality. He left accompanied by approximately eighty other like-minded members and was cheered by the multitude that had assembled in Parliament Square. He was then sent to London by this group of Scottish noblemen with a letter of complaint to Queen Anne which contained the reasons for the illegality. The Queen refused to accept the letter but granted Lord Blantyre a private audience.

Alexander was described as 'a very busy man for the liberty and religion of his country yet whatever party gets the better, he can never get into the administration. He was very zealous of the Revolution. He could start the hare but hath no other part in the chase. Very short of stature, and short-sighted and fair complexioned.' Alexander had two marriages, the first, to Margaret, daughter of John Henderson of Fordel, being without issue. His second marriage was in or before 1683, to Anne, sister of John, the 2nd Lord Belhaven. He died on 20 June 1704.

Walter, 6th Lord Blantyre

Walter was born on 1 February 1683. He voted against the Union of Parliament but was one of the 31 Scottish Commissioners who, in 1706, signed and applied their seal to the Articles of Union of the Scottish and English Parliaments. The Treaty of Union commenced on 1 May 1707. The vast majority of the Scottish people deeply resented the secretive manner in which these long and protracted negotiations took place. The Commissioners representing both countries in the discussions were selected by Queen Anne. It was thought, probably correctly, that although the Scottish nobility appeared to argue Scotland's case for better conditions, in the end they succumbed too easily to English demands, and were in fact in the pockets of the English before discussions commenced. Riots erupted throughout the country against the contemptuous terms in which Scotland was spoken of by many of the leading members of both houses of the English Parliament and the neglect of the interests of the Scottish nation. Members of the Scottish Parliament, which was mainly composed of the Scottish nobility, were accused of accepting English bribes to satisfy their own self interests and feather their own nests.

Walter Stewart was one of the 16 Representative Scottish Peers selected at the general election in 1710. He died, unmarried, at Westminster, of a fever on 14 June 1713 and was buried in the Richmond vault in Henry VII's Chapel in Westminster Abbey. He was succeeded by his younger brother, Robert.

Robert, 7th Lord Blantyre

Robert was in Minorca serving as a Captain of a Regiment of Foot when he inherited the title. He had two marriages, the first to Helen, daughter of the Earl of Strathmore. His second marriage was to Margaret, daughter of the Hon. William Hay of Drumpellzier and he had 10 children by her. He died at Lennoxlove, Haddington on 17 November 1743 and was buried in the family vault, which was probably within the original Parish Church at High Blantyre Cross. A plaque indicating the site of the family vault of the Lords of Blantyre can still be seen in the Old Kirkyard.

Walter, 8th Lord Blantyre

It appears that Walter spent most of his life abroad. In 1747, while in Utrecht, Holland, Lady Jane Douglas wrote that, 'Among the rest of the British, young Lord Blantyre deserves the greatest praise. He has extreme good sense, the best scholar, the greatest application, a vast pleasure in reading and the best taste in books, is free from all manner of vice, and has the sweetest temper in all the world, and to all appearance will be a very great honour to his country.' He died unmarried on 27 May 1751, aged 25, and was buried in the family vault at High Blantyre. Two poetical tributes to his memory were published in the *Scots Magazine* 1751.

William, 9th Lord Blantyre

William succeeded his brother Walter and was a Colonel in the service of the States of Holland. He died, unmarried, in an old family mansion on his estate at Erskine on 16 January 1776.

Alexander, 10th Lord Blantyre

In 1776 Alexander became the third son of Robert Stewart to inherit the title. Like his brother before him, he resided at Erskine and took great interest in the management of his estates and in all aspects of agriculture. He was described by his tenants as a very humane man, and was a highly respected nobleman. He saw the interests of both proprietor and tenants as being reliant on each other, which in turn was of great benefit to the country in general. He married Catherine, daughter and heiress of Patrick of Eaglescairnie, by whom he had five children. He died at Clifton on 5 November 1783.

Robert Walter, 11th Lord Blantyre

Robert Walter was born on 26 December 1775 and inherited the title in 1783. He was educated at Eton. He was Ensign in the Third Foot Guards in 1775 and later a Captain in the Thirty-First Foot and Seventh Dragoons and Lieutenant Colonel of the Forty-Second

Highlanders. He had a distinguished military career and served in various countries including Holland in 1799, Egypt in 1801, Pomerania and Zealand in 1807, and in the Peninsular War in 1809. He attained the rank of Major General, and was made a Companion of the Bath on 4 June 1815.

Robert was elected as one of the 16 Scottish Representative Peers to the House of Lords in 1806 and was for sometime Lord Lieutenant of Renfrewshire. He returned to his Erskine estate in 1811 and in 1828 began to build the magnificent Tudor-style Erskine House (q.v.), better known today as Erskine Hospital for wounded soldiers. Robert never saw the completion of his fabulous new home as he was accidentally killed on 22 September 1830 by a stray shot as he stood at a window in his hotel observing the Brussels Revolution. He married Fanny Mary, a daughter of the Hon. John Rodney, and had 11 children by her.

Charles Walter, 12th Lord Blantyre

Born 21 December 1818 died 15 December 1900. Charles was elected as a Representative Peer to the House of Lords during 1850-92. On 4 October 1843 he married Evelyn Sutherland Leveson-Gower, second daughter of the Duke of Sutherland, and had six children, five daughters and one son, by her. The barony became extinct on the death of Charles due to the fact that he was predeceased by his son and heir, Walter, Master of Blantyre (q.v.), who died unmarried on 15 March 1895.

Thus ended the lineage of the house of the Stewarts of Blantyre who were of the royal blood of that name. With the death of the last Lord Blantyre, on 15 December 1900, all property and superiority of the parish passed into the hands of his third daughter, Ellen, who married Sir David Baird. Their youngest son, William Arthur Baird, later inherited the property and superiority of the parish in 1910.

After the Reformation, when Walter Stewart was created the first Commendator of Blantyre Priory in 1580, it was his duty to ensure that all tenants' rents and other monies previously paid to the Prior of Blantyre from land that had belonged to the Catholic Church, were delivered to the King's Treasury. In 1598 Walter purchased the lands of Blantyre from John Dunbar of Enterkin and feued the lands to local families.

In 1599 'The king gave to Walter Lord of Blantyre, the King's treasurer, the lands and barony of Blantyre which formerly belonged to David Dunbar of Dalderk.

Arms of the Lord of Blantyre.

Also the King granted to Walter the right of patronage of the cell or Priory of Blantyre ... The King also dissolved the Priory of Blantyre from the monastery of Jedburgh ... All to be united into a free barony to be called the burgh of Blantyre.' It is not known how many Lords of Blantyre resided at Blantyre Priory, which in its day was a very impressive structure perched high on top of Blantyre Craig directly opposite Bothwell Castle, but the 7th Lord Blantyre, Robert Stewart, died at Lennoxlove, so it may well be that he moved from Blantyre Priory some time after he inherited the title from his brother.

The 7th, 8th and 9th Lords of Blantyre were buried in the family vault, which probably lay inside the original Blantyre Kirk in the old Graveyard at High Blantyre Cross. When the Old Kirk was demolished in 1793, the vault was adjacent to the new church, but it was later protected from the weather by a small stone structure constructed over its site. The small structure fell into disrepair and was later removed, and a plaque that can still be seen to today was placed over the tomb. Some time later, the three coffins of the Lords of Blantyre were removed and interred elsewhere, probably in the family vault at Bolton Church near the family home in Lennoxlove, Haddington. Charles, the 12th and last Lord, was buried in the family vault at Bolton Church and his son, the Master of Blantyre (q.v.), is also buried there.

The Duke of Hamilton purchased Lennoxlove in 1948 and the house is open to the public. A fire caused by a cigarette dropped by a tourist on 21 May 1997 seriously damaged the Blantyre/Stewart Room and most of the magnificent paintings of the Stewarts of Blantyre were destroyed or severely damaged.

DESCRIPTION OF THE ARMS OF THE LORD BLANTYRE
Or, a fess chequy azure and argent surmounted of a bend engrailed, and in chief a rose gules.

CREST
A dove with an olive leaf in its mouth proper.

SUPPORTERS
Dexter, a savage wreathed about the head and middle with laurel, holding in his right hand a baton, all proper: sinister, a lion rampant gules.

MOTTO
'Sola juvat virtus'.

TRANSLATION
'Virtue alone delights'.

Low Blantyre Primary School
SEE STONEFIELD PARISH SCHOOL (S)

Low Blantyre Station
Low Blantyre Station was originally a goods yard constructed by the Caledonian Railway Company and opened on 17 September 1849. It was located in the area directly beyond the current Hamilton-bound platform and the site is now occupied by new houses in Rosebank Avenue. The passenger station, pictured here, was added a short time later.

Low Blantyre Station, c.1910.

Main Street.

Mains

Mains was the original name for Old Place House (q.v.), constructed in 1762, which is located in Janefield Place. The original entrance was close to Greenway Lane, along a track off Hunthill Road. At one time the house was hidden behind the old Caledonian Railway line that ran parallel to the top section of Stonefield Crescent.

MacDonald, Margo

Margo MacDonald MP was married to the late Peter MacDonald, the proprietor of the *Barnhill Tavern* (the *Hoolet's Nest*) (q.v.) in Bardykes Road. She won a sensational victory for the Scottish National Party in the 1973 by-election at Govan, but failed to retain the seat in the 1974 General Election. She was elected Deputy Leader of the Scottish Nationalist Party and held the post between 1974-9. In 1997 she was elected as an MSP in the new Scottish Parliament in Edinburgh. Since 2003 she has served as an Independent MSP. Through her appearances on television and radio programmes and her regular articles in the press, Margo continues to

Margo MacDonald, MSP.

be a well-known personality throughout Britain and is highly respected in political circles.

MacDonald, Rev. Robert

Rev. Robert MacDonald was the second minister of the Free Church (Anderson Church), Stonefield Road. In 1873 he was elected a member of the first Blantyre School Board.

McAlindon and Sons

McAlindon and Sons were tailors and outfitters whose premises were at 116-18 Glasgow Road. The shop was located in the tenement that stood where the east end of Devlin Grove (q.v.) now stands.

McAlpine, Robert

Robert McAlpine was a Hamilton builder who, in 1878, constructed and gave his name to McAlpine's Building, that stood on the corner of Glasgow Road and Alpine Street, almost directly opposite Logan Street. He also constructed a tenement called 'McAlpine's in the Park' at Calder Street, opposite the car park of the new Health Centre where the dentist's surgery is at present located.

McClelland, Hugh

Hughie McClelland was a local character who lived in the Model Lodge in Burnbank near Springwells. He roamed around the Blantyre and Burnbank areas living on handouts from local inhabitants. He was tall, had long unkempt hair, wore a ragged coat, and the legs of his trousers were ragged and frayed, all of which gave him a wild appearance. When drunk, he would rant and rave at the top of his voice. Not knowing he was harmless, strangers would run away from him in terror, but it was claimed Hughie was a well-educated and knowledgeable man who had turned his back on the world.

McConell, Mary Ann

Mary was the daughter of the gardener of Craighead House (q.v.) in Whistleberry Road and was born at the lodge house there on 29 September 1828. After marrying her second husband, a gentleman named Dixon, in 1853, she emigrated to America. Their son William Brown Dixon became the Vice-president of the United States Steel Corporation and was instrumental in reducing the twelve-hour day worked by the employees. He put forward other proposals that would have been beneficial to the workers, but when these were rejected he resigned in 1912. Little did he know that Philip Murray (q.v.), a Blantyre man born close to his mother's birthplace at Craighead Lodge, would, in later years, take up his quest and succeed.

McDonald, Joe

Born in Blantyre, Joe McDonald played football as a youth for Saint Joseph's Boys Guild. He later played professional football for Aberdeen FC and Falkirk FC and gained one international cap for Scotland against Ireland.

McKerrell, Danny

Danny McKerrell attended Calder Street School where he played for the football team. He played professional football with East Fife and was a member of the team that won the Scottish Cup at Hampden in season 1937-8 when it defeated Kilmarnock 4-2, after a 1-1 draw. Danny assisted with the training of the Blantyre Victoria (q.v.) football team that won the Scottish Junior Cup (q.v.) in 1949-50. He died on 3 June 1950.

McKinlay, Ken

Ken McKinlay, known as 'Hurri-Ken' to speedway enthusiasts, was regarded as one of the greatest speedway riders of all time. Born in Blantyre in 1928, he was a grocer and farmer before taking up the dangerous sport of speedway whilst a dispatch rider in Germany just after the Second World War. He returned to Scotland and joined the Glasgow Tigers (q.v.) in 1949, soon becoming a regular, and within a few seasons was challenging another Blantyre man, the great Tommy Miller – one of the best riders in the world – for top spot within the club.

During the 1950s and '60s Kenny made regular visits to compete in Australia where, strangely, he represented England in a Test series between the two countries. When Glasgow Tigers folded in 1954, Kenny signed for Leicester and out-scored many of the world-class riders against whom he competed. He competed in 12 world finals, his best performance being when he was in a run-off for third place. Kenny spent three years riding for Coventry from 1962, after which he captained West Ham to the treble in 1965 after the amalgamation of the National and Provincial Leagues. West Ham had had a successful run under his captaincy, winning the league, the London Cup and the Knock-Out Cup.

At the age of 40, Kenny returned to Coventry. He later moved to Oxford where he was forced to retire in 1974 after a particularly bad crash in the Division Two Riders' Championship. He represented Scotland, England and Great Britain, and rode in Holland, Denmark, Germany, Sweden, Poland, Australia, New Zealand and South Africa. As well as his 12 world final appearances, he was the first to win the Midland Riders title three times, and was Australian champion in 1964. He also held the British, Scottish and Division Two Match Race championships.

Ken McKinlay died in February 2003 and will be remembered as one of the greatest riders in the history of speedway racing and one who never rode an unfair race, not even in retaliation.

McLean, Rev. Duncan

Rev. McLean was a preacher of the gospel at Blantyre Works Chapel-School (q.v.). He was buried in the old Works graveyard located on the Clyde Braes, where Caskie Drive is now situated.

Madder Mill

The Madder Mill was one of a number of large factory buildings within Blantyre Works and was situated directly below the rear of the Shuttle Row (q.v.).

The Shuttle Row was one of the original buildings constructed between 1775-8.

Malcolmwood Farm

In old maps of the area the spelling of Malcolmwood Farm is 'Milcolmwood'. The farm is situated at the top of Lindsay Hill above Millheugh Bridge (q.v.). It is thought the old road from Glasgow came down from south-west of Dechmont Hill towards the farmhouse. At a point about one hundred metres north of Malcolmwood it crossed the present Loanend Road, continued through Dysholm field and crossed the River Calder at Pattonholm Ford, where it entered the Parish of Blantyre. This route was taken by Mary Queen of Scots (q.v.) and her army on their way to defeat at the Battle of Langside in 1568.

The architecture of Malcolmwood farmhouse suggests that it was constructed in the 16th century. The London-bound mail coach passed the front door as it made its way down Lindsay Hill to the Millheugh Bridge.

Marshall, John

John Marshall was a printer in Glasgow Road, Stonefield who printed the booklet commemorating the Golden Jubilee of the Anderson Church.

Mary Queen of Scots

Legend has it that Blantyre is named after a horse called 'Blanc' ridden by Mary Queen of Scots as she passed through the town. When her horse paused she is reputed to have said that Blanc was tired, hence the name Blantyre. Of course, we know that the name is recorded in ancient Scottish documents as early as 1175 and had probably existed for a considerable time before that. It is claimed that Mary's army passed through Blantyre the day before her defeat in 1568 at the Battle of Langside and she is reputed to have drunk from a spring in Dysholm field after crossing the River Calder by way of the Pattonholm Ford directly below Barnhill. The spring thereafter was called 'Queen Mary's Well' (q.v.).

Masonic Orders

Lodge 599 was originally located in a hall above the *Livingstonian Public House* that stood on the corner of Glasgow Road and Forrest Street. The building was constructed in 1888. The day before the laying of the foundation stone on 9 May of that year, a jar containing newspapers of the day and other documents was meant to be sealed in the cavity behind the stone but by some strange omission the usual coins of the realm had been neglected. Major Ness came to the rescue and immediately offered a commemorative set of coins presented to him during the Jubilee of Queen Victoria, a great sacrifice as the coins were of value and could not be replaced. It is not known if the jar containing them was ever recovered when the old hall was demolished.

A new Masonic Building was constructed on Glasgow Road between two existing tenements on the corners of Church Street and Logan Street, and was opened on 28 June 1903. Lodge 557 is located at Main Street, High Blantyre and was instituted in 1884.

Master of Blantyre

Walter Stewart, the Master of Blantyre, only son of Charles Stewart, the 12th Lord Blantyre, would have inherited the title on the death of his father. Unfortunately he predeceased his father, dying on 15 March 1895, and when his father died on 15 December 1900 the title became extinct.

As a young man, Walter went round the world, climbed the Rocky Mountains, met with a few adventures, had some narrow escapes, and saw some of the finest scenery in America, New Zealand, and many other countries. He returned to Scotland and settled near the north-east coast, as tenant of a large sheep farm called Sciberscross in the parish of Rogart, Sutherland, a few miles west of Dunrobin Castle, where he remained for 12 years. He took a great interest in all parochial matters and was warmly accepted into the community, being elected to the School Board and made captain of the Rogart volunteer company. After his acceptance of the captaincy the strength of the company advanced rapidly until it became numerically more than double what it previously was and by far the strongest company in the battalion. His kindness and unwearying helpfulness to the poor, and his frequent assistance to others in need of aid, secured for him the warm regard and sincere respect of all sections of the community.

In the winter and spring of 1879-80, phenomenal snowstorms raged throughout the Highlands and were considered the worst weather in living memory. Many in Rogart, as in other localities, experienced great difficulty in procuring fodder for their cattle, and even if it had been available, did not have the means to pay

Master of Blantyre.

for it. Many families found themselves on the verge of starvation and Walter was their means of survival as he battled throughout the winter to provide people with the essentials to see them through their suffering. Later, at a public meeting in Rogart, he was presented with an illuminated address and a silver salver with suitable inscriptions as tokens of heartfelt gratitude and the deep regard felt towards him by all classes in the neighbourhood.

Walter then purchased Eilanreach farm in the village of Balmacara on the north shore of Loch Alsh, directly opposite the Isle of Skye. He resided there for ten years until his death at Balmacara House. He served the community as a member of the Glenelg Parochial School Board, as a County Councillor and a Justice of the Peace. After his death many ordinary people came forward with recollections of his kindness towards less fortunate townsfolk. Fishermen spoke of the many times he had taken their small boats in tow behind his, the *Eilanreach*, as they struggled to return to Glenelg with their catch. When his shepherd, Ewen Cameron,

lost his wife, the Master sailed his yacht to Loch Hourn and brought back the funeral party, with the mourning husband and his children, and showed the kindest sympathy towards poor Ewen afterwards, even during his long last illness.

The purser of a steamer related the following story regarding the kindness of the Master of Blantyre: 'On a cold winter's day, a number of years ago, as the ferry-boat of Glenelg was waiting to take passengers ashore, a gentleman followed by his highland servant came along. As he was stepping into the boat, he saw a poor woman and her child crouched and shivering upon the deck. He at once took off his plaid and threw it over them, going ashore himself with only a light coat as protection. On making inquiries afterwards as to who the gentleman was, I learned that it was the Master of Blantyre.' Crofters also talked of his kindness and the consideration given to them in times of need. Two Glenelg shepherds remembered the time when the Master, sailing home down Loch Alsh, observed them and their dogs trudging along with tired feet many miles from Balmacara. He sent a boat to bring them on board the *Eilanreach*, and save them the toilsome walk over the mountains to their homes.

The Master of Blantyre was a very religious man and was missed not only at Glenelg, but throughout the Highlands, Inverness and elsewhere. He did much to improve Glenelg in the ten years that he lived there. He made a post-path from Ardintoul, kept it in repair, and also got a daily post provided. He secured a telegraph wire by giving a large guarantee to the company. He built good houses for his shepherds and kept three pairs of horses that he did not require for himself, but used to plough the crofters' lands for them. He also grew potatoes, oats and turnips to give people employment, even though it would have been cheaper had he bought them.

Notice that the Master of Blantyre's funeral would leave Eilanreach at six o'clock on the Monday evening was given in all the different churches in the district and a large gathering assembled, notwithstanding a continuous downpour throughout the day. Tea was prepared for all, it having been the Master's express wish: 'Now mind, no whisky.' At the appointed hour, the coffin was brought out and set down on the grass in front of Balmacara House amongst the people. Rev. Watson, minister of Kintail, offered a prayer in Gaelic and after readings from the scriptures by other ministers, the coffin covered in his green plaid was carried by 24 men, in sets of eight, and followed by his household and friends, to the *Eilanreach*, which was berthed at Quarry.

Three ministers led the funeral, which was followed by schoolchildren from the Master's school and over 200 people from the surrounding districts. There would have been many more mourners in attendance but for the terrible weather conditions which prevented those from around Loch Alsh getting over the water. Many tears were shed as the white boat sailed into the darkness on her way to Glasgow, from where the coffin was conveyed to the burial place of the family at Bolton, near Haddington. The Master of Blantyre was buried in the sarcophagus that stands in the Kirkyard of Bolton Church, close to the Blantyre's family home at Lennoxlove House (q.v.).

Mathieson, J.F.

J.F. Mathieson was a watchmaker and jeweller whose shop was in the Masonic Building at 155 Glasgow Road, directly opposite the top of the original corner of John Street.

Mavis Mill

Mavis Mill was situated at the 'West End', directly across the River Calder, between the present Priory Bridge

Mavis Mill, c.1900.

Estate and what used to be the Spittal Pit (now Doonin of Bardykes). The last miller to own the mill, which closed in the 1930s, was Thomas Stratton. Thomas told of how, when his wife was kicked in the face while milking a cow, he pulled a hair from the tail of a horse, threaded it on an ordinary needle and proceeded to stitch the deep wound. It seems that this was the way country people treated such wounds in those days.

Mayberry, Hugh

Hugh Mayberry was employed by Lord Blantyre as Commissioner of the Blantyre Estates. It was he who first thought it necessary to mark the place of David Livingstone's birth, and to this end he commissioned a plaque in 1897, which can still be seen on the gable of Shuttle Row. Major Ness (q.v.) presided over the installation ceremony in front of over 3,000 people. Mayberry was instrumental in the construction of Low Blantyre railway station, which was considered the finest in the district at that time. He also raised funds to erect a railing round the old burial ground at Blantyre Works, in which many of the earlier residents of the village were interred, some of whom were the forefathers and family of David Livingstone. The cul-de-sac at Caskie Drive was constructed on the old burial site.

Two tenements bearing Mayberry's name were constructed in Blantyre. The first was behind Ulva Place, adjacent to the Cross Row at Blantyre Works. The second, which is extant, stands on Glasgow Road between Livingstone Memorial Church and St Joseph's RC Church, and is amusingly known as 'Purgatory'.

Merry & Cunningham

Merry & Cunningham were the proprietors of Auchinraith Colliery (q.v.) and constructed houses in Elm Street and Auchinraith Road for their employees.

Merry's Rows

These houses, latterly referred to as 'Murray's Rows' locally, were constructed in 1876 by Merry & Cunningham for the miners employed at their colliery at Auchinraith Road. Elm Street replaced Merry's Rows, seen here in this picture *c.*1880, which shows members of the Salvation Army at what is now the junction of Elm Street and Auchinraith Road. Merry's Pit was situated adjacent to the east side of the timber house at 121 Auchinraith Road and occupied the land between there and Parkville Drive, Springwells. At the time of writing the site is being used for the construction of houses. The new street leading into the estate will be called Victoria Gardens.

Another small miners' row, named the 'Auchinraith Row' (q.v.), was situated at this point on the old pit road. This was a cul-de-sac before the present road was extended to the top of Logan Street to eliminate a bad bend at the railway bridge adjacent to Auchinraith School (q.v.) at the top of Craig Street.

Merry's Rows, c.1880.

Mid Row

The Mid Row was the smallest of four rows of houses built by Henry Monteith (q.v.) at Blantyre Works Village.

Mill Dam Court Case

Robert Wallace of Kelty, MP for Greenock, raised an action in the Sheriff's Small Debt Court at Glasgow on December 1838 against Henry Monteith, the proprietor of Blantyre Mills, for violating his rights as a proprietor of 'salmon fishings'. Wallace claimed compensation amounting to £8 8s. 6d. for loss and damage to his fishing at 'Weems' (Wemyss) Bay, 'four miles distant from the Blantyre Dam', by illegal obstructions to the course of the salmon up the River Clyde caused by collection of water to supply Monteith's cotton works at Blantyre. (It is worth mentioning that Wallace may have misled the court in stating that his fishing rights at Wemyss Bay were only four miles down river from the Blantyre Dam by claiming that his rights on the Clyde extended to this point.)

Mr Wallace, who brought the action not only on his own behalf but also as a representative of other proprietors, one of whom was the Duke of Hamilton, stated that the salmon fishing at Weems was out in the sea and that any fisherman on the coast could, in theory, come forward with a similar claim. He also maintained that, unlike other proprietors, such as the Duke, he did not want the removal of the dam, as he knew the value of water power to the country, and only requested that the fish should have access to their natural habitat. While the Blantyre Company took enough water to keep their works going, they should leave the comparative 'driblet' which would allow the fish to pass up and down the river. He claimed that the present sluices and Salmon 'chace' were unsuitable, and that poachers from near and far were 'cleeking the fish' as they lay dead or dying below the dam. Some poachers who stayed all day at the dam had their meals brought to them by their families.

The court was informed that the original 1790 dam was 16.5 metres wide and it was extended in 1796 to 63 metres in width, in 1814 to 109 metres in width, and in 1836 to 127.5 metres in width. The dam was broken down in a severe flood in the spring of 1834 and repaired.

After hearing all arguments for and against the dam, the Sheriff of Lanarkshire declared that he found that salmon got past the dam easily during rains and floods. On five or six runs a year the salmon could not get past the dam, and so the dam, as it stood, was an illegal erection. The Blantyre Company had unquestionable right to use the dam for the purpose of their machinery, and, therefore he could not have it stopped or find a way to preserve the breeding of salmon in the river by the upper and lower heritors. The Sheriff awarded compensation to Mr Wallace but found that for eighty to one hundred days a year the fish got over the Blantyre dam easily. He noted that the company would make alterations at their own expense to secure a passage for fish to the upper reaches of the river.

In the end the court case resolved nothing, because the dam was modified and raised to its present height, which restricted, even more, the free passage of salmon up river and eventually they stopped returning to their ancient spawning grounds on the upper reaches of the Clyde. In the 1960s salmon were released in the Clyde in an attempt to reintroduce the species to the river. The venture was successful, and today the number of salmon has returned almost to the levels that existed at the time of the court case.

Before the construction of the Blantyre Mills commenced in 1785, a dam had been built at this section of the river by Lord Blantyre and was known as the 'Small Waulk' or 'Fulling Mill', for the thickening of the 'Hodden Grey' of the Lairds of Blantyre, which was preceded by the 'Little Cotton Mill' first built, and that through the 'Triffing Dam Dyke', then existing, plenty of water flowed for salmon to pass freely up river.

Mill Houses

The painting below shows the ruins of the Bottom Row at Blantyre Mills, on the right of the picture, with Shuttle Row at top left. The building at the extreme right of the Bottom Row was originally the boardroom of the Blantyre Mills and is now a private house occupied by Mr and Mrs A. Walker. Most of the Mill factories and buildings were demolished by 1904, the remainder by 1912. The window of the room where David Livingstone was born in the Shuttle Row is at the top left of the painting.

Miller, Professor John (1735-1801)

John Miller was born in Shotts and inherited Millheugh House and Estate at Barnhill. It is said that the lands of Millheugh had been owned by the Miller family

Bottom Row and Shuttle Row.

Millheugh House.

since the 14th century. The house was situated adjacent to the waterfall on the River Calder above Millheugh Bridge. Miller became an advocate in 1760, and in the following year was appointed Professor of Law at Glasgow University. He wrote two books, *The Origin of the Distinction of Ranks*, in 1781, and *Historical View of the English Government from the Settlement of the Saxons in Britain to the Accession of the House of Stewart*.

Miller, Tommy

Tommy Miller, born and bred in Blantyre, is regarded as one of the all-time greats of speedway racing. As a youth he raced at Bothwell racing track, and signed for Glasgow Tigers (q.v.) in 1949 and made his debut at the White City Stadium in Glasgow. Such was his ability that he was promoted almost immediately to the senior team and made his debut for them on 5 April 1950 in a Northern Cup match against Newcastle.

Racing against the top riders in the country improved Tommy's undoubted abilities and he was soon recognised as one of the top riders within the sport. In 1951 he scored over 300 points and broke a number

Tommy Miller.

Millheugh Bridge, 1925.

of track records in the process. It was during the 1951 season that he gained his first ever trophy when he won the Hamilton Cup, the first of many. He was the first Tiger to be nominated to ride in the prestigious Silver Helmet Match Race Championship, which he won. In 1952, during a Scotland versus England International match, his 76.0 seconds was the fastest ever recorded at the White City Stadium. Tommy achieved the magical 1,000 points for Tigers in only his third season. Glasgow Tigers sold Tommy to Motherwell Eagles in 1954 for £15,000, a huge sum at that time. He continued to pull in the crowds in the Motherwell colours as he kept up his high standard of riding.

Tommy was the proprietor of motorcycle and car establishments in Motherwell and Glasgow. In 1964 he suffered a heart attack and his health gradually deteriorated until he died at Hairmyres Hospital in East Kilbride on 12 June 1975. He is still regarded as one of the biggest stars in the history of speedway racing.

Millheugh Bridge

It is thought that the original Millheugh Bridge was constructed in the 13th century. It is almost certain that it fell into disrepair on several occasions and had to have major repairs carried out to its structure, but it is thought that the arch demolished in 1952 was that of the original bridge.

It was believed that the arch had twisted due to underground workings but this was not the case. The arches of a medieval Scottish bridge, unlike those of a Roman bridge, were not perfectly curved as they were constructed in a different manner. The Romans used a centrally located keystone, whilst the Scots built the bridge on top of a timber structure. When an arch was completed the timbers were pulled down and the arch fell in on itself, giving the bridge an irregular appearance. The old Millheugh Bridge was a perfect example of this method, as can be seen in this photograph. The arch was of such strength that it survived and repairs to the old bridge throughout the centuries were carried out on top of it. The photograph also clearly shows that the old bridge had been 'capped'. When repairs or reconstruction were being carried out to Millheugh Bridge, carriages such as the London stage-coach would revert to using the adjacent Pattonholm Ford (q.v.).

Millheugh House

SEE PROFESSOR JOHN MILLER (M)

Millheugh Mill

The old Millheugh Mill was attached to the south side of the original Millheugh Bridge. The small arch of the present bridge was constructed over the site of the original lade. The miller was authorised by Lord Blantyre to operate the mill, which was normally handed down through the generations. As part of the agreement for their lease, the farmers of the parish were directed to bring their corn to the mill and a percentage of the end product was given to Lord Blantyre as part of their rent, making the landlord, the miller and the farmers interdependent.

Monteith, Henry (1764-1848)

Henry Monteith was regarded by his contemporaries as one of the giants of business in the commercial community of Glasgow during the second half of the 18th century. As a young boy he was apprenticed to a master weaver, and through his expert knowledge of the craft, together with his business acumen, he successfully managed his father's company at Anderston in Glasgow. In partnership with his brother, James, he purchased the Blantyre Mills (q.v.) from David Dale (q.v.) in 1792. Shortly after the transaction, the French Revolution disrupted trade in the country and brought Henry and James to near bankruptcy. Henry and his brother asked David Dale to rescind the contract, but he refused and declared the contract binding. Henry and James managed to survive the depression by selling their stock of yarn at an auction in London and amassing a fortune of £80,000 over a period of five years.

Henry continued to manage his father's weaver's business in Anderston, Glasgow, and set about expanding that company. The firm was badly hit by the American War of Independence but, undeterred by the slump, Henry moved the factory to Barrowfield, Bridgeton. The firm of Monteith & Bogle was established and became known throughout Europe when, in conjunction with Blantyre Mills, it was the first European company to manufacture the famous 'Turkey Red Dye', a colour which at that time was the height of fashion for garments, and had to be imported from Far Eastern countries. Dyed calico yarns, hankies and hatbands using the formula discovered by Henry and James were manufactured at Blantyre Works and the company cornered the British and European markets, which amassed another great fortune for the Monteiths.

When James died in 1802, Henry devoted himself entirely to the running of the Blantyre Mills. He constructed more houses for the ever-expanding work force and a row of houses behind the Shuttle Row adjacent to the Madder Mill had an end section used as the company boardroom. The boardroom building still stands today and is now a beautiful private house.

Further expansion necessitated an extensive project of house building. A large complex of homes was built at Station Road on land now occupied by Anderson Gardens, Fagan Court and Caskie Drive. Four rows of houses were constructed at Station Road, the largest being the Fore Row, which ran up Station Road, and the Mid Row located immediately behind it. The Cross Row was the smallest row and ran from Station Road to the edge of the Clyde Braes. The fourth row, the Waterloo Row, ran along the top of the braes from the present Anderson Gardens to where Caskie Drive is now located. A school was constructed in 1828 on the

Model of Blantyre Works.

site of what is now Anderson Gardens and the layout now formed a large quadrangle, in the centre of which was a large well, as the accompanying picture shows.

The houses now situated at the top right of Caskie Drive, above the Braes, stand on the site of the old graveyard of Blantyre Works. Around this time a beautiful villa was constructed for the works manager on the land where the African Pavilion now stands in the David Livingstone Centre. This mansion was known locally as 'Jolly's Lodge' and named after one of the managers who once lived there. As the mills expanded and diversified, the name of the Blantyre Mills gradually disappeared and was replaced by Blantyre Works.

At the completion of this building project, the Monteiths had created a self-contained village with tollgates and tollhouses at the corners of Knightswood Avenue and Rosebank Avenue (see illustration on p.151). Most of the houses were 'single ends' (one room) and lacked basic services, but Blantyre Works Village was considered a model complex for employees and was years ahead of its time.

With his growing wealth, Henry, along with two associates, James Oswald and James Ewing, established the Glasgow Bank in 1809. In 1816, following the slump in the cotton industry after the Napoleonic Wars, he sold off his interests in the weaving manufactories at the Works to a gentleman named Kerr, but retained his interest in the profitable Turkey Red Dye side of his business. He was elected Lord Provost of Glasgow in 1819-20, and in 1821 was elected as MP for Lanarkshire Burghs, holding the seat for ten years.

Henry, who had two marriages, purchased a large estate in Carstairs and constructed a magnificent Tudor/Gothic-styled house. At the age of 66 he retired and spent his remaining years living in splendour on the estate. It is recorded that on 13 January 1837, aged 73, he was called out of retirement to preside over the largest civic banquet ever held in Glasgow to honour Sir Robert Peel, who had been elected in 1836 as the Dean of Procurators of the University of Glasgow. Peel later became Prime Minister of Great Britain.

Monteith, James

James Monteith's father, John, worked on a loom in his small cottage, like all other weavers at that time. He taught his son the skills of his trade and James, who was a great innovator, took it upon himself to import finer yarns from Belgium and produce muslin that was regarded as in equal quality to the finest East Indian fabrics. Such was the demand for this product that the business prospered and James soon introduced cotton into his weaving. Later he formed a partnership with David Dale, and although Dale is generally regarded as the founder of the Blantyre Mills (q.v.) in the 1770s James was as deeply involved in its conception and construction. His two sons, Henry and James Monteith, purchased the Mills in 1792.

Moore, Lieutenant Colonel John Wardrop

John Wardrop Moore of Greenhall was one of the heritors of the Parish of Blantyre. He was born in 1862 at Greenhall House, which was constructed by one of his forefathers c.1760. The Greenhall Estate consisted of 332 acres between Stoneymeadow Road and the River Calder. The house was demolished in the 1960s and later Greenhall Estate was landscaped and linked by footpaths to the neighbouring estate of Millheugh, then opened to the public. Wardrop Moore joined the local militia volunteers in 1883 and rose to the rank of Lieutenant Colonel.

A decision was taken in 1850 to repair and partially rebuild the perimeter wall of the Old Kirkyard at High Blantyre Cross. Moore took the opportunity to construct a commemorative arch within the wall, adjacent to the Kirkyard gates, and dedicated the structure to the inhabitants of Blantyre. A horse trough was originally constructed within the arch, but motorised transport caused the demise of horse-drawn carriages and the trough was removed and replaced by a stone seat.

Mount Pleasant

The name Mount Pleasant originally belonged to the small building that stood adjacent to Robertson's Aerated Waters, Springwells. The present row of cottages was then built along Glasgow Road, as far as the bridge that carried the railway across the road at the corner of Whistleberry Road, and this attractive row took the name of the small tenement, which is still at the east end, opposite the Springwells housing estate.

Murphy, Jimmy

Old Jimmy Murphy was the bellman at Blantyre Works. He had no formal education and, as Jimmy himself said, had great difficulty in 'reading the words'. It is doubtful if he had ever been to school. Part of his duties was to go round the village and call out the time and place of any function within the Works Village; he was, one could say, the 'Town Crier'. Blantyre Works' Literary and Scientific Institute met weekly in the School Hall during the winter months and 'men of letters', personal friends of Major Ness (q.v.), gave the lectures. Major Ness told the story of the occasion when Jimmy was entrusted to go round the village and cry out the subject for a forthcoming event, 'Development', and Jimmy set off on his rounds. Major Ness was sitting in his house, which at that time was in the Shuttle Row, when he heard Jimmy shouting out 'Deevilment'. This particular word in those days covered all sins known to man so Ness rushed out of his house and asked, 'Jimmy, what is that you are saying?' 'Whit is it Maister?' asked Jimmy. 'What is the name of the subject of tonight's meeting?' asked the Major. 'Deevilment,' replied Jimmy. 'Jimmy,' said Ness, 'it is not about Devilment, its Development.' He then spent a considerable time trying to get Jimmy to pronounce the word correctly and thinking that he had succeeded, allowed Jimmy to proceed on his round. Jimmy had no sooner left the Major when he found himself tongue-tied again and reverted to announcing the subject of the meeting as 'Deevilment'. Major Ness declared that, thanks to Jimmy Murphy, the particular meeting was the best-attended in the history of the Blantyre Literary and Scientific Institute!

Murray, Philip (1886-1952)

Philip Murray was a miner born in Baird's Rows (q.v.), Blantyre, although some say he was born in Bothwell Park. His father, also a miner, moved the family from Blantyre to Bothwell for a short time, probably to work in Bothwell Castle Colliery. After the death of his mother his father remarried and returned with the family to Blantyre, where Philip was educated at Saint Joseph's School. On leaving school he gained employment in local collieries until he emigrated with his father to America, arriving there on Christmas Day, 1902 with the rest of the family following in 1903.

Once again he got employment in the coal industry. During a dispute he struck a weigh-man whom he claimed cheated the miners when noting their production quotas, and things came to a head when he organised a strike and led a deputation to the manager of the Keystone Coal & Coke Company. The next day Philip and his family were evicted from their tied house and banished from the area by the County Sheriff. These

events were to be a turning point in his life. Philip studied and improved his technical knowledge of all things pertaining to the mining industry. A staunch socialist, he joined the Pittsburgh United Mine Workers Union and was elected in 1912 to the executive board and to other prominent positions within the labour unions, including Vice-President of the United Mine Workers (1920-40), Chairman of the Steelworkers Organising Committee (1936-42), President of the Industrial Organisations of America (1940), and President of the United Steelworkers of America (1942-52).

Murray was appointed to the National Mediation Board created by President Roosevelt in 1940 to prevent labour disputes during the Second World War.

President Harry Truman with Philip Murray.

He also worked closely with William Bauchop Wilson (q.v.) another Blantyre man, who was First Secretary of the Department of Labour during President Woodrow Wilson's term of office, on co-ordinating the labour movement in America during the production of armaments in the First World War. It was even said that the efforts of the two Blantyre men in this field were probably the main reason that the allies won the war!

Philip Murray fought tooth and nail all his life with the steel barons and mine owners of America for better pay and working conditions for his fellow men. American President Harry Truman (pictured here with Murray), paid tribute to Philip when he died in 1952, comparing him with Britain's renowned politician Ernest Bevin. President Roosevelt's wife, Eleanor, stated, 'We are poorer because of his passing.' Murray donated a large sum of money towards the construction of the Blantyre Miners Welfare.

'Murray's' Rows

SEE MERRY'S ROWS (M)

High Blantyre Cross.

Names From The Past

A number of inhabitants of the ancient village of Blantyre have been recorded in old Scottish documents which, like all official records of that time, are written in Latin. One such document records that Stephen de Blantyre witnessed a grant to the Abbey of Cambuskenneth *c.*1200. Another from around 1248, states that 'Maldwin, Earl of Lennox grants to Stephen of Blantyre, a complete half-three times a ploughland measure of Killearn, namely that half in which the church was established and the appointment of Stephen de Blantyr as Prior of Killearn Church'.

An inquest of mortancestery of Patrick Blantthyre, son of Stephen de Blantthyre, dated 1263, is recorded in an Act of Parliament. Mention is also made of Patrick de Blauntire of Stirlingshire, who rendered homage in 1296 to King Edward I of England. At that time Stirlingshire extended further west than its present boundary. The seal of 'Patricii de Blauntir' contained a boar, a crab and a serpent. The Bishop of Durham, in 1304, issued a writ to restore to Agnes de Blantyr her dower lands of Norham Liberty. Walter de Blanctire is mentioned as a friar preacher and the King's confessor in 1343. John of Blanteir, a Scottish merchant, was issued with a safe conduct to enter England in 1426. In 1531 David Blantyre had a gift of the escheat of Alexander Abirkeirdo in Angus.

Ness, Major John (1833-1908)

Major John Ness was born in the village of Kingston, which later became the site of the great Kingston Docks in Glasgow. He commenced his duties as headmaster at Blantyre Works School on 1 June 1856. He married his wife, Mary Reid, in 1858, had five sons by her and lived in Waterloo Row overlooking the River Clyde and the Braes at the bottom of Station Road.

Ness found much disobedience in the school when he first arrived in Blantyre but soon established a reputation as a strict disciplinarian. Once a code of obedience had been established, his pupils and their parents grew to love and admire their 'Dominie'. Ness' word was law inside and outside of the school, and if any parent attempted to question or complain about any punishment of their child administered by the headmaster, the child's father would be threatened with dismissal by the company. This took place on a few occasions in his early days at the school, until it was recognised that here was a man of authority. It was claimed that Ness and the Works Manager – one in the Mills, the other in the Schoolroom – were a sufficient guarantee for the good behaviour of both young and old and the services of a policeman were quite unnecessary for the upkeep of order within the Works Village.

Mr Ness was informed by the firm of Messrs Henry Monteith & Company on 1 April 1873 that his services would be no longer required as headmaster of Blantyre

Works School because a School Board was about to be formed in Blantyre for the purpose of looking after the educational affairs of the parish and they could not carry on with their school at Blantyre Works any longer.

The Blantyre School Board was elected in April of 1873 and advertised for two teachers – one for High Blantyre and the other for Stonefield – to take up the duties of headmasters of schools erected by the Board in these districts. At the meeting to select the headmasters, the Clerk announced that he had received three petitions in favour of the appointment of Mr Ness to the headmastership of Stonefield Public School, and asked if he should read out the petitions first or open the applications. The Chairman requested that the petitions be read first. They were from Messrs Henry Monteith & Company, the Blantyre Works Sabbath School Teachers, and from the scholars of the Blantyre Works Sabbath School. After the petitions had been read the Chairman said, 'Gentlemen, it seems as if it is the unanimous desire of the ratepayers that Mr Ness should be appointed to the position of headmaster of Stonefield Public School and I think we cannot do otherwise than appoint him to the position.' Without opening any of the other applications the Board voted unanimously to appoint Mr Ness and immediately informed him of his appointment and of his salary, which was £120 per annum.

Ness was headmaster at the Works School for 18 years and 32 years at Low Blantyre Primary School which, as indicated, was originally known as Stonefield Parish School. It can only be assumed that he continued his duties at the Works School until the Stonefield Parish School was opened.

The character reference given for Mr Ness by Messrs Henry Monteith & Company read as follows:

> We have very great pleasure in bearing testimony to the admirable manner in which our school has been conducted by Mr John Ness for the past sixteen years. We consider Mr Ness a most experienced teacher in all branches suited to a Parish School. While possessing the faculty of gaining the affections of his pupils, he at the same time maintained exemplary discipline in the classroom. We much regret parting with Mr Ness, and we can with every confidence recommend him for the situation of Headmaster of Blantyre School, for which he is now a candidate.

At the demise of the Works School there were 180 pupils on the register. Owing to over-crowding, the school had for some time used one of the toll gate houses and the old original school room in Shuttle Row to accommodate the pupils. On the morning of the transfer to the new Stonefield Parish School, all the pupils gathered together in the old Works School and were addressed by Mr Ness. A prayer was said, and then 'Auld Lang Syne' sung. The staff and pupils then marched in procession the half-mile up Station Road to their new school. From that first day to the day it was demolished in 1978, to make way for the Clydeview Shopping Centre, the school was affectionately known as 'Ness' School'.

David Livingstone returned home only twice from Africa. His first visit was to his mother's house at Peacock Cross in Hamilton, where she had lived prior to his leaving for Africa towards the end of 1856. Mr Ness wrote to Dr Livingstone, who was in London lecturing and attending functions given in his honour, to ask him to give an address at a soirée of the members of the Blantyre Literary and Scientific Institute. Livingstone replied to Ness' request:

> Ship Hotel,
> Charing Cross,
> London.
> 19 December 1856
>
> My Dear Sir,
> I beg leave to return my warmest thanks to the gentlemen comprising the committee of the Blantyre Works' Literary and Scientific Institute for their polite offer of a soirée in my honour, and kind and obliging letter which accompanied it; but I am unable to afford myself the treat of a visit to my birthplace and my friends who may still be in the land of the living. My work is by no means finished, and I must be back in my adopted country before May next year. I cannot speak well in English now, and have no wish to learn again. Probably when I reach my dotage and become garrulous I shall tell my adventures. In the meantime, I desire to spend my short in England in retirement.
>
> With good wishes for the prosperity of the Institute, believe me, Sir, yours and so on.
>
> DAVID LIVINGSTONE

But Ness was not about to give up on his quest to get the great man back to his roots so he went to visit Livingstone's mother, who by this time lived in a cottage near Peacock Cross, Hamilton, and asked her to use her influence to persuade her son to visit Blantyre. Mrs Livingstone agreed to help and in due course sent Ness a letter informing him that David had arrived the previous night, and that Mr Ness might try again to get him to visit Blantyre. Ness immediately wrote another letter to Livingstone, which he sent with a man named Archie Campbell, an old playmate of the explorer. Livingstone at last agreed to come to the meeting and wrote in reply:

Hamilton
27 December 1856

Dear Sir,

As my mother and sisters, seconded by Mrs Livingstone, think that I ought to gratify my friends in Blantyre, and myself, by attending the soirée mentioned, I think I must act the part as the good son, brother and husband, and come to my old haunts for an hour or two in the beginning of next week. I am somewhat tired by the excitement of public meetings and private gatherings in England, and was glad to get away as I am anxious to avoid speechifying for having repeated attacks of clergyman's sore throat in Africa, and am far from fluent in my native tongue. I hope the arrangements will be made with a view to comparative silence on my part. The above will show that the deputation need only name the day and the hour by letter, and no exposure made of themselves in this miserable cold weather.

Yours most truly,
DAVID LIVINGSTONE.

Mr Ness immediately went to Glasgow and saw the partners of Messrs Henry Monteith & Company and informed them of the visit. Mr James Hannah, the principal partner in the firm and at that time a Bailie in the City of Glasgow, agreed to preside at the meeting. The date was fixed for 31 December 1856 and the following wording appeared on the ticket that was issued:

BLANTYRE WORKS LITERARY AND
SCIENTIFIC INSTITUTE SOIREE.
IN HONOUR OF DR LIVINGSTONE,
ON THE OCCASION OF HIS VISIT TO HIS
NATIVE PLACE,

ON WEDNESDAY, THE 31 DECEMBER 1856.
* * *
JAMES HANNAH, ESQ., IN THE CHAIR.
* * *
DOORS OPEN AT HALF-PAST FIVE:
TEA TO BE SERVED AT SIX PRECISELY.

Blantyre was the residence of many prominent Glasgow businessmen, and representatives not only of Blantyre but also of the surrounding districts, attended the Livingstone meeting. On the platform that night were Livingstone's mother, Sheriff Gardner of Hamilton, and other notables.

After various speeches of welcome Dr Livingstone was asked to address the audience. The great explorer, while relating some of his experiences and adventures, suddenly came to an abrupt halt and stood looking at his audience in a dazed frame of mind. The silence was painful, and, by means of encouragement, someone shouted out, 'Speak it out Dr Livingstone!' Livingstone said, 'Excuse me ladies and gentlemen, but you do not know the mental agony I am suffering. I am speaking to you in English, but at the same time I am thinking my subject in African, and I am translating my words from African into English. I have been 16 years in Africa, and during that time I have scarcely looked upon the face of a white man. Do you wonder that I have almost forgot my mother tongue?' He then continued with his talk and described Africa from a map that he himself had drawn.

The soirée, which was Livingstone's first public meeting in Scotland, was a resounding success and all felt honoured to have been in the company of possibly the most famous man of their time. Mr Ness subseqently attended a great meeting held in the City Hall, Glasgow, over which the Duke of Argyle presided. In the course of the Duke's speech he remarked that Dr Livingstone was at present home from Africa, and referred to his visit to Blantyre. He said that Livingstone was born in Hamilton and that he came to Blantyre every morning to work in the mills there, and Ness felt the urge to interrupt the Duke and point out his error but he restrained the impulse. On coming home that night, he immediately sat down and penned a letter to the Duke at Inveraray Castle pointing out that he was wrong when he said Dr Livingstone had been born in Hamilton, and suggested that if his Grace could spare the time, he would be only too pleased to show him over Livingstone's old haunts. A few days later a letter arrived from the Duke thanking Mr Ness for pointing out the mistake that he had made but adding that it had been pointed out to him immediately after the meeting, and he deeply regretted his error.

When the world feared that Livingstone was dead, no word having been heard of him for a number of years, Mr Ness helped to raise funds locally for the 'Livingstone Search Expedition'. He also raised money to send a deputation from Blantyre to attend Livingstone's funeral at Westminster Abbey and Ness gathered a group around him for the purpose of forming a 'Livingstone Monument Fund', but early funds deposited in the City Bank in Glasgow were lost when the bank failed, and the proposed scheme had to be abandoned. Ness did not give up the idea of identifying Livingstone's birthplace and, after a report in the *Glasgow Herald* regarding his quest, his ambition was achieved in the summer of 1897. Lord Blantyre's Commissioner, Mr Hugh Mayberry (q.v.), responded and erected a marble plaque on the gable of Shuttle Row at Blantyre Works. A brass band and a crowd of over 3,000 people witnessed the unveiling. Mr Ness presided and in his address recalled his meeting with the great explorer. The plaque can still be seen today on the east gable of Shuttle Row.

Because of the unsettled situation in Europe at the time, a local 'Volunteer Force' was established by Ness in 1859, equivalent to the 'Home Guard' during the Second World War, to protect the country in the event of a foreign invasion. Ness rapidly attained the rank of major due to his enthusiasm within the voluntary movement. Promotion carried him beyond the confines of his own parish, and rarely did a volunteer gathering of any kind take place in the county without the presence of the gallant Major. The following circular was written by him and posted throughout Blantyre:

BLANTYRE PARISH RIFLE CORPS

A Public Meeting of the Inhabitants will be held in the Free Church, Blantyre, on the evening of Saturday first [*sic*], 10 December, at six o'clock, for the purpose of making the necessary arrangements for organising a Rifle Corps. The present unsettled aspects of Europe, as well as the opinions of many of our highest military authorities, cannot fail to bring us to the conclusion that such an event as an invasion of this country is possible. It has therefore been considered by a number of the influential gentlemen connected with this Parish, that the Inhabitants of Blantyre should form themselves together into a Rifle Corps, to act together, in case of emergency, with our Fellow-Countrymen who have already enrolled themselves in many parts of the country, and by these means to strengthen the hands of our Government. We have only to cast a retrospective glance at the history of our country, to find many noble and heart-stirring examples of the patriotism and self-devotedness of our Forefathers, and the perseverance and determination that invariably characterized their struggle for liberty – an inheritance which is now our duty to protect. It is therefore confidently expected that every one who is at all able will come forward and lend a helping hand in this great national movement, so that Blantyre may stand second to none in Loyalty to Queen and Country.

Eighty-nine volunteers came forward and formed themselves into the Blantyre Rifle Corps, which was recognised as one of the strongest groups of its kind in the county. Ness was appointed Secretary to the new Corps, and in this capacity he wrote to the Duke of Hamilton, who was Lord Lieutenant of the County of Lanark, informing him of the formation of the Blantyre Corps. He asked the Duke to take the necessary steps to enroll the Company, to consist of 100 effective members, as 'The Lanarkshire Rifle Volunteers, Blantyre, Bothwell, and Uddingston, District, No. 1'. He also informed him that when they received the government arms there would be a need for safe and sufficient ranges for rifle practice. In due course a reply was received, recognising the formation of a corps, commencing 10 December 1859, which was to be known as the 'Blantyre Rifle Corps, No. 44'. This later became 1st Company, Blantyre, of the 2nd V.B. Scottish Rifles. Ness attained the rank of major on 10 June 1886 and it was by this title that he was known locally until his death in 1908.

An attempt was made on three occasions to form Blantyre into a burgh. In 1887 a number of local businessmen formed themselves into a committee to carry out the necessary arrangements. Major Ness and Mr John Clark Forrest (q.v.), a banker and large landowner in the parish, were two of the most prominent men. Local ratepayers voted in the first referendum, which took place in Stonefield School. At the closing of the poll the Sheriff announced from the door of the school that the proposal had been defeated, much to the disappointment of Major Ness, who pointed out that Coatbridge and Hamilton, which were not much larger than Blantyre, owed their prosperity to the fact they had created themselves into burghs and said that the rejection

Nicholson's Shop, on the corner of McLaughlan's Building, Station Road, 1960.

of the proposal by the ratepayers was a retrograde step. Another attempt made in 1891 was again defeated. A third and final attempt was defeated in 1894.

The Works Bell was located in the belfry on the roof of the Wages Building and rung at 6a.m. every morning, except Sunday, to start the working day. When the building was being partially demolished in 1904, Major Ness had high hopes that the bell would be acquired by the School Board for use in the empty belfry of Stonefield Parish School, but it was gifted to Stonefield Parish Church. In 1922, 14 years after his death, Major Ness (as usual) achieved his aim when the church spire collapsed and the bell was gifted to the school. When Low Blantyre Primary was demolished in 1975, the bell was relocated to its present position on the west wall of Shuttle Row, approximately 100 yards from its original position. All that remains of the Wages Building is the gable end at the bottom of Station Road, adjacent to the David Livingstone Memorial Bridge, which is now a listed building.

The Major was a member of Lodge Livingstone, No. 599. On four occasions he held the office of R.W.M., and he also held important positions within the Provincial Grand Lodge. Burnbank, Lodge Major Ness, No. 984, honoured him by naming their lodge after him.

A meeting was held on 1 June 1906 to celebrate the jubilee of Major Ness as a headmaster in the Parish of Blantyre. Many distinguished persons, former pupils, friends and family attended, and many examples were given of the public service he had given the community. Major Ness must surely rank as one the most dedicated men who ever resided in Blantyre. Throughout his life he strived to improve the conditions, welfare and quality of life of his fellow inhabitants. It was said that there was hardly a public event or function held within the parish in which the Major was not involved.

He was a deeply religious man and he was at the forefront in raising funds for any worthwhile event. On his arrival at Blantyre he became a member of the

Bothwell United Presbyterian Church, the only church of his persuasion in the locality. This was originally called Wooddean United Free Church (q.v.) and was built for the use of the workers of Blantyre Works. He was the leading light in the effort to raise funds to construct the Livingstone Memorial Church, although he remained a member of Bothwell Church.

Twenty-nine years after the Blantyre Explosion, Ness related his recollections of that terrible morning to an audience gathered in the Old Works' School to celebrate his jubilee:

> Between nine and ten o'clock our school work was interrupted by the sound of a far-off explosion. An hour later all the doors of the school were besieged by grief-stricken women who, between their sobs said, 'Oh, Mr Ness, let the weans oot the school, their faithers are awe deid.' One woman, even more excited than the others, cried, 'Oh, Mr Ness, let them oot. Five hunner men have been killed at the pit.' My reply was that it would be better to let the children remain because no good could be done by their running about. Next morning the school resumed as usual, and in the course of the day, I had a visit from Dr Middleton, who was the school inspector at the time. He expressed that in a time of such disaster I should have dismissed the scholars from the school, and at the same time he added that Father Frawley, who was the priest in charge of the Catholic school, had adopted that course. My reply was firm, that Father Frawley was not a master, while I was under a School Board, who were my masters. Until, I said, I got orders from the Board, I could not close the school.

Nicholson's Piggery

Nicholson's piggery was located on the Clyde Braes overlooking the river. Access was gained by passing under the railway bridge at the bottom of John Street and turning right. The Nicholsons had a grocer's shop on the corner of McLaughlan's Building (see illustration opposite), which stood on Station Road at the corner of Woodburn Avenue close to the station gates.

Norris, Dewar

Norris the Grocer was a prominent name in Blantyre. Dewar Norris had two shops, one at the bottom of Stonefield Road, and the other adjacent to the Picture House Cinema at Glasgow Road by the bus stop at present situated in front of the Blantyre Sports Centre.

O

Stonefield Parish Church (left) and Batters, Ironmonger, Glasgow

Old Craighead Road to Bothwell Bridge

An old medieval road to Bothwell Bridge was located adjacent to where the west side of the East Kilbride Expressway now crosses Glasgow Road. Originally it was part of an ancient track from the River Clyde to Blantyre Village at Kirkton; later the top section became our Auchinraith Road. A section of the old road was still visible and in use until it disappeared during the construction of the Expressway extension in 1978.

This small section gave access into Baird's Rows (q.v.) (Craighead Rows) and Blantyre Celtic's football ground at Craighead Park, adjacent to Blantyre Greyhound Stadium, which also disappeared under the Expressway. It was probably the construction of Craighead House and its estate some time in the 18th century that caused Whistleberry Road to replace the old Craighead Road. In the photograph opposite, looking along Glasgow Road towards Burnbank, Auchinraith Road is in the

Old Man's Rest, Stonefield Public Park.

Construction of East Kilbride Expressway across Glasgow Road.

right foreground and Whistleberry Road is at the bottom of the hill. The medieval road would have been on the immediate left.

Old Man's Rest

'Old Man's Rest' was a glass enclosed shelter and stood on the main footpath through Stonefield Public Park that ran from the entrance at Hastie's Farm, Glasgow Road to the gate in Station Road. It was adjacent to the rear gardens of Nos 56 & 58 Station Road. Senior citizens would gather there and play chess and dominoes. My parents lived at 56 Station Road, and my brother and I were born there. My father was a pigeon fancier and the small black marks seen against the sky in the photograph are corks threaded on the telephone wires so that the pigeons would avoid hitting them when approaching the loft.

Old Place

The ancient site of Old Place, which was also recorded on early maps as 'Mains', is the possible location of the mysterious 'Blantyre Castle' (q.v.). It is now the site of

the houses in Janefield Place and its adjoining streets. Old Place House, at No. 12 Janefield Place, is all that remains today to remind us that this historical site ever existed. An ancient Blantyre family named Coats were descendants of Robert Coutts (Coats), Prior of Blantyre *c*.1520. It was a branch of this family that constructed Old Place House in 1762 on a site now thought to have been previously inhabited. Various branches of the family also owned large areas of land within the parish: there was a 'Coats of Blantyreferme', and 'Coats of Thornhill', whose house gave the name to Coatshill Avenue. Coatshill House, demolished in the 1980s, was situated directly across from local shops at the foot of Coatshill Avenue and David Livingstone Primary School. A William Coats built the mansion called Woodhouse that once stood on the present site of the east wing of St Joseph's School at Station Road. This family, or a branch of their descendants, founded the famous Coats Thread Mills of Paisley. A gravestone marking the burial place of James Coats of Old Place can be seen in the Old Kirkyard at High Blantyre Cross.

Hasties Farm, Glasgow Road.

Parkneuk

SEE AUCHENTIBBER (A)

Parochial Board/Parish Council

The Parochial Board was established in 1848 and was involved in all matters and decisions concerning the community until Blantyre Parish Council succeeded it in 1895. The Parish Chambers building situated in Cemetery Road was opened in 1901. Before its demolition in March 2001, it was used as a day centre for the care of the elderly and disabled.

The Parish Council ceased to exist after the introduction of the Local Government Act (Scotland) 1929 and from April 1930 became part of the 5th District Council of the County of Lanark. Further changes took place with the introduction of the 8th District Council in April 1964 and the reorganization of local government in May 1975, when Blantyre became part of Hamilton District, Strathclyde Region. On 31 March 1996 Hamilton district joined with the surrounding areas of East Kilbride, Clydesdale, Rutherglen and Cambuslang to form the present authority of South Lanarkshire.

Parish Chambers, Cemetery Road.

Blantyre, Lenox, Massachusetts.

Blantyre Lenox, Massachusetts

Parochial Library

The Parochial Library was located in Blantyre Works Village.

Paterson, W. Robert

As a young boy, Robert Paterson emigrated with his parents to America. He became a successful businessman and made his fortune in the production of turpentine.

Robert Paterson.

In 1902 he constructed a magnificent mansion in Lenox, Massachusetts as a present to his wife and claimed that the structure was an authentic replica of the baronial Blantyre Castle that once stood in his birthplace in Lanarkshire, Scotland. There are references in some ancient Scottish documents to the existence of the Castle of Blantyre at Old Place/Mains (q.v.), but no description of the structure or its accurate location has ever been found. Knowing that nobody in America would ever obtain enough knowledge of the subject to dispute his claim, Robert probably felt safe in giving his house the grand title of 'Blantyre Castle'. The house was later sold and converted into a five star hotel which retains the Blantyre name to this day. The painting of Paterson seen here hangs in the hotel lounge.

Pathfoot

Pathfoot is the bottom section of the Peth Brae that takes the road to Millheugh Bridge (q.v.). This photograph shows the two cottages that stood there. The one on the right had stables at the rear where the London stage-coach changed its horses before continuing up the Peth Brae on its way to its next stop at *Hamilton Inn*, now the Hamilton Museum.

Paton's Barber Shop

James Little of Crossbasket constructed the 'Wooden Hut' which stands at the corner of Stonefield Road and Broompark Road as an ironmonger's shop. It is currently a florist's. The business was intended to occupy his father, who was a political activist for the Liberal Party. James felt that at times his old father was rather too outspoken and, indeed, prone to giving street speeches on the benefits of Liberalism. The ploy worked and Mr Little spent more time on his new business venture, his political preaching gradually ceasing. In November 1938 James Little sold the premises to a local hairdresser named James Paton for £114. Paton fitted out the hut as a barber's shop and served the male population of the Larkfield area for many years.

Pathfoot, c.1900.

Picture House Cinema, The 'Doocot', c.1947.

Pattonholm Ford/Mill

Pattonholm Mill was situated on the Calder Braes and was so called because of its location adjacent to Pattonholm Ford, which carried the medieval road, through Dysholm field from Loanend Road and across the River Calder, past the mill and up into the old village of Blantyre. The mill, also known as Dysholm, stood directly below the Cottage Hospital (q.v.) and Aggie Bain's Cottage (q.v.) in Bardykes Road.

Peesweep

Peesweep was a tenement building that stood on the Sydes Brae at Auchentibber.

Pettigrew, William

At the time of the Blantyre Explosion (q.v.) at Dixon's Pit in 1877, William Pettigrew owned Malcolmwood Farm located above Millheugh Bridge, at the junction of Lindsay Hill with Loanend Road. When the destitute 'Blantyre Widows' were evicted from their tied miner's houses at Dixon's Rows, six months after the explosion, it was William Pettigrew who came to their assistance by constructing huts to accommodate them and their children. It is not known where these huts were erected.

Picture House Cinema

The famous circus family, Messrs E.H. Bostock & Sons, opened the Picture House Cinema in May 1913. The cinema, known locally as 'The Doocot', replaced the Blantyre Electric Cinema (nicknamed the 'Fleapit') located above the Livingstonian Bar at the corner of Glasgow Road and Forrest Street. It stood on Glasgow Road where the main entrance to the Blantyre Sports Centre is now. Silent films had been shown in the Co-op Hall in Herbertson Street prior to its opening. The front stalls were long benches without arms onto which people were packed until it was impossible to move. The mid-stalls occupied the middle third of the floor space. A barrier separated the 'posh' seats at the back.

The last, and best known, manager of the cinema was Mr Jack Brown, who during his management at the Picture House was promoted to the position of general manager of the Hamilton Hippodrome Theatre and the Playhouse Cinema in Quarry Street, Hamilton. He lived with his family in a house above the two shops

Demolition of Blantyre Gaol, Glasgow Road.

adjacent to the cinema on the corner of Alpine Street. Jack started his career doing odd jobs in cinemas at the age of nine, during the era of the silent movies, and was in show business for more than 60 years. Through his connections in the theatre, he persuaded the great Harry Lauder to perform at the Picture House in aid of local charities. He was manager of the 'Doocot' from 1939 until it was closed by the owners, due to dwindling attendance. It was converted into a ten-pin bowling alley in 1960 but destroyed by fire in 1967.

Police Station

The original gaol stood on Glasgow Road at the corner of Herbertson Street, almost directly opposite the top of Forrest Street, at the rear of the Co-op Hall, seen here being demolished. The Telephone Exchange in Forrest Street can be seen on the right across Glasgow Road. The small Auchinraith Industrial Estate at Rosendale Way now stands on this site.

Polk, President James Knox (1795-1849)

James Knox Polk, the 11th President of the United States of America from 1844 to 1849, was the grandson of William Pollock, a Blantyre blacksmith. According to the old Blantyre parish register, William was born at Kirkton on 27 December 1735. He followed his father's trade and worked as a blacksmith at his Smiddy at Kirkton. William emigrated in the mid-1700s to America, where his son, Samuel Pollock, a planter farmer, was born on 5 July 1772 in Tryon, North Carolina. Samuel married Jane Knox, who was born on 15 November 1776.

Their son, James Knox Polk, was born near Pineville, Mecklenburg, North Carolina on 2 November 1795. He married Sarah Childress, who was born on 4 September 1803. A successful lawyer, he entered politics as a representative in the Tennessee legislature from 1823 to 1825 and was elected Governor of Tennessee for 1839 to 1841. He served as a representative in the United States Congress for fourteen years, and as Speaker of the House from 1835 to 1839.

On 29 May 1844 he became the first politician to receive news by telegraph when he heard that he had been nominated by the Democratic Party to stand for the Presidency. He was elected President in 1844. During his term of office he expanded the nation by 800,000 square miles to the Pacific Ocean as a result of the Oregon Treaty and the Mexican War. He retired in

Douglas Street, c.1880.

1849 due to ill health and died on 15 June 1849, at his home in Nashville, Tennessee.

The American version of his ancestry is different from the above but our information is taken from the Rev. Wright's account in *The Annals of Blantyre*, where he states that he was quoting from an old letter he had in front of him. The letter, written on 15 April 1782, was from William Pollock (the president's grandfather) to his father Archibald Pollock, residing at Kirkton Smiddy, Blantyre, and stated that for many years he had followed in his father's trade of blacksmith, and prospered so well he had amassed a considerable fortune, bought an estate, married a wife and had seven children. He went on to inform his father that he had 14 Negro slaves, 12,000 acres of land and a large stock of flour and meat cattle. Rev. Wright states that Archibald received a second letter from his son on 18 March 1790, but does not give any information regarding its contents.

The old pronunciation of the name Pollock in the Blantyre dialect, even in the early part of the 20th century, was Polk, and it would appear that the President's forefathers decided for some reason or other to use the Scottish version of the name. I would suggest that William Pollock would have been illiterate, like most of the lower classes at that time in Scotland, and when William reached America and gave his particulars to immigration personnel, he pronounced his name in the broad Scottish dialect which would have sounded like Polk. It is possible that his name was written down just as it sounded to the person who took his particulars. If in fact William Pollock were illiterate, he would not know that his name had been spelt wrong by looking at his documents. The family name would become Polk without anyone being any the wiser.

It was once thought that the thatched cottage that stood adjacent to the Old Parish Church, on the corner of Craigmuir Street and Main Street, was the birthplace of William Pollock. A deputation from the American Consul visiting the site to ascertain whether this assumption was correct must have realised that the house was constructed after William had emigrated to America, although the house was built by a member of the Pollock family, as the year 1777 and the initials J P were carved on the lintel above the front door as was the custom at that time. When the cottage was demolished in the 1950s the lintel was inserted into the kerb of the path behind the gate of the Old Parish Church, where it can still be seen today.

The Kirkton Smiddy where William Pollock was born stood in Douglas Street and backed on to the Old Kirk/Graveyard wall. The cottage seen on the left of this photograph of Douglas Street *c.*1880 is probably the original Kirkton Smiddy.

Population

Before the construction of the Blantyre Mills, which commenced in 1775, the population of the parish of

Blantyre was 496, the bulk of whom resided at Kirkton and Priestfield (at High Blantrye Cross). The majority of the remainder resided at the hamlets of Hunthill, Barnhill and Auchinraith, and possibly at Springwells. After the construction of the Mills, the population rose rapidly. The population increased thereafter as follows: The entire Parish: 1801: 1,751, 1811: 2,092, 1821: 2,630, 1831: 3,000, 1878: 7,619, 1885: 10,000 plus, 1902: 14,382.

In 1841, the population of the High Blantyre area was 261; by 1891, following the discovery of coal in 1871, it had increased to 7,836.

Another example of the rapid increase between the years prior to the construction of the Blantyre Mills and those following the discovery of coal and the opening of various collieries can be seen in the statistics for births, deaths and marriages in the town:

	(1773-1783)	(1875-1885)
Births	17	440
Deaths	?	180
Marriages	6	78

The population rose to approximately 22,000, its highest level after the Second Word War. It dropped dramatically during the 1960s, owing to the demise of the coal industry within the town. The present population of the town is approximately 18,500.

Post Offices

The earliest post office was probably the one located in the tollhouse at the entrance to the Blantyre Works Village at Station Road. The post office that served the High Blantyre District was in a tenement situated at Main Street, on the east of Cemetery Road. Stonefield was originally served by a post office that was located in a tenement at the foot of Stonefield Road. These premises closed when the post office was transferred to a tenement in Glasgow Road, opposite the Bethany Hall. This office closed when, in 1953, a new post office was constructed further along Glasgow Road on the corner of Logan Street, and this office was demolished in 1997 after the post office transferred to premises in the Clydeview Shopping Centre.

Power, Mary

Mary Power was the proprietor of a small wooden hut at Station Road that she used as a grocer's shop. Originally the shop was aligned with the front of the adjacent houses on Station Road but it had to be relocated when the construction of prefabs (q.v.) commenced in what were the fields of Forrest's farm and the yard of Hugh B. Kerr of Station Road. When building began at Park Lane, during the 1950s, Mary's shop was placed on rollers and pushed uphill to receive its new address, No.1 Park Lane.

Prefabs

After the Second World War there was great demand for housing. A quick solution was the construction of prefabricated houses throughout the country that were quickly manufactured and relatively cheap to produce. All were provided with a fridge and a toilet which was separate from the bathroom. Four prefab sites, each of a different style, were chosen in Blantyre, three of them with prefabs made of asbestos panels.

The largest estate was on what is now the site of Ballantrae Road, opposite the High Blantyre Industrial Estate. It had eight streets whose names were associated with Robert Burns: Alloway Street, which led into the prefabs from Main Street, Afton Street, Armour Street,

Post Office, corner of Glasgow Road and Logan Street.

High Blantyre Prefabs, c.1949.

Burns Street, Ellisland Street, Lochlie Street, Mossgiel Street and Nith Street. The photograph (p.129) shows Ellisland Street, looking towards Mossgiel Street, with the Auchinraith Colliery 'bing' in the background. At the time of writing, a new housing estate is under construction on the site of the 'bing' which will be known as Victoria Gardens, the entrance to be off Auchinraith Road at the top of Craig Street. Another prefab site was located at Parkville Drive and Auchinraith Terrace, Springwells, around the base of the Auchinraith 'bing'. A third was at the foot of Station Road, on the original location of the Mill Rows, and is now occupied by the houses of Anderson Gardens, Fagan Court and Caskie Drive. The postal address was Station Road.

The best quality prefabs, which were known as 'Tehrans', were constructed in an area off Station Road on a large yard owned by the builder Hugh B. Kerr (q.v.), and in the fields of Forrest's farm between St Joseph's School, Thornhill Avenue, Farm Road, Kerr Street and the rear of the houses at Station Road. The names of the streets of the site were: Park Lane, Clyde Crescent, Kerr Street and Centre Street, which was located at the top of Kerr Street and was a cul-de-sac that linked Park Lane and Clyde Crescent via a lane at either end of the street, so providing a more direct route through the site to the Thornhill housing scheme and Bruce Terrace. Tehran prefabs were constructed with sections of pebbled panels and were of such good quality that many local authorities took the decision not to demolish them but to brick around the outer walls and make them permanent houses. The Tehrans that were removed to allow redevelopment were carefully dismantled and sold as summer homes and offices.

14 Centre Street, c.1967.

No. 14 Centre Street (my former home, pictured here) was the last of the four houses that stood on the lane from the end of the cul-de-sac linking Park Lane and Centre Street with the foot of Clyde Crescent. In the background, the trees of Thornhill Avenue can be seen approximately fifty metres above Bruce Terrace.

Primitive Methodist Church
SEE BETHANY HALL (B)

Priory Bar
The Priory Bar was located at the west end of the Masonic Buildings on the corner of Glasgow Road and Logan Street. The Masonic Building was the central part of three separate sections, the east and west buildings constructed in 1875 and the main central section, known as the Masonic Halls, built in 1903.

Priory Bar, 1979.

Priory Pit
SEE COLLIERIES (C)

Priour Walter de Blanctire
Walter of Blantyre succeeded William as Prior. It is recorded that in 1343 Prior Walter de Blanctire was the confessor to King David II of Scotland. He was a person of considerable importance during King David's reign. Another ancient Scottish document mentions the fact that 'Priour Walter de Blantir' acted as one of the Scottish Commissioners appointed to negotiate the ransom of King David Bruce, who was taken prisoner by the English in the Battle of Durham in the year 1346. The Prior and other commissioners had a 'safe conduct' from the English King, permitting them to

travel through England with one hundred horsemen. King David was liberated in 1357. The fact that the Prior was involved in this negotiation indicates the stature of the early Priors of Blantyre within the realm of Scotland. Walter had another safe conduct through England which permitted him and three companions to study at Oxford University. Like his predecessors, he would have taken a prominent part in any decisions made by the Scottish king and his Parliament. After many years of involvement at the highest level in Scottish affairs, Prior Walter seems to have returned to the quiet and regular life at Blantyre Priory (q.v.) and in 1350 the Pope granted him, 'plenary indulgence at the hour of death'.

Priour William de Blantir (c.1296-1340)

The first prior that we know of was William. Like all the early Priors of Blantyre, he was the equivalent of a present-day Member of Parliament and would have played a part in all the important events that shaped Scottish history in the mid- to late 13th century. The following is a brief account of some of the political intrigues that existed during his time as 'Priour de Blantir', and of the outcome of events in which he would, no doubt, have been involved.

On 8 July 1249 Alexander III inherited the throne of Scotland on the death of his father Alexander II. He married Margaret, the sister of Henry III of England, at York, on 20 December 1251. With this marriage it was hoped that peace would prevail between Scotland and England. Alexander had estates in England and, as duty demanded, paid homage to Henry for those lands. Henry insisted he was superior to the King of Scotland, an opinion that he implanted in the mind of his son and heir, Prince Edward, later known as the 'Hammer of the Scots', and so began the wars that lasted for centuries over the independence of Scotland.

King Alexander III and Queen Margaret were visiting London when the Queen gave birth to a daughter at Windsor in February 1261 and named her Margaret. In 1281 she was married to King Eric of Norway. Disputes raged at this time between Scotland and Norway over territorial demands in the Western Isles. A Scottish army defeated the Norwegians at the Battle of Largs in 1263, but it was the marriage of Margaret to King Eric that finally brought the hostilities to an end. In 1282 Alexander, the 19-year-old Prince of Scotland, was married to Margaret, daughter of Guy, Earl of Flanders.

But Scotland's prospects of prosperity and security were dashed with disasters which followed each other in rapid succession and spread dismay throughout the kingdom. Alexander had lost his Queen after a sudden illness and his second son, David, died when a boy. His daughter Margaret, Queen of Norway, died during childbirth in 1283, leaving an only child named after her mother and known as the 'Maid of Norway'. The death of Queen Margaret was followed by that of her brother Alexander, the Prince of Scotland, on 28 January 1284. The Scottish King was thus in a few months bereft of all his children.

These calamities rendered it necessary that immediate measures be taken for the settlement of the crown. A Parliament was quickly assembled at Scone on 5 February 1284, when the nobles of the realm solemnly bound themselves to acknowledge Margaret, Princess of Norway, as their sovereign, failing any children whom Alexander might have in any future marriage. Alexander, still a relatively young man, took a second wife, Joleta, the daughter of the Count of Dreux. Within a year of his marriage, on 16 March 1286, the King was killed. On a dark night, as he was riding between Kinghorn and Burntisland on the northern shore of the Firth of Forth, his horse stumbled over a rocky cliff at a place now known as 'King's Wood End'. His death was, perhaps, the greatest calamity that has ever befallen the kingdom of Scotland. He died aged 46, in the 37th year of his reign.

The four-year-old Princess Margaret of Norway, recognised as heir to the Scottish crown in 1284, was residing in Norway. It was necessary, owing to her infancy and her absence from the kingdom, to appoint a regency and a Parliament was held at Scone on 11 April 1286, when six guardians of the realm were chosen to carry on the government of the country.

By this time Prince Edward had inherited the English throne, and like his father before him, declared his superiority to the Scottish monarch. In 1289 Eric, King of Norway, opened negotiations with Edward regarding the affairs of his infant daughter and her kingdom of Scotland, which was precisely what the English king wished for. He had in mind a marriage between the young Queen of Scots and his only son, Edward, Prince of Wales, which would bring the realm of Scotland under the banner of England. He had secretly procured a dispensation for the marriage from the Pope and drawn up a treaty.

In the meantime, the Scottish nobles had foolishly asked the English king to act as umpire in the dispute that had arisen between the Scottish nobles regarding the succession of a female monarch. The final arrangements for the proposed marriage were agreed at a Scottish Parliament that met in Brigham on 18 July 1290. The treaty was known as the 'Articles of the Treaty of Brigham', and was signed by the guardians of Scotland, clergy, earls, and barons on behalf of the whole community. It was agreed that the rights, laws, liberties and customs of Scotland were to be observed at all times throughout the whole kingdom, and that the kingdom of Scotland was forever to remain separate from England, and it was to this treaty that Priour William de Blantir attached the seal of Blantyre Priory.

All the scheming and treachery of the English king came to nothing when the infant Queen fell sick after setting sail from Norway and, at the age of eight years, died in Orkney about the end of September 1290. King Edward conquered Scotland and the nobles, clergy and others paid homage to him in 1296. In the following year Sir William Wallace (q.v.) began the great struggle for national independence and among his active supporters was Prior William of Blantyre, who had no hesitation in breaking his oath of fealty to the English King.

After the Battle of Falkirk, in 1298, Edward practically completed his second conquest of Scotland and the Prior of Blantyre was one of the many prisoners of war taken after the defeat of the Scottish army. When Comyn and his followers surrendered to Edward in February 1304, a general amnesty was declared. This included the Prior of Blantyre but, as he was still being unlawfully held prisoner, the following command was later issued by King Edward:

> The K. to the Sheriff of Lanark.
> Among the conditions of the late agreement between his envoys and Sir John Comyn of Badenaghe, all prisoners were to be released, except Sir Hubert de Morham and his father. The K. hears that Robert de Barde who lately took friar William de Cokeburgne, warden of Blantyre Priory, is distraining him and his pledges for ransom, in violation of the treaty. He commands the sheriff instantly to stop this and allow nothing of the kind in future in his bailliary.
> Wemyss, 5 March 1304

The Sheriff of Lanark, Robert de Barde, was none other than Robert the Bruce, who appears to have been removing items from Blantyre Priory as a means of enforcing payment of the ransom for his release.

Among those who were excluded from the amnesty was Sir William Wallace, who never swore allegiance to the English King.

The insight into this old document shows us how the Priors of Blantyre and their monks would, at time of war, abandon their peaceful pursuits and take up arms in defence of their country.

High Blantyre Cross.

Quarries

In the past there were many stone quarries throughout the parish of Blantyre, the vast majority located in fields surrounding Auchentibber and Calderside. On maps of around 1900, over a dozen stone quarries and six limestone quarries can be seen. Dykehead Limestone Quarry was the last to close and was located behind the cottages at the top left of Sydes Brae. The eastern edge of the field at Dykehead runs along the parish boundary with Hamilton and it was from Earnock Road, at the Hamilton side of Dykehead field, that access was gained.

One old stone quarry which can still be seen in Low Blantyre is located in the 'Dandy' (the local name for woods which run along the banks of the River Clyde) adjacent to the playing fields of the David Livingstone Centre. Stone from this quarry was used by David Dale to construct the Blantyre Mills.

Queen Elizabeth, The Queen Mother

During the Second World War the King and Queen toured the country to help keep up morale. The Queen is seen here throwing a bowl at the opening of the new season at Blantyre Miners Welfare Bowling Green in 1942. King George VI is standing in the centre of the second row.

The Queen Mother first visited Blantyre, as the Duchess of Kent, when she opened the David Livingstone Memorial in 1929. She also opened the Africa Pavilions in 1977.

Queen Mary's Well

During the march with her army to the ill-fated Battle of Langside in 1568, Mary Queen of Scots and her army camped, on the day before the battle, on the Calder

Queen Elizabeth, The Queen Mother at Blantyre Miners Welfare, 1942.

Scottish Quoiting Cup Winners, 1928.

Braes below Bardykes Road. Then the army proceeded into Dysholm field, crossing the Calder via Pattonholm Ford. A spring of water rises from the ground here which was used as a well by travellers on the old road from Blantyre to Glasgow. It is said that the Queen refreshed herself by drinking from the spring, and from that day it was known as 'Queen Mary's Well'. Today the spring is in the centre of an area of marshy ground opposite Malcolmwood Farm (q.v.).

Quoits

Before the First World War, and for a few decades after, the game of quoits was a very popular sport, especially among the working classes. The aim was to throw a number of metal rings, about the size of a large horseshoe, over a small pole placed in a circular clay pit from a distance of approximately twenty-five feet. Quoiting pitches were relatively easy to construct and there were several throughout Blantyre. One was on the Clyde Braes between the rear of the houses of Rosebank Avenue and the railway bridge at the bottom of John Street. There was another between Broompark Road and Cemetery Road, High Blantyre. Smith's garage was constructed on the site. The most prominent was the magnificent Auchentibber Quoiting Green (q.v.), surrounded by beautiful gardens, which was reputed to be the best quoiting arena in Scotland. Traces of the old green can still be seen today behind the War Memorial. The photograph shows the Auchentibber team that won the Scottish Cup in 1928.

Blantyre Works from The Braes.

R

Rae, William

William Rae, born in 1840, was a miner who discovered that he had 'healing hands' and was known throughout Scotland and large parts of England as the 'Bloodless Surgeon'. He lived in Raploch Cottage, 7 Station Road, Blantyre from 1902 until his death there on 28 July 1907. Thousands attended his funeral and it is said that people from all areas of Britain packed the streets from his home in Station Road to the cemetery in High Blantyre.

'Ragman's Roll'

In the 13th century a list of Scottish Roman Catholic benefices was drawn up as a basis for taxation. Baiamund De Vicci, an emissary of the Pope, was sent to Scotland with the document that became known as the 'Ragman's Roll'. It contained the names of religious properties in Scotland, such as Blantyre Priory (q.v.), that could be taxed by the Pope to finance the crusades. As a receipt of payment, the seal of the institution was attached to the document by a strip of fabric, hence the name.

Railways

The Caledonian Railway Company constructed a goods yard in Low Blantyre adjacent to their Glasgow-Hamilton railway line, which opened on 17 September 1849. It was situated on the land between Rosebank Avenue and the present station. A passenger station was then constructed, adding Low Blantyre to the line

William Rae.

later owned by the London, Midland, Scottish Railway Company (L.M.S.). In 1863 the Hamilton-Strathaven Railway was extended to High Blantyre and a station constructed adjacent to the Old Parish Church at Craigmuir Road. This line and High Blantyre Station (q.v.) were taken over by the Caledonian Railway in 1864.

In 1882 the Auchinraith Spur was laid by Caledonian Railways to link Low Blantyre Station (q.v.) with High Blantyre Station and provide a direct line to Strathaven from Glasgow. This gave direct access from the north to the Earnock Iron Works and the sidings at Dixon's Collieries, and the LMS took over this line from 1945 until it closed in 1953. Hunthill Junction (q.v.), from the corner of Hunthill Road and Stonefield Crescent to the viaduct over the River Calder, was constructed in 1885 to connect Glasgow with East Kilbride. This line closed in 1935. High Blantyre Station and Goods Yard closed in 1960.

Randolph, Thomas, 1st Earl of Moray

Thomas Randolph, Earl of Moray, was a nephew of King Robert the Bruce. Moray and the famous Black Douglas were the highest-ranking soldiers in the Scottish army at the Battle of Bannockburn. For his outstanding service and gallantry, the King gifted the Barony of Blantyre to Randolph.

Randolph was a brave and fierce warrior whose fame was known throughout Europe. It is said that before the Battle of Bannockburn Robert the Bruce had deployed Randolph, with a body of horse, near to the church of Saint Ninians, with instructions to prevent the English from relieving Stirling Castle, which was besieged by the Scots. A short time later Bruce observed a body of 800 enemy horse under the command of Lord Clifford approaching Stirling Castle from the east and turned to his nephew, saying 'There is a rose fallen from your chaplet,' meaning that Randolph had lost some honour by allowing the enemy to pass. Randolph rushed to resist the English advance on Stirling with little more than half their number, but, being on foot, the Scots were at a disadvantage when the English turned and charged them with their lances. Randolph drew his troops into close order to receive the onslaught.

Douglas, observing the danger that Randolph was in, asked the King's permission to go to his assistance. The King refused, saying, 'Let Randolph redeem his own fault. I cannot break the order of battle for his sake.' The danger seemed to increase as the English horse completely surrounded the small body of Scottish infantry. 'So please you,' said Douglas to his sovereign, 'my heart will not suffer me to stand idle and see Randolph perish, I must go to his assistance,' and he rode off. As he and his troops approached the scene

of combat, they observed the English horse ride off in disarray, many with empty saddles. Douglas halted his men declaring, 'Randolph has gained the day; since we were not soon enough to assist him in the battle, do not let us lessen his glory by approaching the field.'

After the death of Bruce and during the minority of his son David, Randolph was elected to act as Regent of Scotland. He proved to be a wise and just ruler and his death was regarded as a national catastrophe. It was rumoured that the English had poisoned him, but no proof was ever found to justify this claim. His two sons, Thomas and John, successively became the 2nd and 3rd Earls of Moray, and were therefore Lairds of Blantyre. They both died without issue and their vast estates passed into the possession of their sister, the Countess of March, better known in history as Black Agnes of Dunbar.

The Earl of March was a treacherous and unreliable noble during the wars with England, but not his wife Agnes. She inherited the spirit of her father, who spent his whole life in service to the nation. On one occasion, when her husband was absent from the Castle of Dunbar, she was besieged there for 19 weeks by the Earl of Salisbury and Arundel at the head of a large army. When large military siege engines were used to batter the walls, the Countess and her maids would wipe the sections struck by the missiles with napkins, suggesting that the only inconvenience caused was a little dust. The English brought forward an even larger siege engine known, to the soldiers as 'The Sow', and sheltering beneath its roof proceeded to attempt to gain entrance with hammers and pick-axes. Agnes instructed a large boulder to be dropped from the battlements onto The Sow, which broke its back. The English soldiers fled in panic as arrows from the walls showered upon them.

The Earl of Salisbury admired the bravery and resistance that Agnes had shown and reluctantly lifted the siege after weeks of fruitless effort. Black Agnes, the Lady of Blantyre, was hailed as a hero throughout the nation, and many poetic tributes were penned regarding her exploits during the siege of Dunbar Castle. One verse, expressing the frustration felt by the Earl of Salisbury, read:

> She kept a stir in tower and trench,
> The brawling boisterous Scottish wench:
> Came I early, came I late,
> I found Agnes at the gate.

Before the deaths in 1369 of both the Earl and Countess of Dunbar, they gifted the Barony of Blantyre to their son George, who later inherited the Earldom. Before his death he disposed of the Barony of Blantyre to his kinsman David de Dunbar of Enterkin (q.v.) whose descendants continued as proprietors of Blantyre Barony for over 200 years, before it was purchased by Walter Stewart, who later became first holder of the title Lord Blantyre.

Reddendo

'Reddendos' were levies imposed on nobles and landed gentry as a token of their loyalty to the crown, and the lord of the manor was bound, with his retainers, in times of war, to join the sovereign's army. These reddendos were levied at all levels of society. For example, Jackson of Bardykes was duty bound to present, on request, a red rose to Lord Blantyre. They were written into the lease whenever land was given to a particular family, but were only meant to signify a symbolic gesture of loyalty to one's superiors. Nobles and landed gentry, on the other hand, usually made an annual payment of gold in some form or another, such as a necklace or a chain, to the sovereign.

Reid, Andrew

With one exception, during the latter part of the 1600s, the ministers at Blantyre were 'Prelates', who obeyed the laws of the parliaments of the Stewart dynasty, and accepted the rule of bishops and the Episcopal form of government. The people of Blantyre appear to have kept well clear of the Battle of Bothwell Bridge, which was fought between the Episcopalian government and the Presbyterian Covenanters. After the battle, in 1679, a 'Fugitive Roll' was drawn up, and the name of only one man in the parish of Blantyre was included in it and denounced as a 'Rebel and Fugitive'. He was Andrew Reid, servitor to Robert Smith at Blantyre Kirk.

After the Battle of Bothwell Bridge many men were captured and banished to America or the West Indies. Some were executed in neighbouring towns and villages such as Hamilton, Bothwell, East Kilbride, Glassford and Strathaven, but it is claimed that Claverhouse and his men executed only one man in Blantyre, and if this were the case it has to be assumed that the unfortunate man was Andrew Reid. No record exists that I know of that states that Andrew Reid was ever captured, far less executed.

It is said that late one night, when the victorious army was scouring the surrounding areas for the remnants of the defeated Covenanter army, Maxwell, the Laird of Shott, who was an officer in Claverhouse's regiment of dragoons, was roused from his bed by his captain shouting, 'Come along Maxwell, we have at last ferreted out the fox', presumably Andrew Reid. Maxwell rose and made ready his horse but his young wife pleaded with him not to be part of such a cruel and unrighteous expedition, throwing herself down in front of his horse and declaring, 'If you will go, it must be over my dead and mangled body, for I too will suffer with this persecuted people.' Maxwell eased his horse past his prostrate wife and rode after his captain and troopers to apprehend and execute the unfortunate man.

Riot Act

During the General Strike, which commenced on 1 May 1926, the working class of Britain suffered appalling hardship. The mining communities, in particular, stubbornly refused to go back to work until the recommendations made by a government committee in 1917 were implemented. After eight months of suffering and deprivation, emotions ran high and on 23 October, eight months after the 'Lock-Out', the miners of Blantyre took to the streets and serious disorder broke out. Rioting and looting took place and the police, with batons drawn, charged the mob which numbered nearly seven hundred. Although seven men were arrested, the police were unable to control or subdue the miners and were forced to call in the army to restore order. Militia were rushed from Hamilton Barracks and, for the last time in British history, the Riot Act was read. With drawn sabres the mounted cavalry dispersed the rioters, but still the mood of discontent continued. On hearing of what had taken place, miners from surrounding communities rushed to support their colleagues in Blantyre. A meeting took place in a field, probably adjacent to Dixon's Collieries at Priestfield, and was the largest number of miners that ever assembled in Blantyre. It took place amid a very large number of police but the gathering broke up without further disorder.

Robertson's Building

This three-storied building stood at the top of Stonefield Road on the ground now occupied by the shopping precinct and houses between Burnbrae Road and the corner of Broompark Road. A number of shops in Robertson's Building served the Larkfield district. The most important to the children of the neighbourhood was Caldwell's ice-cream shop!

Rosendale.

Rodger, Martin

Martin Rodger was an early proprietor of a chemist's shop located on Glasgow Road adjacent to the Picture House Cinema. The last chemist there before the redevelopment of the east end of Glasgow Road was a Mr Paterson.

Rolls-Royce

After the end of the Second World War, industrial estates were constructed throughout the country to provide premises for manufacturing companies and give employment to local populations. The first factories at High Blantyre Industrial Estate were constructed in 1948 and expanded rapidly thereafter. The Rolls-Royce factory opened in 1952 during the Korean War to provide support to the British Army engaged in that conflict. On average 500 people were employed, but at one time the number reached approximately eight hundred.

Blantyre Rolls-Royce manufactured parts for various aircraft engines including the famous Merlin and Griffin piston engines used in the famous Spitfire and Hurricane fighter planes and the Shackleton reconnaissance aircraft. They were also used by the navy in their Motor Torpedo Boats and rescue Speed Boats.

The Avon, Dart, Conway, Tyne, Spey and the RB 211 all, with the exception of the RB 211, were named after British rivers and were produced for commercial jet aircraft.

Blantyre Rolls-Royce closed in 1977 and manufacture transferred to Hillington, Glasgow. All employees were offered jobs at Hillington but some declined due to the increase in travel.

Rosendale

Rosendale tenement sat on the corner of Auchinraith Road and Glasgow Road between the Caldwell Halls (q.v.) and the *Horse Shoe Pub* ('Kelly's Corner'). The access road to the front of the tenement extended diagonally behind the Caldwell Halls away from Glasgow Road.

Blantyre Bowling Green.

S

St Andrew's Church

St Andrew's Church was constructed as a replacement for Stonefield Parish Church (q.v.), which was destroyed by fire in 1979. The Rev. John Handley, Moderator of the Hamilton Presbytery, opened the church on Sunday 21 March 1982. St Andrew's stands on the site of the original church.

Saint Joseph's School-RC Church

With the demand for labour at the Blantyre Mills from 1785, Roman Catholics were recognised for the first time since the Reformation 300 hundred years earlier as part of the community of the Parish of Blantyre. In part of the Statistical Account for 1835, the population of Blantyre is given as 1,821, of whom 149 were Roman Catholics. If we assume that the average family consisted of five persons, this gives a total of 30 families, the majority residing at Blantyre Works Village. There were no religious or educational facilities for Catholic families within the community at that time, the Catholic Emancipation Act of 1829 not being fully implemented at the time the Statistical Account was published.

After the construction of St Andrew's Cathedral in Glasgow in 1816, the Roman Catholics of Blantyre probably made their way there to attend mass. The spiritual needs of the local Catholic community were met by Father Danaher of Hamilton, who hired Hope Hall (q.v.), located down a small path off Glasgow Road, directly opposite Victoria Street, and held mass and taught Catechism to the young members. Father Danaher was ably assisted in his work by a small group who later formed a committee and approached Mr Watson, the manager of Dixon's Collieries, with the view to obtaining a row of four houses that had recently been constructed at the top of Hall Street, adjacent to Stonefield Road. Their request was granted and the committee removed the internal dividing walls and soon converted the row into a church. A small room was retained to act as a school and a Miss Diegnet educated the pupils. The converted property was known as the 'Chapel Row'.

In 1877 the Catholic community rejoiced on being informed that Father John Frawley (q.v.), who was 27 years of age, would be the first permanent priest in their

Chapel Row, Dixon's Rows, c.1950.

newly restored parish, now named St Joseph's. Father Frawley was installed in a cottage in Glasgow Road, directly opposite Mayberry Place, which he used as a presbytery. He was born in Buttevant, County Cork and ordained at the Irish College, Paris in 1875, before serving for one year at St Margaret's, Kinning Park, Glasgow. Because of ill health, he was moved to 'the country' to serve at St Margaret's, in the parish of Airdrie. On 16 September 1877 Father Frawley was transferred from Airdrie to establish a Roman Catholic church in Blantyre and become the first priest to serve in the parish for over 300 years. Within five weeks of commencing his appointment, Father Frawley was confronted with the human tragedies caused by the Blantyre Explosion at Dixon's Colliery. Rev. Stewart Wright spoke very highly of the actions of Father Frawley during and after the 'Calamity'.

Work commenced on the construction of Saint Joseph's School-Chapel in April 1878, on the site where the present parish hall now stands. Under the guidance of Father Frawley, it was built on land purchased from John Clark Forrest (q.v.), a local landowner, but owing to the distress caused by the of the explosion at Dixon's Collieries only a small portion of the funds required to construct the property became available. Father Frawley intimated in the *Hamilton Advertiser* that the school would open in the summer of 1878 and that the church, which formed the upper floor of the structure, would be completed by October 1878. The school and the chapel, with over 600 seatings, was completed and officially opened on 24 October 1878. One of the earliest headmasters was a Mr McDade.

Father Frawley's health once again deteriorated and he had to resign his post after serving the parish for three years. He emigrated to Australia in June 1880 but died the following year on 28 April at Inglewood, Victoria, aged thirty. The Roman Catholic community rightly holds his memory in high esteem for his remarkable achievements in the three short years he served in the parish that he established.

There are many Blantyre parish priests of the past worthy of a mention within this book. I have noted a few who served our community and rose to positions of distinction within the Catholic Church in Scotland and further afield. During the early years of St Joseph's Church, between 1895 and 1926, there were 11 curate assistants to the parish priests, nine of whom were Irish, who eventually returned to their homeland to continue their calling.

Rev. Peter Donnelly
Father Donnelly, aged 27, succeeded Father Frawley in May 1880, and served the parish of St Joseph's for almost eight years. In that time he established a small school in Auchentibber for the children of Catholic families who worked in the limestone quarries in the district. Forty-one pupils attended this school. Father Donnelly was transferred to Hamilton where he preached until he died on 20 November 1902, aged 49 years.

Canon Thomas Hackett DD
Father (later Canon) Hackett was a teacher before entering a college in Belgium where he studied for three years. Later he attended college in Rome where he successfully took his Doctor of Divinity. After completing his studies he was ordained in 1882 and in 1884 was

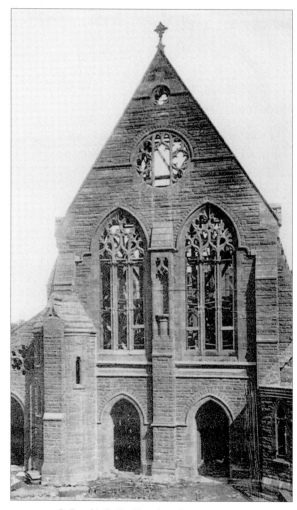

St Joseph's R.C. Church under construction.

Salvation Army Citadel, c.1960.

assigned as assistant at St Patrick's in Anderston, a post he held for four and a half years. He was appointed parish priest of Blantyre in 1888, a position he held for 33 years. It was Father Hackett who set in motion the construction of the present church and chapel-house. Due to the rapid rise in the Catholic population within the parish, the original church proved inadequate to serve the congregation. When the congregation was shown the plans for the present St Joseph's Church, many within the impoverished Catholic community thought the project on too grand a scale, and felt that a temporary building should be constructed. Father Hackett declared that it was to be 'the real thing or nothing' and opposition to his project was withdrawn.

In 1889 an extra 81 feet of ground, adjacent and west of the existing frontage of the original church, was purchased. A decision to convert the old church on the upper floor into classrooms and expand the school on the ground floor was approved by the Archbishop of Glasgow, and work soon began on the fine Gothic-style church, which measures 43.59 metres long, 19.07 metres wide and 18.46 metres high, and can accommodate over 1,000 people. Messrs Pugin & Pugin of London designed the church at an approximate cost of £10,000, a considerable sum at that time. St Joseph's was solemnly opened on 10 June 1905, the opening sermon being preached by the Most Rev. John A. Maquire, Archbishop of Glasgow.

Rev. Hackett served the parish of St Joseph's until his death on 5 March 1921. Affectionately known throughout the Catholic community as 'The Doc', he was buried at Dalbeth Cemetery, Glasgow. At the cost of £1,500, his parishioners installed a new High Altar in St Joseph's as a fitting memorial to their beloved priest.

Rev. Canon Robert Paterson PhD

Canon Paterson, born *c.*1870, was parish priest of Blantyre from 1923 until 1945. He carried out extensive interior work in the church in 1928, including the installation of a new marble altar.

Right Rev. Monsignor Canon John Ash

The Right Rev. Monsignor Canon John Ash was appointed parish priest of Blantyre in 1945. Prior to his appointment to St Joseph's he was parish priest at Christ the King, Glasgow. When the Diocese of Motherwell was established, after it split from the Glasgow Archdiocese in 1943, he became the diocesan treasurer. When the Motherwell Chapter was established in 1952, he was installed as one of the canons. After the Golden Jubilee celebrations of St Joseph's in 1955, Monsignor Ash carried out extensive renovations to the church and had

Location of School Lane

School Lane.

the present mortuary-chapel constructed in memory of the much-loved Father Thomas O'Halloran. His final appointment took him to Rome in 1957 where he was installed as Vice-President of the 'Association for the Propagation of the Faith', reporting on behalf of the Scottish committee. On 26 March of that year he was honoured by the Pope and made Domestic Prelate with the title of Monsignor. When his health failed, he moved to Bon Secure Hospital, Tralee, where he died on 11 June 1958. The parishioners of St Joseph's donated a marble cross which was engraved on his tomb.

Salvation Army

The Citadel (p.141) of the Salvation Army stood opposite the main gates of Castle Park (Blantyre Victoria's football ground) at Forrest Street and was demolished in the early 1990s. On Sundays the Salvation Army Band was a regular sight in the town, accompanying the preachers as they gave sermons on street corners.

School of Dance

SEE DAISY BROWN (B)

School Lane

School Lane was a street at High Blantyre Cross, the top of which can still be seen adjacent to the entrance door of *Carrigan's Pub* (formerly Logan's). The road was located between the pub and a long row of old houses to the east. At one time an old school was located at the present park gates at the bottom of the old lane.

Scottish Junior Cup

Blantyre Victoria Football Club (q.v.) won the Scottish Junior Cup at Hampden Park in 1950, the year of their jubilee. Vics returned in triumph to the town, sitting on top of a bus and displaying the famous trophy to the thousands who lined Glasgow Road to welcome them home. They were cheered by men, women and children who stood up to six deep on the pavements from the West End to the Community Centre, opposite Livingstone Memorial Church, where a reception was held in their honour. The Scottish Cup was later displayed in the window of Sandy Thomson's newsagent's shop, located directly opposite Church Street in the tenement that ran from the corner of John Street to Clark Street. Headlines in all the national newspapers were gained when, early one morning, the shop window was smashed and the Scottish Junior Cup stolen. Searches were carried out throughout the town but to no avail. Later the police, acting on information, dug up the cup from where it had been buried on the Clyde Braes at the bottom of John Street below Nicholson's Piggery.

Shanks' Pub

Shanks' Pub occupied the gable of a tenement adjacent to the Kirkyard gates. The pub is to the left of the water fountain in the photograph.

Shott House

Shott House/Farm is situated on the Stoneymeadow Road directly opposite Ellisland Drive. The house was constructed in 1603 but the farmhouse and its outbuildings are much older. Four thousand-year-old Bronze-Age graves were uncovered in the fields surrounding the farm.

The story is told of a Laird of Shott who, on returning home late one evening from a function in Hamilton, fell from his horse because he had consumed too much alcohol. He was found lying in the gutter by some passers-by, who enquired what had happened to him. He replied, 'I'm Shott.' Alarmed at hearing this, they ran to fetch a policeman who, on his arrival at the

Shanks' Pub.

scene, recognised the Laird and quickly established that he was obviously very drunk. With the help of the others, he lifted the old man back upon his horse and sent him on his way towards Blantyre knowing that the horse would deliver its intoxicated master to Shott House.

Shuttle Row

It is thought the Shuttle Row tenement was constructed *c.*1780 as part of the housing complex built by the Blantyre Works Company (q.v.) to accommodate the families of employees. A plaque to mark the birthplace

Shuttle Row, c.1880.

of David Livingstone (q.v.) was inserted into a gable wall of the tenement at a ceremony held in 1898. The property was purchased in 1927, when it was in a dilapidated condition, and converted into the original museum established to commemorate the memory of the great man. The museum, now called the David Livingstone Centre, was taken over by the Scottish National Trust which is at present carrying out extensive redevelopment work to the property. The Shuttle Row contained 27 homes, each of which consisted of one room with no running water or toilet. The accommodation was known as 'a single-end' and it was in one of these homes that David Livingstone was born. The well used by the inhabitants of Shuttle Row can still be seen at the front of the tenement.

Slag Road

The Slag Road got its name from the fact that ash and slag from the 'bing' of a local colliery was laid down to create a path that ran through the fields between Glasgow Road and Auchinraith at Main Street, High Blantyre, before the construction of the houses in Craig Street. The old track ran parallel to the Clay Road, another dirt track which in turn became Victoria Street.

Slaughterhouse

The Blantyre Slaughterhouse was located at the bottom right side of John Street, now the site of the John Street Industrial Estate. The sound of gunshots could be heard throughout the Stonefield area when animals were being slaughtered.

Small, William

SEE BLANTYRE RIOTS (B)

Small Waulk

SEE MILL DAM COURT CASE (M)

Smith, A. & J., Motor Hirer and Undertaker

This well-known family business was established in 1877 and based until recently at Broompark Road at the corner of Main Street, having originally been located at Clyde Cottage, Glasgow Road. In those early years, before the invention of the motor car, two magnificent black Belgian horses drew the hearse, which was a beautiful ornate carriage. It was customary to use completely black horses to observe the solemnity of the occasion.

Sneddon's 'Laun'

Tenements were usually known by the name of the owner of the building and the land upon which they stood. The word 'land' was pronounced in the local dialect as 'laun' and 'Sneddon's Laun', was located on the corner of Main Street and Craigmuir Road, adjacent to the gates of Blantyre Old Parish Church, the end section of a row of separately owned tenements. The east end of the tenements was adjacent to the gates of the Old Kirkyard and Craigmuir Road and the Blantyre Explosion Centenary Monument and gardens now occupy this site. The dirt road between the monument and the church wall is the original road from the Kirkton to Crossbasket and Greenhall House at the General's Bridge on the Stoneymeadow Road.

Sodger's Hole

At one time there was a very deep pool directly under the Millheugh Bridge (q.v.). A soldier, home on leave during the First World War, was swimming in the pool with friends but got entangled at the bottom of the river and was unfortunately drowned. The pool became known as the 'Sodger's Hole' (Soldier's Hole). When the old Millheugh Bridge was demolished in 1948, the deep pool was filled in with rubble from the old bridge and a concrete surface created before construction of the present bridge began.

Spiers' 'Laun' and Spiers' Restaurant

Spiers' Restaurant was situated on the corner of Main Street and School Lane and was known as 'Spiers' Laun'. It was part of an impressive building, possibly designed by a local architect named Robert Thomson, the entrance of which was flanked by two large columns. The restaurant was also known at one time as the Station Café. The building also contained Malcolm's fruit shop, William Wilson the tailor, a butcher's shop, and a barber's shop. There were three houses at the east end of the tenement and houses above the shops. School Lane ran between the restaurant and *Logan's* (now *Carrigan's*) *pub*.

Spittal Bridge

The Spittal Bridge spans the River Calder at the West End of Blantyre and is in fact three bridges. The

Station Café, Spiers' 'Laun'.

original bridge was a medieval structure, widened in 1844 by local unemployed weavers. It was widened again when a metal structure was added in 1907 to connect the Glasgow Tram Company tramline with the Lanarkshire Tram network. The three bridges can be seen in the accompanying photograph. The bottom dark arch is the medieval bridge, the lighter arch of the 1844 reconstruction above it. The metal bridge is now in a very dangerous condition and is hidden amongst trees under the high wall west of Callaghan Wynd.

Approximately fifty metres downriver from the Spittal Bridge are another two tunnel bridges constructed to span the Calder when the Cambuslang Road was realigned in 1928. Most locals are unaware that they exist. The old Bardyke Mill can also be seen in the photograph at the bottom right of the bridge.

Priory Spittal Bridge.

Sproat's 'Laun' (Kidd's Building), Glasgow Road, c.1960.

Low Blantyre Primary Infant School ('Wee School') and Dining Hall.

Sports Centre

The Sports Centre is seen here under construction at the corner of Greenside Street, behind the last Glasgow Road tenement, which was demolished in 1981. The tenement was situated directly opposite the eastern section of the present Clydeview Shopping Precinct, Glasgow Road. The Sports Centre, costing £2.2 million, opened in March 1982.

Springfield Cottage

Springfield Cottage stood on the corner of Broompark Road and Springfield Crescent and was demolished in the mid-1990s. The gates of the cottage had a set of beautiful pillars with approximately ten figureheads, carved around the ornate tops, obtained from Hamilton Palace after its demolition.

Sproats 'Laun'

Sproats 'Laun' was a small tenement that stood on the south side of Glasgow Road between Elm Street and Jackson Street. It was known latterly as 'Kidd's Building' after Kidd's fish and chip shop located on the eastern corner of the building on Jackson Street. In the view, looking west along the south side of Glasgow Road, a car is passing Elm Street at the right of the photograph.

Station Cafe

SEE SPIERS' 'LAUN' AND SPIERS' RESTAURANT (S)

Stein, Jock

Jock Stein's cottage, seen here in the foreground, was attached to the north end of a row of thatched houses situated opposite the *Barnhill Tavern (Hoolet's Nest)* (q.v.) at Barnhill. Jock's house was very small and he bred pigs at the rear.

Jock Stein's Cottage, Bardykes Road, c.1890.

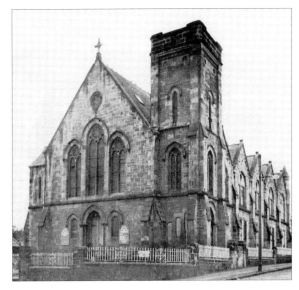

Stonefield Parish Church, 1960.

Stewart, Francis Teresa

SEE BRITANNIA (B)

Stewart, Walter, Master of Blantyre

SEE MASTER OF BLANTYRE (M)

Stonefield Parish Church

In the past it was the custom in churches that families paid a subscription for a personal seat in a particular pew but, due to the rapid increase in population, seating had become limited in Blantyre Old Parish Church. Even before the increase, resulting from the sinking of new collieries in the Low Blantyre (Stonefield) area, it had become apparent that a second parish church would be required. The foundation stone of the new church, originally known as the 'Chapel of Ease', was laid in May 1878 by the Rev. Stewart Wright (q.v.) of Blantyre Old Parish Church and Provost John Clark Forrest (q.v.). The Provost donated the land, between Elm Street and Church Street, upon which the church was built. It was completed in 1880. It was 24.61 metres long and 14.46 metres wide and was of Norman-Gothic design. It cost £5,000 to build and seated 900 people but was destroyed by fire on 3 September 1979 when a plumber left a blowlamp burning on the roof while he had lunch. The church was demolished in 1980 and the new church, St Andrew's (q.v.), constructed on its site.

Stonefield Parish School.

Stonefield Parish School

The Education Act 1870 stipulated that schools be built in every parish throughout the country. Stonefield Parish School was constructed in 1873 to seat 400 children. An extension, which was urgently required, was added in 1892 to accommodate a further 500 pupils, such was the increase in the population caused by the ever-expanding coal industry within the town. The name of the school was changed to Low Blantyre Primary School, but was always known affectionately as 'Ness School' after its first headmaster, Major John Ness (q.v.). The ASDA store now stands on the site of the school at the corner of Glasgow Road and Victoria Street.

Strathern, John

John Strathern was the Dyemaster at Blantyre Works in 1873.

Struthers, J.B.

J.B. Struthers was a publican who owned various public houses in Blantyre at the turn of the 20th century. It was at the rear of his pub, the *Auchentibber Inn* (q.v.), that J.B. encouraged the miners of the hamlet to construct a quoiting green, adjacent to the Sydes Brae, that was reputedly the finest in Scotland. Struthers died in 1939.

Subterranean Tunnel

It is claimed in the book *Scottish Chiefs*, that there is a tunnel hewn out of the bedrock under the River Clyde that links Blantyre Priory and Bothwell Castle. Ever since I can remember, speculation has insisted that the huge boulder blocking what appears to be the entrance to a cave in the corner of the ravine directly under the priory site is the entrance to the mysterious passage.

Sullivan, John L.

See Wellington Bar (W)

Suspension Bridge and School viewed from Bothwell.

Suspension Bridge

Henry Monteith (q.v.) & Company, the proprietors of Blantyre Works, constructed the Suspension Toll Bridge in 1849. It was built to give easier access to the Works for those employees who resided in Bothwell and the surrounding areas and had previously to be ferried in a rowboat across the river. When the River Clyde was in spate, workers were unable to cross due to the cancellation of the ferry service. Carts could ford the river at a point directly below the present David Livingstone Memorial Bridge (q.v.) when the river was running low, or when the sluice gates were opened to direct the Clyde along the lade to turn the turbines. The 73 metre long Suspension Bridge was constructed approximately 100 metres upriver from the weir, directly below the present Anderson Gardens, which are opposite the main entrance gate of the David Livingstone Centre car park. It was the last toll bridge built in Scotland until the construction of the Forth Road Bridge in 1964. Later, it passed to the colliery owners William Baird and Company who had sunk two pits in Bothwell and

another two in Blantyre, including the 'Priory Pit'. It was known locally by several names such as the 'Pey Brig', the 'Ha'penny Brig' (because a charge of an old ½d. was levied on the general public who crossed) and the 'Swing Brig'. A special token was given to the employees of Blantyre Works and, later, to miners who worked at the Priory Pit allowing them to cross at a cheaper rate.

The toll to cross the bridge with a barrow was 2d., and Bothwell grocers who brought their wares to sell in the Works Village paid 4d. for a weekly ticket. The selling of the tickets was put out to franchise and the best known owner was old Jock McBain and his family, whose house in the Waterloo Row at Blantyre Works overlooked the bridge and the river. Youngsters through the years avoided paying the toll money by crawling on hands and knees below the small aperture of the 'pay-bowl', unseen by the occupant. Happy days!

Swiss Cottages

Swiss Cottages were the last two original houses in the area known as Priestfield. They had thatched roofs and were located in Priestfield Street. One of them was demolished in the early 1990s and the other in 1999. It is thought they were constructed in the late 16th century. New houses (Douglas Gardens) are at present being constructed on this site, which is adjacent to High Blantyre Cross.

Sydes Brae

The top of Sydes Brae has not changed much over the years but the foot of the road was realigned during construction of the East Kilbride Expressway. Sydes Brae originally ran from Auchentibber to Loanfoot (q.v.), where it crossed over the High Blantyre-Strathaven railway line, and continued to the bottom of the hill at a level crossing that took a spur line into Dixon's Collieries. The foot of the Sydes Brae was originally located at the electricity pylon directly opposite No. 13 Douglas Street at the Hamilton access ramp to the East Kilbride Expressway.

T

Blantyre Works.

Taylor, Thomas

SEE AEROPLANE I (A) AND BARNHILL SMIDDY (B)

Teddy's Bar

The *Stonefield Tavern* pub at the corner of Glasgow Road and Priory Street is better known as 'Teddy's' after Teddy McGuiness who was once the proprietor.

Telegraph Station

High Blantyre Post Office (q.v.), which was located in the tenement that stood on the corner of Main Street and Cemetery Road, was connected to the National Telegraph system in 1878.

Telephone Exchange

A Telephone Exchange was constructed at Herbertson Street, adjacent to the Burleigh Church Hall and almost directly across from the entrance doors of the Co-op Hall, now the car park of Reid the Printers. In 1958, a new exchange was built in Forrest Street, adjacent to Blantyre Victoria's Castle Park football ground.

Templeton, James

James Templeton was the last blacksmith to work and own the Barnhill Smiddy (q.v.) at Broompark Road adjacent to High Blantyre Primary School. Barnhill Engineering now occupies this old property.

Ten Pin Bowling

After the closure of the Picture House Cinema (q.v.) at Glasgow Road in the 1950s, two local men, Ian Liddell and William Paul, converted the property in 1959 into a ten pin bowling alley and named it 'The Blantyre Bowl'. The property was destroyed by fire in 1966. Ten pin bowling proved to be very popular and a number of the players were successful at national level, John Keenan winning the British Under-21 Championship.

Thomson, Charles

Charles Thomson was the Manager of Dixon's Collieries and was elected Chairman of the first Blantyre School Board in 1873.

Thomson, Robert

Two Blantyre brothers were members of the Scots Greys at the Battle of Waterloo when the infantry of the 92nd Highlanders, so keen to engage Napoleon's troops, broke ranks and grabbed the stirrups of the Scots Greys in order to join the charge. One of the brothers was a sergeant and the other was a corporal. Robert Thomson was so tall and heavy that a special horse had to be found to take his massive frame. During the famous charge of

First tram from Motherwell to Blantyre, 6 October 1903.

the regiment, Robert's horse was killed by an exploding shell which also wounded the corporal. He fell to the ground and lay trapped under his dead horse until he was found after the battle with three other comrades wounded by the same shell. Two of them were soldiers who had been clasping his stirrups. Robert was awarded the Waterloo Medal. After his discharge he returned to his family home in Blantyre but his brother settled in London.

Tollbooths

SEE TURNPIKE ROADS (T)

Tramcars

The Hamilton, Motherwell & Wishaw Tramways Company line was opened on 22 July 1903 and provided an excellent means of travel from Blantyre to Hamilton, Larkhall, Motherwell and Wishaw. The western terminus at Blantyre was situated 65 metres west of Stonefield Road at Livingstone Church. The company extended the line in 1907 to create a new terminus at Dunallon Loop (q.v.) at the West End, Glasgow Road, where passengers wishing to continue to Glasgow disembarked and

travelled into the city on trams belonging to the Glasgow Corporation Tram Company, which terminated at Priory Bridge. The Hamilton, Motherwell & Wishaw Company constructed further lines within Lanarkshire to include within its network Newmains in 1909 and New Stevenston in 1911, making it possible to travel in a circular route around various districts of Glasgow and return to Blantyre via Newmains.

The Company later changed its name to the Lanarkshire Tramways Company but closed on 10 October 1930 and the old 'Shoogly Trams' disappeared from the streets of Blantyre. The picture was taken at Motherwell Cross as the first tram set out on the inaugural run to Blantyre on 6 October 1903.

Turkey Red Dye

SEE BLANTYRE MILLS/WORKS (B)

Turner's Building

When the old post office located at Glasgow Road opposite the Bethany Hall Church was closed, a new post office was constructed on the site of Turner's

Blantyre Works Tollgates.

tenement, which stood adjacent to the Central Building at the corner of Glasgow Road and Logan Street.
See Post Offices (P)

Turnpike Roads

In 1750 a main road known as the Turnpike was constructed through the original village of Blantyre (High Blantyre Cross). The turnpike road replaced the old 'pack road', which was a simple dirt track that linked the east coast with the west along the high ground adjacent to Stoneymeadow Road, behind Greenhall House and Crossbasket House then continued to Ayr. Later, another turnpike road was constructed through Stonefield, improving the journey from Hamilton to Glasgow. Landowners, property owners and shopkeepers paid contractors to construct the turnpikes within the parish, which in turn enabled them to erect tollhouses and collect a levy on every carriage, or other form of transport, that used the roads within their town or village.

There were two main tollbooths located within Blantyre: the tollhouse of the Stonefield Turnpike was located at Glasgow Road adjacent to what is now Station Road; the other was at Main Street adjacent to Broompark Road. The roads through the open land between settlements remained dirt tracks that had been used for centuries and were sometimes impassable in winter. The Blantyre Works Company erected gates across the road between two tollhouses either side of Station Road at the corners of Rosebank Avenue and Knightswood Terrace. These were closed at 10p.m. each evening to prevent traffic entering the village after that time. In 1850 the government abolished tollbooths from the roads and highways throughout the country.

Typhoid Fever

In 1878 there was an outbreak of typhoid fever throughout the county. Two residents of the hamlet of Springwells died after catching the disease. The epidemic was blamed on poor sanitation and bad supplies of drinking water.

U

High Blantyre Primary School, c.1875.

Udston Colliery Disaster

Ten years after the 'Blantyre Explosion' (q.v.) another calamity hit the people of Blantyre when many local miners were victims of the Udston Colliery Explosion. The blast occurred on 28 May 1887 and took the lives of 73 miners, the majority of whom resided in Auchentibber. The Udston Colliery was located in Hillhouse close to the No. 3 pit of Dixon's Colliery and, like the Blantyre Explosion, a naked light ignited high levels of gas and coal dust thus causing the disaster. By 1922 most of the seams of Udston were abandoned and the colliery closed in 1934.

The Village.

Village

The houses of the old Blantyre Works were known simply as 'the Village' and the area beyond the station, on Station Road, is still known by this name today. Blantyre Works erected gates between two tollhouses at the entrance to the Village (see photograph on p.153 and above). The Shuttle Row, the Wages Building, the house behind the David Livingstone Centre, and the white gable of the old row containing three shops, seen here in the centre right of the photograph below, are the only buildings still standing today that were once part of the large village at Blantyre Works.

The Village above the Dye Works.

Church Street/Glasgow Road.

Waddell Family

John Jeffrey Waddell, IAFSAScot, was an architect and archaeologist who resided at Caldergrove House, Hallside, situated on an estate on the River Calder adjacent to the Spittal Bridge at the West End, directly opposite Bardykes House. As the house was some distance from the village of Hallside it was generally regarded

Etching of Blantyreferme by John Jeffrey Waddell.

as a Blantyre house. Waddell was born in Glasgow in 1876 and educated at Glasgow High School, Technical College and the School of Art. Early on he found his life's work in architecture and went into partnership with Dr P. McGregor Chalmers, and together they designed and built factories, mansion houses and many well-known cinemas and churches throughout Scotland and Northern Ireland. When Waddell became the sole partner, he specialised almost entirely in church work, particularly the restoration of ancient buildings such as Dornoch Cathedral, Iona Cathedral, the Town Church of St Andrews and the Parish Church of Bothwell. He also designed and built the Scots Church in Brussels. Some of his buildings have been called 'poems in stone'. He was responsible for the fine Adam's Interior in Banff Parish Church and a beautiful example of the Norman style in St Modan's Church, Falkirk.

Waddell's other passion was archaeology and he was a leading member in the Archaeological Society and St Andrew's Society. He discovered many ancient carved stones, one of his most notable finds being the Cross of St Ninian, which now stands in the forecourt of the Parish Church in Hamilton (off Cadzow Street) and is well worth a visit. He also sketched many local scenes, two of which can be seen here. After a short illness John Jeffrey Waddell died at Caldergrove House in December 1941. He had two daughters, Bertha and Jenny, who became well-known in their own right. In 1927 they formed a theatre company to entertain children and such was their success that in 1935 and 1937 they were invited by Queen Elizabeth to entertain Princess Elizabeth (the present Queen) and Princess Margaret at Glamis Castle. In 1953 and 1955 they were invited by the Queen to entertain Prince Charles and Princess Anne at a garden party at Buckingham Palace. In 1967 they also entertained Prince Andrew and Prince Edward. Bertha was awarded the MBE in 1963 and died in 1983.

I met Bertha and Jenny Waddell in the late 1970s when I was researching Caldergrove House. When Bertha answered my knock at the front door, she peered through the small gap she had made to establish who the stranger was on her doorstep. I explained my reason for disturbing her and she slowly opened the door and invited me into a house that seemed to have become trapped in time. The large entrance hall was packed with antique furniture which, to my untrained eye, was pre-Victorian. In the two corners of the rear wall from the ground floor all the way up to the ceiling of the upper hall, were two triangular display cases behind round bevelled glass. Within these units, which must have been at least ten metres high, were hundreds of stuffed exotic birds arranged on branches of trees, a truly amazing sight. The contents of the cases could be viewed from each floor level as you ascended the winding staircase. Each room was furnished, like the hall, with unusual pianos, ornate sideboards, dining tables and chairs,

Etching of the Old Boat House at Blantyreferme by John Jeffrey Waddell.

beautiful fireplaces, drapes, and so on. It was obvious that the house was too large for two elderly ladies to maintain.

After Bertha's death the house was sold to the National Coal Board and stood unoccupied for some time. A large collection of miscellaneous architectural papers, personal papers, household accounts and papers relating to architectural works *c.*1918-1922 are now in the possession of the National Monuments Records of Scotland. Shortly after the house was sold, it mysteriously burned down. One can only hope that all the wonderful furniture and other contents had been removed before it was destroyed.

Wallace, William

A local legend claims that the great Scottish patriot, William Wallace, sought sanctuary in Blantyre Priory (q.v.) when the English were scouring the countryside in search of him. Acting on information, soldiers surrounded the Priory on three sides but did not guard the sheer Blantyre Craig, which towers over 32 metres above the River Clyde, as they thought that no escape could be made from such a great height. Wallace jumped over the Craig and made his escape. Legend is often based on fact, and it interesting to note that the prior at the time was 'Frere William Priour de Blantir' (q.v.), a friend and loyal supporter of William Wallace. Legend also states that water once sprang from a shape imprinted in the bedrock directly under the cliff, which was caused by the foot of the Scottish Martyr after his mighty leap.

Warnock's 'Laun'

Warnock's 'Laun' was a small tenement that stood on Broompark Road between Springfield Crescent and the corner of Stonefield Crescent.

Water Supply

A water supply was introduced in 1880 at a cost of £10,000, and directed at first to communal wells throughout the parish, where it was collected in pails and containers. It was not until the early 1920s, in Dixon's Rows for example, that water was supplied directly into houses.

Waterloo Row

Waterloo Row, constructed by Henry Monteith & Company in 1822, was a two-storied tenement, erected

Waterloo Row.

to provide houses for the majority of early employees at Blantyre Works. It overlooked the Braes and the River Clyde and formed one side of a large quadrangle of buildings which included the tenements of the Fore Row on Station Road, the Mid Row, behind and parallel to the Fore Row, and the Cross Row between the Waterloo Row and the Mid Row at the top end of the quadrangle. The work's school formed the bottom side of the quadrangle (see photograph on p.113). All of these houses were demolished in 1929 after a fire had destroyed many of the houses in the Fore Row in 1928. Most of the inhabitants were rehoused in the new council houses at Knightswood Terrace, Station Road and Viewfield Avenue which were being constructed at that time.

Webster, Jan

The novelist Jan Webster (née Jenny McCallum) was born on 10 August 1924 in the manager's house at Loanend Colliery. This was situated adjacent to the Loanend Rows on the Loanend Road between Malcolmwood Farm and the Dalton. The McCallums were allocated a house in Morris Crescent, where Jenny attended the nearby Calder Street School. She qualified to attend St John's Grammar School in Hamilton and later continued her studies at Hamilton Academy where she excelled at English. On leaving school she went into journalism.

The coalmining environment of her childhood in Blantyre created a lasting impression on Jenny, who made good use of her observations and knowledge of colliery life. She wrote 14 books, the best known being *Colliers Row*, published in 1977 as the opening part of a trilogy which follows the life of a young Lanarkshire woman and her children who emigrate to New Zealand and America. Jenny married fellow journalist Drew Webster and moved to London and, in the 1980s, to Macclesfield where she died in November 2002.

Glasgow Road, looking east from Elm Street, c.1903.

Cowan Wilson Memorial Arch.

Wellington Bar

The *Wellington Bar* was located at the end of a tenement on Glasgow Road at the corner of Clark Street. It was here that the legendary American boxer John L. Sullivan gave an exhibition bout to the inhabitants of Blantyre. Sullivan won the World Heavyweight title when he defeated Paddy Ryan in February 1882 and held the title until 1892 when he lost to 'Gentleman Jim' Corbett. Sullivan then went on stage and toured America and Britain. Regarded as the greatest boxer of his time, he was still a big attraction and drew vast crowds wherever he appeared. It was during his tour of Scotland that Mr McDade, the proprietor of the *Wellington Bar*, invited him to visit Blantyre. He boxed a few exhibition rounds in the rear court of the pub adjacent to Clark Street. In the photograph, *c*.1903, the *Wellington Bar* can be seen to the left of the tramcar at the corner of Clark Street and Glasgow Road, opposite Elm Street.

Wheatlandhead Farm

The farmers of Wheatlandhead owned and worked the land between Broompark Road, Bardykes Road, Stonefield Road and Glasgow Road. Houses now occupy all of the farmland but the house is still extant and is located in Highland Avenue.

Whins

SEE CALDERGLEN HOUSE (C)

Whistleberry Colliery

Whistleberry Colliery was sunk by Archibald Russell in 1891 on his own land of Auchinraith. It was a very deep and wet pit and thrived during the Boer War. Pits Nos 1 & 2, which were situated on the right hand side of Whistleberry Road, opposite Ireland Alloys, supplied vast amounts of coal to Colville's Steel Works in Motherwell.

Whistleberry House

This old mansion is recorded on the Timothy Pont Blaeu map, dated 1596, and stood in the grounds of Auchinraith Estate on the right hand side of Whistleberry Road. The name of the mansion was later changed to Auchinraith House. At one time Captain Lockhart, MP for Lanarkshire in the late 1800s, owned this house.

Wilson, Dr Cowan

Dr Cowan Wilson was born in the Parish of Old Monkland. He succeeded Dr Cooper as the local medical practitioner in Blantyre and for fifty years endeared himself to the inhabitants of the town through

The pond, Stonefield Public Park.

his devotion to the patients at his practice. Dr Wilson was deeply involved in the movement that raised funds to construct the Cottage Hospital (q.v.), the first of its kind in Lanarkshire. In 1935, on the jubilee of his practice, he was presented with £500 in appreciation of his services to the community. Dr Wilson died in 1938 and was buried in Shotts. After his death the inhabitants of the town showed their appreciation of Dr Wilson's

service to the community by donating to a fund to construct a monument to his memory. The photograph, taken before the construction of the sheltered housing at Stonefield Park Gardens, shows the Cowan Wilson Memorial Arch at the entrance to Stonefield Public Park.

Wilson, William Bauchop

William Wilson was born on 2 April 1862 in the Waterloo Row at Blantyre Mills. His parents emigrated to America and settled in Pennsylvania. William was working in a mine when he was only nine years of age. He believed passionately in socialist principles and became involved in the American Labour Movement. He was appointed secretary-treasurer of the United Mine Workers in 1900 and held the post until 1908. Later he stood for election to Congress as a member of the Democratic Party and served from 1907 until 1913. President Woodrow Wilson appointed him as first Secretary of Labour, a position he held from 1913 to 1921. It was Wilson who convinced the President that the department should be established to help unions become involved in advising the government over

Wooddean Church.

William Bauchop Wilson.

legislation and decision-making regarding the labour movement, thereby assisting the economy and also improving the working conditions in America. William Wilson introduced child labour laws, workplace safety, reduced the working day to eight hours and encouraged strong unions.

During the First World War he invited another ex-Blantyre man, Philip Murray (q.v.), to assist him in coordinating the labour movement, Murray being the leader of the American mining and steel unions. His cooperation with Wilson in producing armaments was considered by President Woodrow Wilson, and many others, the main reason that the Allies were victorious in the war. William Wilson died in 1934.

Wooddean Church

Due to over crowding at Blantyre Old Parish Church, a 'Speaker' from the parish church gave 'Relief' services for many years in the Blantyre Mills/Works Chapel-School (q.v.), Messrs Henry Monteith & Co. (q.v.) giving the worshippers free use of the hall. The union of the Secession and Relief Churches formed the United Presbyterian Church in 1847 and the first congregation set up by the united body was the Blantyre United Presbyterian Congregation. Communion was never given during the 60 years that services were held in the Chapel-School, the custom being that all went up to the Old Parish Church on the Sunday after the 'Fast Day' in June, and the communion service was held there. As the church could not hold all those wishing to take communion, a minister preached in the burying-ground and the people went inside in relays, the changing being done to the tune of a psalm.

Though at first subsidised by Monteith & Co., the congregation were determined to be self-supporting. In 1851 they decided it was their duty to maintain the church by their own means and respectfully declined further aid from the Company. A decision was taken towards the end of 1852 to try and obtain a permanent place of worship and, encouraged by generous donations from various bodies, including a gift of £100 from Monteith & Co., they proceeded with the undertaking. As no land was available in the Blantyre Works Village, the congregation accepted an offer of a piece of ground belonging to Mr Robert Monteith within the boundary of property owned by the Works Company on the Bothwell side of the River Clyde, directly opposite the Blantyre Works. Wooddean Church was constructed halfway up Blantyre Mill Road above the David Livingstone Memorial Bridge at a cost of approximately £1,000. The foundation stone was laid on 26 March 1853, and the Church opened on 21 August 1853, when Mr Bannatyne conducted the first service. Later the church changed its name to Bothwell United Presbyterian Church. The manse is still occupied today.

Woodhouse

SEE ROBERT KERR (K)

Wordsworth, Dorothy

When Dorothy Wordsworth visited Bothwell Castle she viewed Blantyre Priory from its battlements and described the scene in her *Journal*:

> On the opposite bank, which is finely wooded with elms and other trees, are the remains of an ancient priory built upon a rock; and rock and ruin are so blended together that it is impossible to separate the one from the other. Nothing can be more beautiful than the little remnants of this holy place; elm trees – for we are near enough to distinguish them by their branches – grow out

Blantyre Priory and Bothwell Castle.

of the walls, and overshadow a small but very elegant window. It can scarcely be conceived what a grace the castle and the priory impart to each other; and the river Clyde flows on smooth and unruffled below, seeming to my thoughts more in harmony with the sober and stately images of former times.

Another description, by an anonymous writer, probably in the late 1700s, of the scenery along the River Clyde as it flowed past Blantyre Woods ('the Dandy'), reads:

The Clyde here is a majestic river of considerable depth and is of a darkish colour, gliding smoothly and silently along the lofty wooded banks, and beautiful and richly adorned undulating fields of Bothwell and Blantyre. Immediately below Bothwell Bridge the banks present a thin sprinkling of wood with occasional orchards. About a mile and a half further down, in a snug retreat almost concealed by the rising ground on either side, the lofty walls of Blantyre Works appear; where a busy population and rushing noise of machinery contrast strangely with the silence and repose of the surrounding scenery, and seem as if threatened to bring into competition the works of Nature and of Art. The lofty woods of Bothwell on the east and of Blantyre on the west, with the magnificent red walls and circular towers of the old Castle of Bothwell, and the shattered remains of Blantyre Priory on the opposite side on the summit of a lofty rock add greatly to the beauty of the scenery. A little further on, the banks begin to decline before they reach Daldowie, and the river leaves the parish amid fertile fields and expanding haughs. The whole on a summer day when the sun is shining is inexpressibly beautiful.

Wright, Rev. Stewart

The Rev. Stewart Wright was born at Inverary on 15 October 1829, the fifth son of James Wright who was at one time provost of that town. His early education was at Inverary and later he attended Irvine Academy and the Universities of Edinburgh and Glasgow. He was licensed by Glasgow Presbytery and for a short time was assistant at Mathews, Glasgow, and was ordained on 23 May 1855 to the charge of St George's in the Field. Following that appointment he was chaplain at Madras from 1858 to 1865 and at Bangalore from 1865 to 1871. Rev. Wright was inducted at Blantyre Old Parish Church (q.v.) on 3 August 1871 and was minister there until his death on 29 November 1887. He married his wife Alice, the daughter of the Rev. Colin Smith DD, the minister of Inverary, on 5 January 1856. They had 12 children, four boys and eight girls.

It is mainly due to the Rev. Stewart Wright and his book *The Annals of Blantyre*, published in 1885, that we are aware today of many of the incidental tales of people and events that occurred within the parish. Wright also gave a vivid description of his experiences during the Blantyre Explosion disaster (q.v.) and the effect of its aftermath on the inhabitants. He will forever be remembered for his untiring efforts during the 'Calamity' and the compassion given to the victims' families during and after the tragic event at Dixon's Colliery. He was the first to appreciate the need to raise funds for the dependents of those killed and his efforts raised many thousands of pounds. Such was his standing within the community that he was appointed Chairman of the Fund Committee to administer and distribute money assist to the destitute families of the victims.

ϒ

Stonefield Road.

Young's Building

Young's Building was a tenement that stood on Broompark Road at the corner of Stonefield Road. Louden, the butcher, had a shop in this building on the site of the present-day car park of *Finbarr's Pub*.

Yuille, Ann

SEE JOHN HUTTON OF CALDERBANK (H)

Old Parish Church and Craigmuir Cottage, 1885, etching from The Annals of Blantyre.

BIBLIOGRAPHY

Bell, Bert, *Still Seeing Red*

Browns, Hugh, Personal Survival Account at the Blantyre Colliery Explosion, 1877

Campbell, James, *Anderson Church Jubilee Booklet*

Coventry, Martin, *Castles of Scotland*, 3rd Edition, Gobblinshead Publishers

Dalbeth Cemetery Interment Lists, Roman Catholic Archdiocese, Glasgow

Davidson, J.M., OBE, FSA Scot., *Bronze Age Burials at Blantyre & Milngavie*

Fordon, John, *Chronicles of the Scottish Nation*

Golden Jubilee, Saint Joseph's Church, Blantyre

Hamilton Advertiser

Henderson, G. and Waddell, J.J., *Bothwell Banks*

Henry, Jim and Moultray, Ian, *Speedway in Scotland*, Tempus Publishing Ltd

John Ness Jubilee Booklet, Wm. Izett, 1906, Hamilton Herald Jubilee Booklet

Marsh, Catherine M., *The Master of Blantyre*, Thomas Nelson & Sons

McGibbon & Ross, *Castellated & Domesticated Architecture of Scotland*, Wylie & Co.

O'Halloran, Rev. Thomas, *Saint Joseph's Parish Blantyre, A Short History*

Page, Arnot R., *A History of the Scottish Miners*, George Allan & Unwin Ltd

Philip Murray Biography, 1953

Statistical Accounts of Blantyre 1791, 1835 & 1952

Stothers, *Glasgow Lanarkshire & Renfrewshire Xmas and New Year Annual 1911/12*

Struthers Lanarkshire 1910/11

The Blantyre Interment Lists, South Lanarkshire Council

The Government Inquiry Report on the Blantyre Colliery Explosion, 1878

The Scotsman

The Sunday Post

Thomson, David and Steel, Ian, *Glasgow Tigers, Into the Eighties*

Webster, Jack, *In the Driving Seat, A Century of Motoring in Scotland*

Wilson, James, OBE MD, *A Contribution to the History of Lanarkshire*, Vol. 1

Wright, Rev. Stewart, *The Annals of Blantyre*, 1885, Wilson & McCormack